Plea Bargaining
Made Real

Plea Bargaining
Made Real

Steven P. Grossman
DEAN JULIUS ISAACSON PROFESSOR OF LAW
UNIVERSITY OF BALTIMORE SCHOOL OF LAW

CAROLINA ACADEMIC PRESS
Durham, North Carolina

Library of Congress Cataloging-in-Publication Data

Names: Grossman, Steven P., 1949- author.
Title: Plea bargaining made real / Steven P. Grossman.
Description: Durham : Carolina Academic Press, 2021.
Identifiers: LCCN 2021010430 (print) | LCCN 2021010431 (ebook) | ISBN
  9781531019914 (paperback) | ISBN 9781531019921 (ebook)
Subjects: LCSH: Plea bargaining--United States. | Defense (Criminal
  procedure)--United States. | Pleas of guilty--United States.
Classification: LCC KF9654 .G76 2021 (print) | LCC KF9654 (ebook) | DDC
  345.73/072--dc23
LC record available at https://lccn.loc.gov/2021010430
LC ebook record available at https://lccn.loc.gov/2021010431

Carolina Academic Press
700 Kent Street
Durham, North Carolina 27701
Telephone (919) 489-7486
Fax (919) 493-5668
www.cap-press.com

Contents

Table of Cases

Cases that are cited in italics are mentioned specifically or discussed in some depth in the text of the book. The non-italicized cases appear in the footnotes.

Introduction

From the criminal libel prosecution of John Peter Zenger when America was a colony through the famous and infamous cases involving the kidnapping of the Lindbergh baby, the espionage charges leading to the executions of Julius and Ethel Rosenberg, the sensational murders inspired by Charles Manson, the less sensational ones charged against O. J. Simpson, and the conspiracy engaged in by the accomplices of President Nixon in the Watergate cover-up, the public's attention to our criminal justice system is dominated by trials. Aside from following the trials themselves with rapt attention, we watch documentaries and dramatized movies and series (some "inspired by a true story") about them. And as we don't seem to get our fill from real trials, we absorb books, movies, and television series in the multitudes that deal with fictional ones.

Judicial opinions in the criminal justice sphere focus on the conduct of trials or the application and interpretation of constitutional and other protections that exist to protect defendants at trial. Decisions such as *Mapp v. Ohio*, applying the rule excluding certain evidence illegally seized by the government, or *Miranda v. Arizona*, prohibiting the prosecution from introducing statements made by defendants if Fifth Amendment protections were not honored, and the many cases interpreting these and other decisions involving legal limits on what evidence can be brought out at trial dominate the legal landscape. This proliferation of trial-related court decisions is even more pronounced when one considers how they are supplemented by the numerous cases dealing with actions by prosecutors and judges during the trial itself which create appealable issues. The curriculum at American law schools reflects this by the attention paid to these constitutional protections as well as to teaching the skills required to become an effective the trial lawyer. Courses in criminal procedure cover trial-related constitutional and other rights, and those in trial practice teach litigation skills for our future prosecutors and defense attorneys. I have taught both types of courses for many years.

And then there is plea bargaining. This is the process in which the prosecutor and defense attorney discuss and arrive at a settlement of the case whereby the defendant agrees to plead guilty to some charge related to the crime in return for a benefit from the prosecutor. These benefits usually involve charge or sentencing considerations. The judge is a necessary party to this agreement, is sometimes involved with the attorneys in its formation, and often plays a key role in its implementation. In large part because, unlike trial convictions, most guilty pleas are not appealed, it is convictions resulting from trials that usually receive most attention from the courts. While it is impossible to ascertain the exact percentage of cases in the criminal justice system disposed of through guilty pleas, there is nearly universal agreement that the number is around 95%.[1] Small wonder that Supreme Court Justice Anthony Kennedy cautioned in 2012 not to ignore "the reality that criminal justice today is for the most part a system of pleas, not a system of trials."[2]

Americans pride ourselves on the protections our laws provide defendants in criminal cases, most especially those rights guaranteed under our constitution that relate to the criminal trial. For example, the Sixth Amendment guarantees the right to have the fate of the accused in all serious cases decided by a jury of one's peers and now requires that all jurors must agree on the defendant's guilt in order for the government to get a conviction.[3] That same amendment guarantees the defendant the right to be represented by competent counsel. The defendant or his attorney has the right to confront and cross-examine witnesses who offer testimony for the prosecution (also under the Sixth Amendment) and the absolute right under the Fifth Amendment to testify or not testify in his defense. Additionally, if he decides not to testify, the prosecutor is forbidden from commenting on that decision and the jury is instructed not to use his failure to testify against the defendant. Last but certainly not least, the jurors will be instructed that in order to convict the defendant, they must find him guilty beyond a reasonable doubt, the highest burden of proof in our law.

---

1. *See, e.g.*, Padilla v. Kentucky, 559 U.S. 356, 372 (2010) (95%); Missouri v. Frye, 566 U.S. 134, 143 (2012) (94% of state convictions, 97% of federal convictions); NACDL Report: The Trial Penalty: The Sixth Amendment Right to Trial on the Verge of Extinction and How to Save It (July 10, 2018) (more than 97%), https://www.nacdl.org/Document/TrialPenaltySixthAmendmentRighttoTrialNearExtinct.

2. Lafler v. Cooper, 566 U.S. 156, 170 (2012).

3. Ramos v. Louisiana, 140 S. Ct. 1390 (2020).

Because Americans have traditionally been so proud of at least the theoretical fairness of our system for handling criminal cases, we have long advocated for other nations to adopt systems that embody rights and protections similar to our own. In reality though, these rights exist more in their potential than in their actuality, or at least as largely unexercised options. This is because the overwhelming number of cases handled by both federal and state courts are disposed of largely without the exercise of these foundational rights–almost always through plea bargaining. Thoughtful people must stop and ask why so few defendants in criminal cases avail themselves of such critical protections.

This surprising result becomes even more anomalous when one examines the nature of our criminal justice process, specifically the adversary system. Our adversary system of justice is based on the concept that the fairest and most reliable outcomes in criminal cases will come from well-armed prosecution and defense teams, each advocating as zealously as possible for its position within the bounds of law and ethics. Those who have participated in the criminal justice process as prosecutors, defense attorneys, victims, witnesses, jurors, or defendants will agree that this notion of zealous advocacy is no mere theory but pervades the conduct of the parties involved. Legal motions and pleadings come from one side and are usually opposed by the other. Witnesses are divided into prosecution and defense witnesses, leading to trials embodying prosecution and defense cases almost always at strict odds with one another.

Given the stakes involved for each side, it is hardly surprising that the nature of this adversarial advocacy often gets intense and highly argumentative. The prosecution might see itself as the voice of the victim of some horrific crime, always representing the interests of the government in seeing to it that a crime is solved and a criminal punished appropriately. The defense attorney is concerned with the loss of freedom for his clients facing serious charges and the severely negative implications of a criminal conviction for everyone he defends. It is not to diminish the consequences of civil litigation to observe that the impact of a criminal case is almost always substantial and significant.

In large part because of these stakes and the highly adversarial nature of the process, there is often little that the prosecution and defense agree upon. It is not unusual to see intense arguments regarding consequential matters such as the suitability of a particular juror or the admissibility of a key piece of evidence as well as on seemingly minor ones such as the positioning of exhibits in the courtroom or scheduling arrangements. Yet despite the inevitable battles fought by prosecution and defense over most everything, somehow they come together to agree upon the most critical of matters — the ultimate resolution of the case, 95% of the time. Without the agreement of both of these highly adverse parties (with the very rare exception of when the defendant pleads guilty to all charges without any promises from the prosecution), no plea bargain can take place.

Add to this the third party who has to agree to the plea bargain — the judge — and the virtual universality of cases disposed of through plea bargaining is even more surprising. While not an adverse party, the judge embodies interests apart from either of the other parties and in many instances is not reluctant to express those interests. As the judge has the right to reject any bargain arrived at between the prosecution and the defense, she too must be on board for the case to be resolved through a guilty plea. This book will examine why it is that all of these obstacles to agreements between the parties regarding the most important aspect of a criminal case, its final disposition, are overcome in such an overwhelming majority of cases and the ramifications of this for the defendant and the system.

The purpose of this book in large part is to provide the reader with a sense of what really takes place in plea bargaining that is different in both substance and language from what can be gleaned from most court decisions. Therefore, following a brief history of plea bargaining in the United States in Chapter I, Chapter II will deal with the largely specious and dishonest justifications used by courts for why defendants who exercise their constitutional right to a trial almost always receive harsher sentences than those which they were offered in exchange for their guilty plea. Seen through a slightly different lens, if two defendants are charged with the same crime and have similar backgrounds, it is almost inevitable that the one who pleads guilty will receive a lighter sentence than the one who rejected the plea offer and was convicted at trial. You may think the reason for such disparate treatment is obvious, and if so, you will be surprised by the entirely different reasons offered by virtually all courts. We will explore how and why the courts struggle so mightily to avoid confronting the reality that giving a break to those who plead guilty inevitably results in punishing those who are convicted after exercising their constitutional right to trial.

Plea bargaining is a process that involves three parties — the prosecutor, the defendant/defense attorney, and the judge. The process by which criminal cases are disposed of through offers, negotiations, and ultimately acceptance of the agreement is a very human endeavor. No meaningful understanding of plea bargaining can come from a discussion that overly institutionalizes these parties and, for example, discounts matters such as the motivations of each to dispose of cases without a trial. An awareness of these motivations allows for a better understanding of the behavior of each of the parties as they engage in plea bargaining. Chapters III, IV, and V therefore explore the roles of the prosecutor, defense attorney, and judge in plea bargaining. By looking at the motivations and roles of these parties, we can better understand why so many cases are disposed of through pleas of guilt. Additionally, these chapters will discuss the ramifications for the defendant and the justice system of the actions taken by each of the parties.

In forming plea bargains, it is typical for the prosecutor to offer a reduced charge or sentence recommendation in exchange for the defendant's surrender of his right to trial and agreement to plead guilty. Most plea agreements therefore stem from negotiations between the prosecutor, the defense, and sometimes the judge, that involve offers, acceptance of those offers, and mutual promises made by the parties. Because these same elements are present in the formation of civil contracts, it is tempting for courts to apply well-established principles of contract law to the less well-developed legal issues involved in plea bargaining. Chapter VI will discuss ways in which courts have attempted to perform this application of civil law to criminal law and whether they have been successful.

While most cases are disposed of through traditional guilty pleas (the defendant acknowledging his guilt for a specific offense he committed), there are several other types of pleas that dispose of cases without trials. Chapter VII will cover pleas that resolve criminal cases but are different from the traditional guilty plea in the manner which the plea is accepted, its consequences for civil cases, or the nature of the crimes to which the defendant pleads guilty.

Next the book will explore the impact of race in plea bargaining. Racism is a problem which pervades society and infects every stage of the criminal justice process. Given this, it is inevitable that plea bargaining is not free from similar kinds of race-based disparate treatment of defendants. Because of the pervasiveness of race-based disparity throughout the system and the relative paucity of empirical evidence related to its effect on plea bargaining specifically, Chapter VIII will begin with a discussion of racism from the initial detention of suspects through their confinement in jails and prisons. Then it will explore the available data regarding racial disparities in plea offers and the ultimate disposition of cases through guilty pleas. The chapter will conclude with suggestions for reducing these disparities.

Finally, in Chapter IX, we will discuss how we can get past the semantics and euphemisms that pervade discussions by courts and others of plea bargaining and begin to enact meaningful reforms to improve upon our system. It is important for the reader to understand that this is not a book strictly on the law of plea bargaining, although many legal issues surrounding aspects of the process will be covered. It is a book focused on what really happens during the process by which American courts handle almost all the criminal cases that come before them. Plea bargaining is a very human and very subjective process. No benefit and much damage has occurred as a result of denying or ignoring this reality.

Judicial opinions attempt to explain the basis for a court's decision. Books and articles about the law often explain or interpret these opinions, sometimes approvingly and sometimes critically. What makes cases involving plea bargaining different is that the decisions more often than not deny, ignore, or mask the actual basis for the opinion. Only by exploring in depth what actually occurs during the plea bargaining process can we get an understanding of the disconnect between the realities of plea bargaining and judicial opinions that cover this area. Only by understanding this disconnect can we reform and improve plea bargaining in meaningful ways.

Acknowledgments

The author would like to thank Eric Easton, Ph.D., J.D, John Maclean, J.D., and Jeffrey Grossman for their invaluable assistance in editing chapters of this book. Additionally, he would like to thank Caterina Quezada Lozano for her help in researching its contents.

Plea Bargaining
Made Real

Chapter I

A Short History of Plea Bargaining in the United States

The history of plea bargaining in America can be summed up by early efforts to create some sort of incentive for defendants to surrender their right to trial, attempts by judges and legislatures to restrict the ability of the parties to bargain toward that goal, and the responses by prosecutors, defense attorneys, and judges designed to avoid these restrictions. The result of this back and forth has been the clear and almost total triumph of plea bargaining in the American criminal courts.

The English criminal law, the basis for much of America's early approaches to adjudicating criminal cases, offered one of the first known examples of a type of plea bargaining with a statute that was passed in 1485. The law, which dealt with unlawful hunting, distinguished between those who admitted their crime and those who denied it. The former were convicted of minor offenses, the latter were prosecuted as felons.[1] In the earliest days of American criminal courts, plea bargaining was rare, but when it did occur, it was most likely to take place regarding penal laws for which there were narrowly prescribed punishments. Because judges had little or no sentencing discretion in these cases, defendants who pled guilty could not hope for a benefit for saving the court from having to conduct a trial. To provide defendants with such an incentive and thereby to ensure a quick conviction, prosecutors would charge crimes at the top end of the relevant criminal statutes and at the lower end as well. This

---

1. Jeff Palmer, Abolishing Plea Bargaining: An End to the Same Old Song and Dance, 26 Am. J. Crim. L. 505, 509 (1999).

would enable them to drop the more serious charges, thus giving the defendant a benefit for his guilty plea. An example of this occurred in early 19th-century Massachusetts involving liquor laws that had such prescribed penalties.[2]

Interestingly, prosecutors in recent times have responded to crimes punished by determinative sentences (such as totally fixed sentences, certain mandatory recidivist statutes, and crimes whose sentences contain mandatory minimums) in much the same way. That is, they have found ways to offer defendants benefits to induce guilty pleas by avoiding the application of those laws in specific cases. As with the Massachusetts liquor laws, one method of achieving such outcomes is to indict for both the charges containing the mandatory punishments and other related crimes not requiring such punishments. The prosecutor would then offer to dismiss the crimes carrying the more serious punishments in exchange for a guilty plea to the other charges.

The attempts by judges and legislatures to restrict plea bargaining has largely failed, as demonstrated clearly by the steady rise in the number of cases disposed of without trials. Professor Lawrence Friedman did a study of inmates in California's Folsom Prison in 1880 and found that one-third of those who pled guilty did so to "mitigate the penalty"[3]—an amount that likely would have seemed shockingly high at the time. Today, one would be hard pressed to find more than a very few prison inmates who would say they surrendered their right to a trial for any reason other than favorable charge or sentencing promises or recommendations.

The steady advance of plea bargaining continued into the 20th century as judicial systems became accustomed to the expeditious manner in which criminal cases could be disposed of through guilty pleas. In New York County at the turn of the century, for example, three times as many felony cases were disposed of through guilty pleas than through trials.[4] In his important article on the history of plea bargaining, Albert Altschuler noted surveys conducted in the 1920s which "revealed a lopsided dependency on the plea of guilty: in Chicago, 85% of all felony convictions were by guilty plea; in Detroit 78; in Denver 76; in Minneapolis 90; in Los Angeles 81; in Pittsburgh 74; and in St. Louis 84."[5] In 1934, The American Legal Institute concluded in a study of the

---

2. Jennifer Mnookin, Uncertain Bargains: The Rise of Plea Bargaining in America, 57 Stan. L. Rev. 1721, 1726 (2005).

3. Lawrence M. Friedman, Crime and Punishment in American History (1993), p. 252n*, cited in Kevin Jost, Plea Bargaining: Does the Widespread Practice Promote Justice?, https://library.cqpress.com/cqresearcher/document.php?id=cqresrre1999021200.

4. Jost, https://library.cqpress.com/cqresearcher/document.php?id=cqresrre1999021200.

5. Albert Altschuler, Plea Bargaining and Its History, 79 Colum. L. Rev. 1, 26 (1979).

federal courts that plea bargaining was "responsible for the prompt and efficient disposition of business," and it was "doubtful if the system could operate without it."[6]

By the 1960s, plea bargaining was so ingrained in our judicial system that in Altschuler's words, "both the American Bar Association Project on Minimum Standards for Criminal Justice and the President's Commission on Law Enforcement and Administration of Justice proclaimed that, properly administered, plea bargaining was a practice of considerable value."[7] During the 1960s and 70s, the Supreme Court handed down a number of decisions (to be discussed later in this book) which either explicitly or implicitly acknowledged or even approved of plea bargaining. The triumph was complete now, both as to its legal recognition and its overwhelming numerical dominance regarding the disposition of criminal cases. That dominance has only increased to the present day.

---

6. American Law Institute, A Study of the Business of the Federal Courts, Part I, Criminal Cases (1934), cited in Jost, https://library.cqpress.com/cqresearcher/document .php?id=cqresrre1999021200.

7. Albert Altschuler, Plea Bargaining and Its History, 79 Colum. L. Rev. 1, 35 (1979), citing ABA Project on Minimum Standards for Criminal Justice, Standards Relating to Pleas of Guilty (tent. draft 1967); President's Comm'n on Law Enforcement and Administration of Justice, The Challenge of Crime in a Free Society 134–37 (1967).

Chapter II

Punishment for Exercising the Right to Trial[1]

No one will be surprised to learn that the American criminal justice system rewards with reduced sentences those criminal defendants who plead guilty rather than go to trial. The result of this is that invariably those who go to trial and are convicted receive heavier sentences than if they had chosen to plead guilty. They also receive heavier sentences than their similarly situated co-defendants who do plead guilty precisely because of the defendant's decision to opt for a trial. This is referred to as differential sentencing. As obvious and inevitable as this cause-and-effect relationship is, American courts at every level have engaged in all sorts of verbal and conceptual gymnastics to avoid acknowledging this reality. This may be due to the poor optics of acknowledging that this difference in the severity of a sentence is primarily the result of the defendant's decision to exercise his constitutional right to trial. Unfortunately, courts have been far more sensitive to these optics than to the dishonesty that attends their decisions and the real consequences created by differential sentencing based on the defendant's choice whether to seek a trial. This response leads not only to absurd and disingenuous opinions attempting to justify differential sentencing but also has frustrated efforts to improve the ever more ubiquitous practice of plea bargaining in the United States.

---

1. This chapter is largely taken from an article I wrote in 2018 titled "Making the Evil Less Necessary and the Necessary Less Evil: Towards a More Honest and Robust System of Plea Bargaining." The parts that are incorporated are done so with the permission of the *Nevada Law Journal*. The article can be found at 18 Nev. L.J. 769 (2018).

This chapter will enumerate and examine the various arguments that courts have made to justify a system in which defendants are in fact punished for deciding to exercise their constitutional right to trial. Those justifications begin with the assertion that while plea bargaining rewards the decision to save the system the time and expense of a trial, it does not punish those defendants who plead not guilty and opt for a trial. This assertion is flawed theoretically, and the flaw is magnified when examined pragmatically. Another justification offered for differential sentencing is based on the theories of sentencing, specifically on the theory of rehabilitation as a factor in sentencing. This justification holds that the defendant's guilty plea represents his first step on the road to rehabilitation and therefore allows for a lighter sentence than had he gone to trial and been convicted. While there is a purely theoretical defense for this justification, the realities of why defendants plead guilty belie its use as a reason for differential sentencing.

The final two justifications for differential sentencing are not fundamentally flawed (as are the reasons above), but they are either numerically insignificant or are beside the point of whether differential sentencing amounts to punishment for exercising the right to trial. Specifically, some courts defend significantly heavier sentences for defendants after trial than the sentences they were offered in exchange for a guilty plea based on what the judge supposedly learned at trial about the defendant's greater participation in the crime or the crime's more serious nature. While this justification may be true in a few isolated cases, it unduly minimizes the information most prosecutors and judges have about the crime and the defendant when a guilty plea is taken. Perhaps more significantly, it fails to account for the near universality of a practice that sentences defendants convicted at trial more harshly than those who plead guilty or than their similarly situated co-defendants receive after having so pled. The final argument as to why differential sentencing is not punishment for exercising the right to trial revolves around the concept of plea bargaining as a negotiation. It is claimed that in plea negotiations, the defendant who chooses not to reach a bargain receives the harsher sentence as a result of these failed negotiations, not as a form of punishment. While there may be some truth to this, it in no way offers a rational justification for differential sentencing that conforms to any of the accepted goals of punishment and how the severity of such punishment is traditionally determined.

Recognizing that the differential sentencing that almost always flows from plea bargaining is punishment for exercising the right to trial does not end the discussion of what type of plea bargaining system the Constitution permits, if any. It begins the discussion. Courts can escape from the flawed and at times shallow justifications offered for differential sentencing without abandoning the plea bargaining system that many regard as essential to the functioning of our criminal justice system. The final section of this chapter will examine the principle that permits the government at times to place a price on the exercise of a constitutional right and just how that principle would apply to plea bargaining. The result of such an application would be a more honest approach to how the criminal justice system operates and provide a vehicle for facilitating positive changes in the system.

A. Differential Sentencing Is Prevalent in Our Criminal Justice System

Criminal defendants who are convicted after exercising their constitutional right to a trial invariably receive harsher sentences than they would have had they chosen to plead guilty.[2] Viewed another way, between two defendants charged with similar crimes and possessing similar backgrounds, the one who

---

2. *See, e.g.,* Correia v. Hall, 364 F.3d 385, 387 (1st Cir. 2004) (Defendant was offered a plea deal of five to seven years. Defendant rejected the State's offer and went to trial, where he was convicted and sentenced to 12 to 17 years); United States v. Thomas, 114 F.3d 228, 272 (D.C. Cir. 1997) (Defendant was offered a plea deal of five years. Defendant rejected the State's offer and went to trial where he was convicted and sentenced to life); Cousin v. Blackburn, 597 F.2d 511, 512 (5th Cir. 1979) (Defendant was offered a plea deal of ten years. Defendant rejected the State's offer and went to trial, where he was convicted and sentenced to 30 years); Walker v. Walker, 259 F. Supp. 2d 221, 223, 226 (E.D.N.Y. 2003) (Defendant was offered a plea deal of eight years to life. Defendant rejected the State's offer and went to trial, where he was convicted and sentenced to 25 years to life); Prado v. State, 816 So. 2d 1155, 1156 (Fla. Dist. Ct. App. 2002) (Defendant was offered a plea deal of four years. Defendant rejected the State's offer and went to trial, where he was convicted and sentenced to 40 years); People v. Dennis, 328 N.E.2d 135, 136 (Ill. App. Ct. 1975) (Defendant was offered a plea deal of two to four years. Defendant rejected the State's offer and went to trial, where he was convicted and sentenced to 40 to 80 years); *see also* Comment, The Influence of the Defendant's Plea on Judicial Determination of Sentence, 66 Yale L.J. 204, 207 (1956) ("The estimates of the extent to which the fine or prison term was diminished for a defendant pleading guilty varied from 10 to 95 percent of the punishment which would ordinarily be given after trial and conviction."); Lindsey Devers, Bureau of Justice Assistance, Plea and Charge Bargaining 3 (2011), https://www.bja.gov/Publications/PleaBargainingResearchSummary.pdf.

chooses to plead guilty will receive a less harsh sentence than the one who is convicted after a trial.[3]

---

3. *See, e.g.*, United States v. Rodriguez, 162 F.3d 135, 152 (1st Cir. 1998); United States v. Stevenson, 573 F.2d 1105, 1106 (9th Cir. 1978); United States v. Wiley, 278 F.2d 500, 501, 503 (7th Cir. 1960). In *Wiley*, the appellate court unsurprisingly found that his decision to go to trial was the apparent motivating factor for the three-year sentence meted out to the defendant, a first-time offender described by the court as an "accessory" in the crime. *Id.* at 503. The court compared Wiley's sentence with that of McGhee, the "principal" offender and "most active participant in the crime." *Id.* The court describes McGhee as a man who "had four prior felony convictions, was the ringleader in this matter, and, subsequent to this offense and while out on bond, committed two other similar offenses." *Id.* After pleading guilty, McGhee received a sentence of two years. *Id.* At other times, courts will strain to justify the disparity in sentences among defendants charged with the same crimes without acknowledging that the disparity was based on the decision of one to plead guilty and the other to go to trial. A blatant example of this occurred in *Jung v. State*, 145 N.W.2d 684 (Wis. 1966). Jung and his co-defendants were charged with armed robbery and attempted murder stemming from a supermarket robbery in which a police officer was shot. *Id.* at 685, 686. Jung was the driver of the getaway car, whereas the two who pled guilty entered the supermarket and committed the robbery. *Id.* at 686. Jung, a married father of five children, had no prior criminal record, whereas the two who pled guilty also pled guilty to several other offenses, one of them to "six other unrelated crimes including armed robbery." *Id.* at 688. The judge sentenced Jung to a total of 60 years in prison and the codefendants who pled guilty to 25 years. The result of these sentences was that Jung's conditional release date was 15 years after that of the other two. *Id.* at 690. In affirming these sentences, the Wisconsin Supreme Court rejected some of the typical arguments used to justify differential sentences, such as that pleading guilty is the first step on the road to rehabilitation or that the codefendants' agreements to cooperate in the case were mitigating factors in the sentencing. *Id.* at 688–89. It then adopted the arguable position that, for sentencing purposes, the driver of the car can be regarded as equally culpable as those who entered the store and pointed the gun at the victims. *Id.* at 690. Far more troubling was the court's apparent disregard of the substantially harsher sentence meted out to the only perpetrator with no other known criminal behavior. In rejecting Jung's assertion that his longer sentence was due to his decision to stand trial, the court described various aspects of the crime. *Id.* at 688–90. None of these addressed in any way why Jung's sentence was longer than his two codefendants. Ultimately, the court seemed to base its decision on the fact that the trial judge did not affirmatively indicate he was punishing Jung for exercising his right to trial. *Id.* at 689.

More recent evidence of this trial penalty can be seen in reports based on findings from the United States Sentencing Commission and Human Rights Watch comparing the 2012 sentences of similarly situated federal defendants convicted after trial with those who accepted plea bargains. Regarding those charged with drug offenses that carried mandatory minimum sentences, those who were convicted at trial received an average of 18 years in prison, while those who pleaded guilty averaged seven years. First-time offenders facing drug charges in which no weapon was present who pled guilty received half the prison term of those who were convicted at trial. Federal sentencing law provides for enhanced sentences of defendants with prior criminal records. Those who were convicted at trial were 8.4 times

One striking example of both of these common plea bargaining based results occurred in the case of Kevin Haynes.[4] A 23-year-old father with no criminal record, Haynes was recruited by Virgil Rivers to participate in four armed robberies over a period of time from 1991 to 1992. The prosecution offered Haynes a guilty plea deal in which his sentence would fall within the range of seven years nine months to eight years five months of incarceration. Haynes rejected the plea offer and opted to exercise his right to trial. In response, the prosecution obtained a superseding indictment as it had indicated it would do if Haynes turned down the guilty plea offer. This superseding indictment involved two statutes which required substantial mandatory prison terms. Haynes then filed a motion claiming the superseding indictment was a vindictive response to his choice to exercise his constitutional right to a trial and therefore a due process violation. The court denied Haynes' motion based on the Supreme Court's holding in *Bordenkircher v. Hayes* (discussed later in this chapter). Haynes was convicted at trial of the robberies and sentenced to 46½ years in prison. In other words, Haynes was to serve almost 40 years longer, or between five and six times as much time in prison, than was considered by the government to be adequate when he was offered a plea to cover all the robberies.

The penalty Haynes received for going to trial can also be seen from comparing his sentence with that of the man with whom he committed the crimes. Not only did Virgil Rivers recruit Haynes for the robberies but Rivers was the principal participant in them, while Haynes (although both were armed) acted as lookout. Perhaps the most significant difference between the two with respect to the factors traditionally used in determining the length of a prison sentence was that unlike Haynes, Rivers had "a substantial criminal record including four robbery convictions." Rivers was sentenced to ten years in prison

---

as likely to have such enhancements applied as those who pled guilty. News Release, Human Rights Watch, An Offer You Can't Refuse: How U.S. Federal Prosecutors Force Drug Defendants to Plead Guilty (Dec. 5, 2013), https://www.hrw.org/report/2013/12/05/offer-you-cant-refuse/how-us-federal-prosecutors-force-drug-defendants-plead. In 2015, the Sentencing Commission found that for most crimes, the sentences of defendants who were convicted at trial were three times that of those who pled guilty. The Trial Penalty: The Sixth Amendment Right to Trial on the Verge of Extinction and How to Save It, Nat'l Ass'n of Criminal Defense Lawyers (July 10, 2018), https://www.nacdl.org/getattachment /95b7f0f5-90df-4f9f-9115-520b3f58036a/the-trial-penalty-the-sixth-amendment-right-to-trial-on-the-verge-of-extinction-and-how-to-save-it.pdf (hereinafter "The Trial Penalty").

4. United States v. Haynes, 93 CR 1043 (RJD), 2020 WL 1941478 (E.D.N.Y. Apr. 22, 2020).

to cover all four robberies. So the man with no criminal record who acted as a lookout received a sentence 4½ times that of the man who recruited him, was the principal participant in the robberies, and had four previous robbery convictions. After serving 27 years in prison, Haynes was ordered free by a federal court granting him the equivalent of compassionate relief.[5]

A study was conducted comparing the sentences in 2015 of those who pled guilty to 36 primary offenses, ranging from murder and kidnapping to tax offenses and drug charges, with the sentences of those convicted of the same offenses at trial. The results showed that the sentences of those convicted at trial were more than three times longer than those who accepted plea bargains.[6] A 2011 article in the *New York Times* reported that in Florida, "felony defendants who opt for trial now routinely face the prospect of higher charges that mean prison terms 2, 5, or even 20 times as long as if they had pleaded guilty."[7] If part of the plea bargain involves the defendant's agreement to cooperate with the prosecution on some matter, the disparity is even more stark. When the guidelines used in the sentencing of federal defendants were mandatory, this difference was reported to be 500%.[8] No one who has practiced law in American criminal courts would be surprised by these results. It should be obvious that this almost inevitable enhancement in sentencing, occurring for the most part when the only variable in the two situations is the defendant's choice to go to trial, amounts to punishment for exercising the right to trial.[9] As one federal judge put it:

> [A]s a practical matter this means, as between two similarly situated
> defendants, that if the one who pleads and cooperates gets a four-year

---

5. *Id.* The federal district court decision granting Haynes the relief referred to contains a fuller description of the earlier court decisions involving Haynes and Rivers and the position in opposition to Haynes' relief requests taken by federal prosecutors. *Id.*

6. The Trial Penalty, Figure 1.

7. Richard A. Oppel Jr., Sentencing Shift Gives New Leverage to Prosecutors, N.Y. Times (Sept. 25, 2011), https://www.nytimes.com/2011/09/26/us/tough-sentences-help-prosecutors-push-for-plea-bargains.html.

8. Berthoff v. United States, 140 F. Supp. 2d 50, 67–68 (D. Mass. 2001).

9. See *State v. Baldwin*, 629 P.2d 222, 225 (Mont. 1981), in which the court wrote:

It may be difficult to distinguish between situations where leniency is offered in exchange for a plea and situations where the defendant is punished for exercising his right to trial by jury. In the absence of clear indications in the record to the contrary, a trial judge could justify any disparity between a sentence offered in exchange for a plea of guilty and the sentence actually imposed following a jury trial simply by characterizing the sentence offered in the plea bargaining process as an offer of leniency — regardless of the judge's true motivations.

sentence, then the guideline sentence for the one who exercises his right to trial by jury and is convicted will be twenty years. Not surprisingly, such a disparity imposes an extraordinary burden on the free exercise of the right to an adjudication of guilt by one's peers. Criminal trial rates ... are plummeting due to the simple fact that today we punish people — punish them severely — simply for going to trial.[10]

Obvious though it may be, the judicial system has struggled to come to grips with this reality for reasons related to the already negative aura surrounding plea bargaining in the United States, the optics of acknowledging our system punishes the exercise of a constitutional right, and the emotional and intellectual difficulty of confronting the real issues surrounding the benefits and problems regarding the manner in which we dispose of 95 percent of the cases in the criminal justice system.[11] If we are to move forward in a meaningful way to address such issues that prevent plea bargaining from working better for all involved, we need to abandon the largely facile defenses and acknowledge the reality that differential sentencing based on the accused's decision whether to plead guilty is as much punishment for exercising the right to trial as it is conferring a benefit for pleading guilty.

B. Justifications for Differential Sentencing

The courts have generally offered defenses of differential sentencing that fall roughly into four categories. They are: (1) the system does not punish those who are convicted after a trial but merely rewards those who plead guilty; (2) there is a difference for sentencing purposes between one who pleads guilty and one who is convicted after trial, in that the former has taken the first step on the road to rehabilitation and therefore deserves a less harsh sentence; (3) after a trial, the sentencing judge learns substantially more about the evil of the defendant and the seriousness of his crime that she was not aware of when there would have been a guilty plea; and (4) the difference in sentences before and after trial results from the give and take of negotiations rather than punishment — in other words: you gambled, you lost. The first two justifications for differential sentencing are seriously flawed both in theory and in practice. The third defense may have some validity in limited cases; however, it does

10. Berthoff v. United States, 140 F. Supp. 2d at 68–69.
11. United States v. Booker, 543 U.S. 220, 276–77 (2005) (Stevens, J., dissenting).

not explain why a sentence after trial is almost always harsher than if the defendant had pled guilty. The final justification is undoubtedly correct, but gambling and losing is inconsistent with the traditional reasons why we sentence those convicted of crimes to greater or lesser sentences.

1. It is a benefit but not a punishment

Perhaps the justification offered most often for differential sentencing is the win/win notion that the criminal justice system offers a benefit to those who plead guilty while merely meting out the sentence the accused deserves if he exercises his right to trial and is convicted. Who can argue with a system that benefits many and harms none? It is likely the simple nature of this benefit/punishment rationale combined with its optimistic vision of the criminal justice system that accounts for its popularity in judicial responses to challenges by defendants to sentences substantially higher after trial than those offered as part of a plea bargain. These challenges stem both from cases in which defendants receive significantly harsher penalties after trial than they were offered in a plea bargain and from those in which the defendant who was convicted after a trial receives a greater sentence than his co-defendants with similar or worse criminal records who were equal or more primary participants in the crime but had the good sense to accept the prosecutor's plea offer.

The benefit/punishment rationale relies on the assertion that the punishment one deserves for criminal behavior is the sentence he receives after being convicted at trial. This would be the "regular" sentence. It follows, therefore, that were he to accept a plea bargain with the virtually inevitable reduced sentence awarded in exchange for his plea of guilt, this discount constitutes a benefit, a departure from the sentence he deserved. However, as one appellate court put it, "[T]he temptation is strong in the area of plea bargaining to assume that defendants convicted after trial receive a 'normal' sentence while those who plead guilty and save the Government the cost of a trial receive special 'leniency' in exchange. If this analysis were valid, some defendants would win and none would lose. But in reality there are winners and losers."[12] The vast and varied ways in which both prosecutors and judges exercise discretion, however, belies the notion of a "regular" sentence. Except when the sentencing options of the judge are limited by crimes that have mandatory minimum sentences, judges rarely have any meaningful limits to the range of sentences they can mete out within the often broad statutory limits of permissible sentences for crimes in most jurisdictions. This in part accounts for the

---

12. Scott v. United States, 419 F.2d 264, 278 (D.C. Cir. 1969).

disparate sentences given to defendants, often with similar backgrounds, convicted of similar crimes. It was the unfairness of this disparity in sentencing that led in part to the implementation of mandatory sentencing guidelines, such as the ones governing federal courts embodied in the Sentencing Reform Act of 1984. Such mandatory guidelines were deemed by many to have significant problems and were ultimately determined to be unconstitutional by the Supreme Court.[13] Although these guidelines still exist and federal judges are instructed to consult them before sentencing, the judge is free to go above or below the guidelines when meting out a sentence.[14] Many states do not even have advisory guidelines, and thus state judges have especially broad discretion in their sentencing practices.

The opportunities within the process of a criminal case for the prosecutor to exercise broad discretion over the eventual sentence the defendant will receive if convicted at trial also detracts from the notion of a regular sentence for a crime. As will be discussed in detail in Chapter III, these opportunities occur at several points during the criminal justice process. The first such opportunity relates to the decision about what charges to bring — a decision over which the prosecutor has broad discretion. If the defendant is convicted of any or all of those charges, the prosecutor's charging decision sets the range of possible sentences. Therefore, sentences for similar crimes will vary in part owing to those charging decisions. The case of William Rummel, which ultimately reached the Supreme Court,[15] is a clear example of the substantial impact of a prosecutor's charging decision and how such broad discretion discredits the notion of a regular sentence for a specific crime. Rummel was charged in Texas with obtaining $120.75 by false pretenses. Apparently Rummel presented himself to the victim as an air conditioning repairman and was paid that amount to provide and install a new compressor. He never did and was charged accordingly. The crime Rummel was charged with was a felony at the time because the value of the fraudulent action was over $50. Texas law required a sentence of not less than two years imprisonment nor more than ten years for this crime. Had the prosecutor so charged, Rummel's sentence upon conviction would have fallen within that range. Because Rummel had two prior felony convictions — one for fraudulent use of a credit card to obtain $80 in services and the other for passing a $28 forged check — the prosecutor chose to charge him instead as a recidivist, which under Texas law mandated life imprisonment. Rummel was ultimately convicted of this crime and received the mandated sentence. He then challenged

---

13. *Booker*, 543 U.S. at 267.
14. *Id.* at 245; Gall v. United States, 552 U.S. 38, 59 (2007).
15. Rummel v. Estelle, 445 U.S. 263 (1980).

this life sentence as violation of the ban on cruel and unusual punishment contained in the Eighth Amendment to the Constitution.

Rummel argued that his sentence was disproportional to the crime he committed and even to the compendium of his three felony convictions (nonviolent crimes adding up to a total of less than $250 in ill-gotten gains) and therefore was cruel and unusual. The Court held the sentence was harsh but not unconstitutional. So what was the regular sentence for felony fraud in Texas at that time? Was it two years, ten years, or something in between? Were they all permissible sentences for a judge to impose should the prosecutor choose not to indict the defendant as a recidivist? Or is the regular sentence the life sentence that Rummel received? Even if you limit the cases to when the defendant has two prior felonies, it is still usually the prosecutor's choice whether to charge the defendant as a recidivist, in which case if convicted he gets life imprisonment, or to charge just the instant crime and argue his previous convictions warrant a sentence close to the statutory maximum of ten years. The answer then is that, in part because of the broad discretion the prosecutor had in choosing how to charge a defendant, there was no regular sentence for fraud in Texas.

The next place where the prosecutor's exercise of discretion makes the determination of a regular sentence for a crime impossible relates to her decision about what bargain to offer and/or accept in exchange for the defendant's guilty plea. The sentencing range agreed to and recommended to the judge as part of a plea bargain is likely to influence the ultimate sentence the judge metes out if the defendant rejects the plea and is convicted at trial. Were the post-trial sentence less severe or equal to the one offered by the prosecutor during plea negotiations, word of that judge's sentencing habits among defense attorneys would create a disincentive for future defendants to accept guilty pleas in that judge's court. Why plead guilty if you can take your shot at a trial acquittal without paying a price for doing so? As one law review article summed it up, "[T]he only way a plea is attractive to a defendant is if it offers a large sentence differential. Thus, judges must increase the cost of going to trial by increasing the post-verdict sentence. One way that many courts have avoided this constitutional conundrum is by classifying the judge's actions (the presentation of a large sentencing differential) as a denial of a benefit rather than a penalty."[16] This is why prosecutors almost never recommend the same reduced sentence after a trial conviction that they offered the defendant as part

---

16. F. Andrew Hessick III & Reshma Saujani, Plea Bargaining and Convicting the Innocent: The Role of Prosecutor, Defense Counsel, and Judge, 16 BYU J. Pub. L. 189, 225 (2002).

of a guilty plea deal. It is also why judges so rarely mete out the same or less severe sentences after a trial conviction than were offered as part of the plea bargain, whether the judge committed to that sentence or not. In the words of one federal appellate court, "If a defendant can successfully demand the same leniency after standing trial that was offered to him prior to trial in exchange for a guilty plea, all the incentives to plea bargain disappear; the defendant has nothing to lose by going to trial."[17] Sometimes the penalty imposed on the defendant for rejecting a plea offer is especially severe and further belies the notion of a regular sentence for a crime.

The situation leading up to the Supreme Court's decision in *Bordenkircher v. Hayes*[18] offers a compelling example of how the prosecutor's choice during plea negotiations further contradicts the existence of a regular sentence. The Kentucky prosecutor offered to recommend a five-year prison sentence as part of Hayes' guilty plea to uttering a forged instrument. He informed Hayes that if the offer was rejected, he would re-indict the defendant as a persistent felon and seek a life sentence. Hayes rejected the offer and was convicted at trial and sentenced to life imprisonment under the recidivist statute. So unlike in *Rummel*, the prosecutor here did not originally charge the defendant as a recidivist but used the possibility as a wedge during plea negotiations. As it did in *Rummel*, the Supreme Court rejected Hayes' argument that his sentence of life imprisonment was cruel and unusual.

Was life imprisonment the regular sentence for defendants charged with $80 forgeries in Kentucky, even for defendants with similar prior convictions? If this case is any indication, that is so only when the prosecutor chooses to respond to the defendant's rejection of his plea offer by seeking such a sentence. Did the prosecutor here withhold the benefit of a five-year sentence recommendation because the defendant refused to plead guilty, or did he punish Hayes with a mandatory life sentence for not doing so? Once again, the absence of a regular sentence for a crime negates the claim that the substantially longer sentence imposed after trial should be regarded as withdrawal of a benefit without also recognizing it as punishment for going to trial.

Perhaps the accused will be persuaded to offer information or testimony leading to the conviction of criminals in the instant case or in other cases. Such a promise by the defendant is invariably induced by the decision of the prosecutor to offer charge or sentencing concessions. Such a decision by the prosecutor in either the charging or plea bargaining phase of the case can

---

17. Frank v. Blackburn, 646 F.2d 873, 883 (5th Cir. 1980).
18. 434 U.S. 357 (1978).

result in the defendant's being charged as a high-level felon facing decades in prison after conviction at trial, a low-level felon likely to receive a lesser prison term, or a misdemeanant, often punished with some non-incarceration sentence such as probation. Again, the prosecutor's discretion negates there being a regular sentence for whatever particular crime the defendant is accused of.

The final time the prosecutor's decision can cause a sentence to vary comes after a trial conviction, when the sentence is about to be imposed. Asked if he has anything to say at that time, the prosecutor can remain silent or choose to recommend a sentence near the maximum allowed for that crime, near the minimum, or somewhere in between. While the judge is not obliged to factor that recommendation into her sentence, judges generally do not exceed that recommendation for fear of appearing unduly harsh.

In almost all non-capital cases, it is the judge who ultimately decides the defendant's sentence. But for the minority of cases in which the judge is limited by mandatory minimum sentencing requirements (and even in such cases, the judge often has discretion about whether and how far to exceed this minimum), the judge still exercises immense discretion regarding the severity of a sentence. So many variables may factor into a judge's sentence that it is impossible to enumerate all of them. Some of these factors are appropriate sentencing factors; others might not be. In the former category would be many of the factors related to the long-accepted theories of why and how severely we sentence people convicted of criminal offenses. Usually, these theories are categorized as retribution, rehabilitation, deterrence, and incapacitation. Retribution calls for a sentence whose severity is commensurate with the seriousness of the crime. It is a morality-based theory that looks to the blameworthiness of the offender and the harm his actions caused. Retribution focuses more on the crime than the criminal and seeks beyond all else to do justice and achieve fairness.

The other sentencing theories are more utilitarian in nature in that their primary goal is to diminish criminal behavior either by the individual criminal or throughout the population as a whole. Rehabilitation as a sentencing theory bases the type and severity of the sentence primarily on what and how long it will take for the defendant to overcome whatever problem caused the commission of the crime. Such a sentence focuses considerably more on the offender than the offense, and values "curing" the offender over proportionality between crime and punishment. Rehabilitation as a theory of sentencing should not be confused with advocacy for the use of rehabilitative programs that are designed to help the defendant overcome any economic, social, medical, financial, or psychological problems deemed to have played a role in his criminal behavior. Such programs are favored even by many people who are opposed to rehabilitation-based sentencing.

Advocates of deterrence-based sentencing seek to use punishment to create a strong disincentive for the particular offender to re-offend (referred to as special or specific deterrence) or to send a similar message to others in the community contemplating committing a similar crime (general deterrence). Such sentences reflect these goals, for example, by conditioning the length of a prison sentence or the amount of a fine to that which the judge believes is likely to deter this offender or other potential offenders from committing a similar crime.

The final theory of punishment, incapacitation, is also utilitarian in that its purpose is to protect the public by separating the most dangerous offenders from society. Sometimes viewed as the dark side of rehabilitation, an incapacitation-based sentence imprisons a criminal offender for as long as it takes for him to no longer be a threat to the public.

Some judges use one or more of these theories to the exclusion of others, while other judges use some or all of the theories in combination, but often prioritize one theory over the others. That the decision about which theories to use or prioritize leads to substantially different sentences for the same crime should be obvious. In fact, two judges who use the same theory still often arrive at different sentences for similar crimes and criminals. Take, for example, the type of case that happens thousands of times in American criminal courts over a week's time. A defendant is charged with selling a small amount of cocaine on a street corner. The crime calls for sentences ranging from probation to ten years' imprisonment. The judge who primarily bases her sentencing decisions on retributionist principles might decide that the defendant may be causing substantial harm to the purchaser (and perhaps his family and community) and is blameworthy for doing so, thus deserving a sentence near the maximum. Or her sentence may embody another principle integral to retributionists — equal and proportionate justice. As most in that state receive short prison terms for such cases, her sentence may instead be near the bottom of the range. The judge focused more on deterrence might want to send a message with his sentence and therefore sentence near the top of the range. Or he may feel that a sentence in this routine case will not be communicated sufficiently to achieve general deterrence and warrant such a heavy sentence. Yet again the judge might be more concerned with special or specific deterrence, designed to disincentivize this particular defendant from ever committing the crime again. Based on the defendant's previous drug charges, the judge may feel a stricter sentence is necessary to achieve this goal.

Judges who look to sentence defendants based on how long it will take for the defendant to overcome whatever personal factors caused him to commit the crime (a rehabilitation-based sentence) may decide the defendant needs many years to overcome these problems or just a few. The judge may know of rehabilitation programs that he believes are likely to help resolve the defendant's drug problem and therefore obviate the need for any incarceration. Unlike a more retributionist judge, these judges look primarily to the individual rather than to the particular crime committed in fashioning a sentence. Given the application of different theories of punishment and varied sentences even by judges applying the same theory, it is impossible to determine what the regular sentence is for a particular crime.

The broad and varied discretion afforded to prosecutors and judges in the vast majority of cases makes it absurd to attempt to claim that there is a regular sentence meted out to defendants who are convicted of similar crimes. Without the ability to make such a determination, one cannot claim the sentence afforded to those convicted after trial is the regular sentence for particular types of crimes or offenders. It follows that if there is no regular sentence meted out after trial, then there is no merit to the claim that the reduced sentence one almost inevitably receives from pleading guilty is a reward while simultaneously denying that the greater sentence meted out after conviction at trial is punishment.[19] The sentences meted out after trial are too fluid to be labeled as regular. Therefore, the difference in the sentences must be regarded as reward and punishment.

Interestingly, the Supreme Court rejected a similarly misguided reward-only rationale when considering the use of the defendant's cooperation as a factor in sentencing. In *Roberts v. United States*,[20] the government asserted that the defendant deserved a harsh sentence in part due to his refusal to cooperate by naming his criminal associates. In response, Roberts argued that although cooperation is "'a laudable endeavor'" that bears a "'rational connection to a defendant's willingness to shape up and change his behavior,'" and therefore warrants a reduced sentence, he should not be punished for his failure to so cooperate.[21] The Court's response to this argument was, "we doubt that a principled distinction may be drawn between 'enhancing' the punishment imposed upon the petitioner and denying him the 'leniency' he claims would

---

19. As one court put it, if anything, "[t]he 'normal' sentence is the average sentence for all defendants, those who plead guilty and those who plead innocent. If we are 'lenient' toward the former, we are by precisely the same token 'more severe' toward the latter." Scott v. United States, 419 F.2d at 278 (D.C. Cir. 1969).

20. 445 U.S. 552 (1980).

21. *Id.* at 557 (quoting Brief for Petitioner).

be appropriate if he had cooperated. The question for decision is simply whether petitioner's failure to cooperate is relevant to the currently understood goals of sentencing."[22] Applied to plea bargaining and embodying that same reasoning, that same sentence would read, "[w]e doubt that a principled distinction may be drawn between 'enhancing' the punishment imposed upon the petitioner who is convicted at trial and denying him the 'leniency' the court claims would be appropriate if he had pled guilty. The question for decision is simply whether petitioner's failure to plead guilty is relevant to the currently understood goals of sentencing." In other words, factoring into sentencing the accused's decision about whether to exercise his right to trial is both benefit and punishment. What matters is whether that decision is an appropriate factor in determining one's sentence.

The assertion that the reduced sentence accompanying a guilty plea is a reward but the harsher post-trial conviction sentence is not a punishment seems even more absurd when viewed in conjunction with the actual extent of plea bargaining in the U.S. Roughly 95%of criminal cases are disposed of without trial in this country. Using this reward-only theory would mean that 19 of 20 criminal defendants receive a "reward" for their guilty plea, whereas the one defendant who is convicted after trial receives the "regular" sentence he deserves and is therefore not being punished for exercising his right to trial. Such a situation is rather like stores that have items "ON SALE" for 51 weeks a year. If you are unfortunate enough to purchase the item during the other week, are you paying the "regular" store price for it? I do not claim this means that differential sentencing reflects only punishment and not benefit, but that it further belies the claim that such a difference is benefit alone.

I tell my law students that it makes me feel good when those in my seminar agree with my point of view. So to reward students who do so, regular agreement with the views of the professor will assure them a grade of "A" or "B". Those who have the temerity to express a viewpoint that disagrees with mine will almost inevitably receive a grade no higher than "C". Grade conscious as law students tend to be, 95% or 19 of the 20 students in my seminar consistently agree with me over the course of the semester and receive the grade I promised. The one student who disagreed with me, as was his right of course, received a "C". Now when he goes to the dean to complain that I punished him for disagreeing with me, I will adamantly deny that I would ever do such a thing. I was merely rewarding the other 19 students for agreeing with me and giving him the regular grade he deserved.

---

22. *Id.* at 557 n.4.

And there, with two differences, you have the argument that the 95% of criminal defendants who plead guilty get a sentence benefit for doing so, but the 5% who get the heavier sentence for exercising their right to trial are not being punished. The first difference between plea bargaining and my hypothetical class (yes, it was just a hypothetical) is that while my grading policy was merely an exercise in ego gone wild, there are some valid reasons why we reward defendants who plead guilty while punishing those who go to trial. The existence of valid reasons or not, however, does not change the fact that like my grading, differential sentencing is both benefit and punishment. The second difference is that unlike during plea bargaining when the judge is precluded from telling the defendant the truth about the harsher sentence he will receive after a trial conviction, I openly tell my students what will happen if they disagree with me so they can make an informed choice.

Therefore, the benefit/punishment distinction rationale commonly offered as a defense to the claim that differential sentencing reflects punishment for exercising the constitutional right to trial is flawed both in theory and in practice.

2. Guilty plea is the first step on the road to rehabilitation

As stated above, there are four traditional justifications for punishment: retribution, deterrence, incapacitation and rehabilitation. The first three of these justifications offer no explanation as to why those who choose to go to trial should receive harsher sentences than those who plead guilty. Retributionists argue for sentences whose severity depends on the extent of the moral wrong committed by the offender and the consequences of his offense. The focus of a retribution-based sentence would be the establishment of a proportional relationship between crime and punishment. Whether a person chooses to plead guilty is irrelevant to this relationship, and therefore no defense of differential sentencing can be based on retributionist principles.

The intent of a deterrence-based sentence is to create a severe enough disincentive to engage in future criminal behavior by either the defendant before the court (specific deterrence) or others who are contemplating committing a similar crime (general deterrence). Whether that sentence results from the offender's guilty plea or conviction after trial has no impact on the degree to which the defendant or another potential offender is likely to eschew future criminal behavior — that is, unless what the sentencer is hoping to deter is the decision to claim one's right to a trial. Deterrence-based sentencing, therefore, offers no explanation for the difference in sentences between those who plead guilty and those who go to trial.

Sentences meted out for incapacitation are designed to separate the most dangerous criminals from the rest of society because of the extreme danger such criminals pose. The goal is to sentence the defendant to enough time to ensure he no longer poses such a danger. The decision to plead guilty or go to trial tells us nothing about how long it will take for a serial arsonist or child molester to no longer be dangerous.

Accordingly, neither retribution, deterrence, nor incapacitation can explain why one who is convicted at trial invariably receives a harsher sentence than the one he was offered to plead guilty. The remaining rationale for punishment, rehabilitation, does offer such a justification theory. Rehabilitation as a sentencing theory conditions the severity of a sentence primarily on the means and the length of time that seem appropriate for "curing" the offender of whatever social, economic, psychological, or other factor is believed to have motivated his criminal behavior. If pleading guilty is viewed as the acceptance of responsibility,[23] such acceptance can be regarded as the first step on the road to rehabilitation.[24] Applying this theory, an offender who pleads guilty requires less time to be completely rehabilitated than one who goes to trial maintaining his innocence.[25] Because this is the only punishment theory that justifies differential sentencing, it too is a popular response to the assertion that such sen-

---

23. *See, e.g.,* U.S. Sentencing Guidelines Manual § 3E1.1 (U.S. Sentencing Comm'n 2016). "Entry of a plea of guilty prior to the commencement of trial combined with truthfully admitting the conduct comprising the offense of conviction, and truthfully admitting or not falsely denying any additional relevant conduct for which he is accountable under § 1B1.3 (Relevant Conduct) (*see* Application Note 1(A)), will constitute significant evidence of *acceptance of responsibility* for the purposes of subsection (a)" (emphasis added).

24. McKune v. Lile, 536 U.S. 24, 47 (2002) ("Acceptance of responsibility is the beginning of rehabilitation."); Blackledge v. Allison, 431 U.S. 63, 71 (1977); Richard Klein, Due Process Denied: Judicial Coercion in the Plea Bargaining Process, 32 Hofstra L. Rev. 1349, 1408 (2004); Hooten v. State, 442 S.E.2d 836, 840 (Ga. App. 1994) ("[G]uilty pleas are recognized as a significant step toward rehabilitation ..."); Jeff Palmer, Abolishing Plea Bargaining: An End to the Same Old Song and Dance, 26 Am. J. Crim. L. 505, 516–17 (1999); Comment, The Influence of the Defendant's Plea on Judicial Determination of Sentence, 66 Yale L.J. 204, 209–10 (1956).

25. In the words of the Supreme Court, "[W]e cannot hold that it is unconstitutional for the State to extend a benefit to a defendant who in turn extends a substantial benefit to the State and who demonstrates by his plea that he is ready and willing to admit his crime and to enter the correctional system in a frame of mind that affords hope for success in rehabilitation over a shorter period of time than might otherwise be necessary." Brady v. United States, 397 U.S. 742, 753 (1970).

tencing amounts to punishment for exercising the right to trial. Unfortunately, the theory breaks down when confronted with the reality of why defendants in criminal cases *actually* plead guilty.

It will surprise no one who has been a defendant in a criminal case, has represented a criminal defendant, or understands human behavior that the vast majority of defendants who plead guilty do so in order to avoid the virtual certainty of the harsher sentence they will receive if convicted at trial. While it is certainly possible (although undoubtedly rare) that the defendant is pleading guilty because he wishes to begin to mend his evil ways, such a reason is likely to be secondary to the understandable human desire to avoid prison or spend the least amount of time there as possible.

Those wishing to disregard this reality must still confront the corollary of the assertion that pleading guilty is the first step on the road to rehabilitation. That is: the decision of those charged with crimes to go to trial manifests a lack of rehabilitative likelihood. In fact, people opt to claim their trial-related rights for a variety of reasons. These reasons generally relate to their belief that they will be acquitted at trial or convicted of a lesser offense. Sometimes this belief is based on a perceived legal impediment to their conviction, such as the government's reliance on a search or seizure of dubious Fourth Amendment legality. Sometimes defendants believe they are actually innocent of the crimes for which they have been charged. Are such individuals likely to need more time to be rehabilitated because they wish to claim the protections afforded to them by law? For example, if a defendant listens to his attorney's advice that the government will not be successful in obtaining a conviction against him, is he less able to be rehabilitated than one who ignores such advice and pleads guilty?

The notion that acknowledging one's responsibility for a negative behavior is the first step toward addressing, correcting, and curing that behavior certainly has support in literature and in practice.[26] The Twelve Step Program, made famous by Alcoholics Anonymous, has this principle as one of its foundations.[27] But that declaration must be sincere and directed — in other

---

26. *See, e.g.,* John Coleman, Take Ownership of Your Actions by Taking Responsibility, Harv. Bus. Rev. (Aug. 30, 2012), https://hbr.org/2012/08/take-ownership-of-your-actions; Seth A. Grossman, A Thin Line Between Concurrence and Dissent: Rehabilitating Sex Offenders in the Wake of *McKune v. Lile*, 25 Cardozo L. Rev. 1111, 1116 (2004); *McKune*, 536 U.S. at 33–34; Raffaele Rodogno, Shame and Guilt in Restorative Justice, 14 Psychol. Pub. Pol'y & L. 142, 143, 154 (2008); John Sabini & Maury Silver, In Defense of Shame: Shame in the Context of Guilt and Embarrassment, 27 J. Theory Soc. Behav. 1, 1–15 (1997).

27. Alcoholics Anonymous World Services, Inc., Alcoholics Anonymous 58–60 (3d. 1976).

words, the desire to correct one's behavior must be the basis, the causative factor, that leads to engaging in the action taken by the subject. It stretches credulity and belies the experience of those engaged in the criminal justice process to believe that the overwhelming number of defendants who plead guilty do so primarily for any reason other than to obtain a benefit in sentencing.[28]

It is apparent then that neither rehabilitation nor any other traditional justification for punishment can be used to support differential sentencing in the plea bargaining/trial criminal justice process.

3. The sentencing judge learns significantly more about the defendant and the crime after trial than she knew during plea bargaining

Some cases have justified harsher sentences for criminal defendants who choose to go to trial because the sentencing judge learns of aggravating factors regarding either the crime or the criminal that she did not know at the time a plea would have been taken.[29] There are several problems with using this as a justification for differential sentencing. As with the first step on the road-to-rehabilitation justification discussed above, this theory rests on a largely flawed premise that belies what actually happens in most cases. Additionally, even if this argument has validity in certain instances, appellate courts too often accept the assertion that information learned at trial was the causative factor in the

---

28. Lloyd L. Weinreb, Denial of Justice 75 (1977). *See also* Defendants' Incentives for Accepting Plea Bargains: Common Reasons Why Defendants Enter into Plea Bargains, Nolo.com, http://www.nolo.com/legal-encyclopedia/plea-bargains-defendants-incentives-29732.html. The Supreme Court noted that "[f]or a defendant who sees slight possibility of acquittal, the advantages of pleading guilty and limiting the probable penalty are obvious — his exposure is reduced, the correctional processes can begin immediately, and the practical burdens of a trial are eliminated." Brady v. United States, 397 U.S. 742, 752 (1970). Even those believing themselves to have a significant chance of being acquitted at trial are incentivized to plead guilty because they know they are highly likely to receive a lower sentence by doing so than if convicted at trial. Jenia Iontcheva Turner, Judicial Participation in Plea Negotiations: A Comparative View, 54 Am. J. Comp. L. 199, 205 (2006).

29. Alabama v. Smith, 490 U.S. 794, 801 (1989); Morales v. State, 819 So. 2d 831, 834 (Fla. Dist. Ct. App. 2002) (noting that because the "trial court, at the time of sentencing, received greater information about the defendant's prior convictions and the extensiveness of this, the third attack on the victim, than was known to the court when the plea was discussed," the harsher sentence was upheld).

enhanced post-trial sentence without any specifics regarding what that information was or whether the information was available at the time of the guilty plea offer. Even when there is some attempt to identify the new information, the explanation of why it led to a significantly greater sentence than the guilty plea offer is often unconvincing.[30]

An example of this can be seen in the 2012 New York case of *People v. Blond*.[31] Blond claimed that the disparity between the final pre-trial plea offer of three-and-a-half years and his ultimate post-trial sentence of 22 ⅔ years of imprisonment plus 20 years of post-release supervision was punishment for exercising his right to trial. In rejecting the defendant's argument, the appellate court conceded that the disparity was "significant" but found no evidence "that the sentences were retaliatory or vindictively imposed as a penalty for defendant's exercise of his right to a jury trial."[32] In support of this conclusion, the court found that "the crimes are of a serious nature, they were committed against a backdrop of physical violence, they involved a vulnerable teenager who was living in defendant's household, he received less than the maximum

---

30. *See, e.g.*, Hampton v. Wyrick, 588 F.2d. 632, 633–34 (8th Cir. 1978). In *Hampton*, the court affirmed the federal district court's denial of a writ of habeas corpus in which the defendant had argued that he was punished for exercising his right to trial. *Id.* at 632. During plea negotiations, the prosecutor had offered Hampton 25 years in prison in exchange for a guilty plea, a sentence that the trial judge indicated was acceptable to him. *Id.* at 633. After rejecting the plea and being convicted at trial, the judge sentenced Hampton to 50 years in prison, double the length, or 25 years more, than what had apparently seemed appropriate to the judge during the plea negotiations. *Id.* In so holding, the federal circuit court noted that although the sentence was "unusual, there exists only speculation that it was vindictively imposed for petitioner's exercise of his constitutional right to a jury trial." *Id.* The court then accepted the basis offered by the state court for why the post-trial sentence was so much longer. *Id.* at 634. "It was within the statutory limits. Further, the trial judge testified at the hearing that he was influenced in the sentencing by the fact revealed at trial as to the vicious nature of the crime and defendant's record of 13 prior convictions." *Id.* at 633 (citations omitted) (quoting Hampton v. State, 558 S.W.2d 369, 371 (Mo. Ct. App. 1977)). That the sentence was within statutory limits sheds no light on the issue of whether the sentence was punishment for exercising the right to trial. No mention is made of whether the trial judge knew of the defendant's criminal record at the time of the plea, but it is hard to imagine the judge approved of a 25-year prison sentence at that time without such knowledge. The final justification for the enhanced sentence relies on the dubious proposition that the judge apparently was also unaware of the "viciousness" of the crime at the time of the plea in a case which involved armed robbery, the taking of a hostage, and the shooting of the defendant by a police officer. State v. Hampton, 509 S.W.2d 139 (Mo. Ct. App. 1974).

31. 96 A.D.3d 1149 (N.Y. App. Div. 2012).

32. *Id.* at 1153–54.

allowable sentence for rape in the first degree, and he has refused to take any responsibility for his conduct or exhibit any remorse."[33] It is hard to imagine that when the plea was offered, the prosecutor and judge were not aware of most of the factors used by the court above to justify the significantly harsher post-trial sentence. The defendant had been indicted on ten counts, including the forcible rape and sexual abuse of a 15-year-old girl. Additionally, he was charged with attempted assault with a brick on his wife, who was the victim's aunt, and property damage he caused to his wife's vehicle when he repeatedly drove his own vehicle into it. When he was arrested and taken into custody, he also caused property damage to a police vehicle "by shattering its window in a violent rage."[34] A pre-trial hearing revealed that the defendant had engaged in previous domestic violence. While undoubtedly the trial judge learned more details about the crimes during the trial, it seems unlikely that such information could justify a prison sentence more than six times that which was offered as part of a guilty plea, given what the parties knew of the defendant and the crime at the time the plea was offered.

Finally, even if this justification applies in certain cases, those cases are likely to be the exception rather than the rule and do not come close to explaining the fact that post-trial sentences of criminal defendants are almost always more substantial than these individuals would have received had they pled guilty.

To understand why this defense of differential sentencing rests on a largely flawed premise, we need to examine the process by which most guilty pleas are entered along with what information about the defendant and the crime are normally available to the prosecutor, defense attorney, and judge before the plea is offered and accepted. Of course, each jurisdiction, and in fact each particular court and prosecutor's office, may have different amounts of material available to them at various times during plea negotiations.

For some minor criminal charges, prosecutors might have a boilerplate policy for plea offers, and therefore the specific details of the crime may not be known to them during plea negotiations.[35] For all other offenses, however,

---

33. *Id.* at 1154.

34. *Id.*

35. Gary Muldoon, Handling a Criminal Case in New York § 17:68 (2017–2018 ed., 2017) (noting that "[i]ndividual prosecutors' offices may have plea policies for various offenses, such as a ban on offering a plea to a lesser offense in a high blood alcohol DWI case, or restrictions post-indictment."); Hadar Aviram, et al., Check, Pleas: Toward a Jurisprudence of Defense Ethics in Plea Bargaining, 41 Hastings Const. L.Q. 775, 837–38 (2014) (quoting Telephone Interview by Deanna Dyer with Assistant Public Defender, Orange County, Calif. (Sept. 3, 2013)) (noting that plea offers for some charges, like a first-time DUI, are standard in the Prosecutor's office, and are not subject to deviation).

it would be the poor prosecutor who offers a plea bargain to a defendant without adequate knowledge of both the alleged offense and the defendant's criminal record. While the computer-generated records of the defendant's criminal history can have omissions or errors, they are generally accurate and likely have already been the basis for determining the defendant's bail and in some cases for what charges were brought. Similarly, when they offer pleas, prosecutors usually know most of the details of the crime charged. For example, not all rapes are the same. While every rape is a serious crime, some might warrant harsher sentences than others because of the degree of violence involved.[36] Of course prosecutors likely would have spoken to the rape victim or at least the investigating officer to learn this detail among others about the rape before determining the extent of the plea to offer the defendant.

It is equally obvious that in most cases no sensible judge would accept a plea of guilty to a lesser charge without knowing the facts of the case.[37] This is true even if the judge only commits herself to dismissing the higher charge as part of the plea deal. Where the judge makes a commitment to a sentencing range or agrees to a specific sentence as part of the deal, the degree to which the judge knows the facts of the case and the background of the accused is likely to be even greater.[38] Still, courts are reluctant to hold that the extra prison time a defendant receives pursuant to a trial conviction that follows the

---

36. This difference in the level of plea offered may stem from just the prosecutor's view of the case or it may be manifested in the law itself. *See, e.g.,* Md. Code. Ann., Crim. Law § 3-303 (West 2017) (rape in the first degree is defined as "vaginal intercourse with another by force, or the threat of force, without the consent of the other" with the use of a dangerous weapon, an infliction of serious injury on the victim, threatening or placing the victim in fear that the victim will be subject to death, suffocation, strangulation, disfigurement, serious physical injury, or kidnapping, committed while aided and abetted by another, or a rape committed in connection with a burglary); *id.* § 3-304 (rape in the second degree is defined as vaginal intercourse by force, threat of force, without the consent of the other, vaginal intercourse with a person who is cognitively impaired, or vaginal intercourse with a victim under the age of 14 when the person performing is at least four years older than the victim).

37. *See* Standards for Criminal Justice 14-1.6(a) (1999).

38. *See* Nancy J. King & Ronald F. Wright, The Invisible Revolution in Plea Bargaining: Managerial Judging and Judicial Participation in Negotiations, 95 Texas L. Rev. 325, 376–77, 379 (2016). Virtually all information that goes into determining the appropriate sentence for a defendant is available at the time that plea negotiations take place. Through interviews with prosecutors, defense attorneys, and judges, the authors describe how judges learn critical information about the defendant at this time. Computer records usually detail the criminal history of the defendant, and the defense attorneys customarily provide personal information about their clients that may be used to mitigate a plea offer.

rejection of a plea offer guaranteeing a lighter sentence is punishment for that rejection. Such a case is the U.S. Court of Appeals decision in *Frank v. Blackburn*.[39] Jimmy Frank was convicted of the armed robbery of a restaurant by a jury in Louisiana state court and sentenced by the judge to 33 years in prison. Prior to the jury verdict, the prosecutor, defense attorney, and judge had engaged in plea negotiations on at least two separate occasions. The first time was before the trial and the second was during the trial when the court took a recess in the middle of the prosecutor's case. On both of those occasions, the judge indicated he would sentence the defendant to 20 years in prison should the defendant plead guilty. Frank challenged the additional 13 years he was sentenced to after the jury verdict, claiming it was punishment for exercising his right to trial. In denying Frank's claim, the circuit court sitting en banc (all the judges in that circuit) reversed the judgment of a panel in that circuit agreeing with Frank's claim. The court did so largely because it found that what the trial judge learned about the defendant during the trial was significant and therefore demonstrated the additional time he imposed was not punishment for rejecting the plea offers. Let's examine that claim.

At the preliminary hearing, the victim of the robbery along with another eyewitness and the arresting officer testified before the same judge in a manner that turned out to be "virtually identical to their testimony at trial."[40] So in addition to the witness identifications, there was testimony from the arresting officer that Frank matched the description of the robber, that he was apprehended a short time after the robbery seven blocks from where it occurred, and that he possessed the exact dollar denominations taken in the robbery. Then, before trial at a conference involving the prosecutor, defense attorney, and judge, the prosecutor "systematically presented the factual merits of this case against the defendant to the Judge, together with the pertinent criminal history of the defendant."[41] It stretches credulity to think that with all this information the judge did not have a very good sense of both the crime and the defendant when he offered a 20-year sentence in exchange for Frank's guilty plea. But there is more. Once the trial started and the victim testified consistent with her previous testimony, the judge renewed his offer of a 20-year sentence in exchange for the defendant's plea of guilty. The defendant again rejected the plea offer and was convicted by the jury.

---

39. 646 F.2d 873 (5th Cir. 1980).
40. 605 F.2d 910, 911–12 (5th Cir. 1979).
41. *Id.* at 915.

In rejecting the decision of its panel, the United States Court of Appeals for the Fifth Circuit accepted the trial judge's assertion that "the Court had more graphic, descriptive, and detailed evidence of the crime and the character of the individual at the time of sentencing."[42] As the trial judge never indicated what was more graphic, descriptive, or detailed about the trial testimony than the "virtually identical" testimony at the preliminary hearing and the prosecutor's recitation about the crime and defendant at the two negotiation sessions, the appellate court apparently thought it had better hedge its bet and offer another reason for its holding. "Even if the trial provided no additional evidence of character, the mere fact that Jimmy Frank refused to acknowledge his guilt and showed no willingness to assume responsibility for his conduct may have led the judge to conclude that this defendant lacked potential for rehabilitation thus justifying the imposition of a greater sentence than that offered in exchange for a guilty plea."[43] So even though Frank had not displayed this so-called assumption of responsibility that indicates a heightened chance of rehabilitation when he was offered the plea before trial, had he pled guilty during the trial after hearing the victim tell the jury that he robbed her at the point of a gun, the court apparently believed that this would have indicated that he was still more likely to be rehabilitated than evidenced by his decision to continue with the trial. As with many courts before and after the decision in *Frank*, this court largely disregarded the record concerning what the judge knew when offering the guilty plea-based sentence twice and preferred to engage in the potential-for-rehabilitation fantasy for a mid-trial guilty plea than to acknowledge that the extra time was punishment for Frank's insistence on a trial verdict.

What is clear is that no responsible judge wants to risk agreeing to a plea to a lesser offense and/or sentence than was embodied in the original charge if it turns out the offense was far worse than she knew. To support the assertion that the increase in sentences meted out after trial compared to those discussed or agreed to during plea bargaining is often due to the additional information judges find out about the crime or the accused during trial requires a belief that judges customarily act irresponsibly in accepting pleas of guilty without adequate knowledge of the critical elements that go into the sentencing decision—the nature of the crime and the defendant's background.

While there are undoubtedly certain situations in which a judge learns something about the crime or the criminal during trial that leads the judge to think the defendant deserves a harsher sentence than she was willing to accept

---

42. 646 F.2d at 885.
43. *Id.*

during plea negotiations, it defies credulity to imagine that the frequency of such situations comes anywhere near explaining why nearly all post-trial sentences are more severe than any proposed plea agreements.

4. Enhanced sentences for those defendants convicted after trial is an essential and inevitable part of the negotiation process that is plea bargaining

The final defense of differential sentencing rests on the recognition that plea bargaining is a negotiation, and the essence of a negotiation is that each side tries to obtain the best outcome possible. In most cases, for the prosecutor that means obtaining a plea of guilty and a sentence commensurate with her assessment of the crime and the criminal. For the defendant, that usually means pleading to the least serious charge and receiving the most lenient sentence possible. Obviously, this often translates to the prosecutor negotiating for a plea that authorizes more prison time and the defendant seeking less time. An essential ingredient in this negotiation is the option each side has to take the case to trial should the negotiations fail to reach an agreed-to plea of guilt.[44] For the prosecutor, this risks the possibility of the defendant's being acquitted. For the defendant, this risks a trial conviction with the almost inevitable result that he will receive a sentence harsher than was offered during the plea negotiations.

In *Bordenkircher v. Hayes*, referenced above, the Supreme Court used this reasoning to dispute the notion that the substantially harsher sentence that Hayes received after his re-indictment and conviction, compared to what was offered during plea negotiations, was in fact punishment for exercising his right to trial.[45] In the Court's words, "in the 'give-and-take' of plea bargaining, there is no such element of punishment or retaliation so long as the accused is free to accept or reject the prosecution's offer."[46] In other words, the process surrounding the decision to plead guilty or go to trial is a gamble for the accused. If you take the gamble, are convicted at trial, and receive a harsher sentence than if you had pled guilty, you cannot come back and say you were punished for that decision.

---

44. Of course, the defendant without the acquiescence of a quid pro quo from the prosecutor or the judge can plead guilty to all the charges he faces, thus eliminating the possibility of a trial. As there is no tangible benefit for their doing so, very few defendants plead guilty in such a manner.

45. 434 U.S. at 362–65.

46. *Id.* at 363.

Nine years before the decision in *Hayes*, the U.S. Court of Appeals for the D.C. Circuit used similar reasoning in *Scott v. United States*.[47] After wisely rejecting the benefit/punishment dichotomy discussed above, Judge David Bazelon offered the following alternative argument for why differential sentencing is not punishment for exercising a constitutional right:

> Superficially it may seem that … the defendant who insists upon a trial and is found guilty pays a price for the exercise of his right when he receives a longer sentence than his less venturesome counterpart who pleads guilty. In a sense he has. But the critical distinction is that the price he has paid is not one imposed by the state to discourage others from a similar exercise of their rights, but rather one encountered by those who gamble and lose.[48]

Similar to what the Supreme Court later asserted in *Hayes*, Judge Bazelon justified differential sentencing as the acceptable price to be paid for taking the risk of going to trial. In so doing, the accused is seeking the reward of an acquittal with the understanding that he will likely receive a heavier sentence should the gamble prove unsuccessful and he loses at trial.

It is reasonable to assert that plea bargaining is a negotiation and that the negotiation inevitably involves a gamble for the accused should he reject the plea deal and be convicted at trial. The advantage of this acknowledgment is at least an implicit rejection of the other (unrealistic) defenses of differential sentencing in recognizing that this difference rests on the defendant's choice to go to trial. The problem lies in its failure to offer a reason — based in any traditional justification for punishment — that explains why defendants who choose the trial option receive or deserve heavier sentences than those who plead guilty. Unlike retribution, rehabilitation, deterrence, and incapacitation, gambling and losing has never been used as an explanation for how long the government should deprive a person of his or her freedom. Clearly the gambling-and-losing argument does not fall within any of the long-accepted sentencing justifications. And, as the Supreme Court said in *Graham v. Florida*, "[a] sentence lacking any legitimate penological justification is by its nature disproportionate to the offense."[49]

Therefore, unlike the other defenses offered, the "give-and-take of negotiations, gamble-and-lose" rationale is a realistic explanation for differential sen-

---

47. 419 F.2d 264 (D.C. Cir. 1969).
48. *Id.* at 276.
49. 560 U.S. 48, 71 (2010).

tencing. However, this explanation offers no sound sentencing basis for why those who go to trial should be imprisoned longer than those who plead guilty. As with all the other justifications, it results in a punishment for the exercise of a constitutional right.

C. That Plea Bargaining Punishes the Exercise of the Constitutional Right to Trial Does Not Make It Unconstitutional — The Government May Place a Price on the Constitutional Right to Trial If the Societal Need It Serves Is Significant

1. Examples of legally placing a price on the exercise of a constitutional right

After acknowledging that the harsher sentence a defendant receives after a trial conviction as opposed to the lighter sentence offered for a plea of guilty is punishment for exercising his right to trial, we must next determine if a person can be lawfully punished for exercising a constitutional right. Cases have held that with appropriate justification and limits, it is permissible to place a price on the exercise of a constitutional right. Some of these cases have involved broad constitutional protections, such as the right to free speech, the free exercise of religion, and the right to bear arms.[50] Notably, other such cases have dealt specifically with sanctioning the inevitable chill on the right to trial that stems from the plea bargaining process itself.[51]

It has been clear since the Supreme Court's holding in *Sherbert v. Verner* that even the most fundamental of constitutional rights, such as the free exercise of religion, can be restricted by government actions, where those actions meet the "compelling state interest" test.[52] In *United States v. Lee*, for example, the appellee claimed his Amish religious beliefs regarding pro-

---

50. *See* Sherbert v. Verner, 374 U.S. 398, 403 (1963) (free exercise of religion); Chaplinsky v. New Hampshire, 315 U.S. 568, 570–72 (1942) (free speech); District of Columbia v. Heller, 554 U.S. 570, 626 (2008) (right to bear arms).

51. *See, e.g.,* United States v. Jackson, 390 U.S. 570, 582 (1968); Corbitt v. New Jersey, 439 U.S. 212, 230 (1978).

52. *Sherbert*, 374 U.S. at 403.

viding for one's own family were violated by the requirement that he pay social security taxes.[53] The Court accepted the sincerity of his claim and concluded that this did involve an interference with the free exercise of his
religion.[54] Significantly, however, the Court said this determination began
rather than ended the inquiry into its constitutionality and reiterated that
such an interference is justified "[if] it is essential to accomplish an overriding
governmental interest."[55]

The government interests pertaining to the nature of the social security system that were enumerated in *Lee* bear a resemblance to the justifications for
the plea bargaining system as well. Specifically, the Court alluded to the nationwide breadth of the social security system, its size, and the benefits that
flow to individuals through social security. Finally, the Court noted that
without the requirement that people contribute to social security, the system
could not function, leading to the conclusion that the governmental interest
was "very high."[56] Similarly, plea bargaining, with the almost inevitable price
it places on the constitutional right to trial, is nationwide in its breadth. The
system by which courts dispose of criminal cases through plea bargaining is
not a unitary system like social security, but it is pervasive in the criminal
justice systems of all 50 states and the federal courts. And while the numbers
vary to some degree, it is generally accepted that close to 95% of criminal cases
are disposed of through plea bargaining. Lastly, it is hard to argue with the assertion that our modern criminal justice system could not function in its
current form without disposing of as many cases as it does through trial-avoid-
ing guilty pleas that save the system time and resources.

As with the free exercise of religion, a person can be punished for exercising
other fundamental protections embodied in the Bill of Rights. For example,
regarding the freedom of speech, the Supreme Court noted in *Chaplinsky v.
New Hampshire*, "[t]here are certain well-defined and narrowly limited classes
of speech, the prevention and *punishment* of which ha[ve] never been thought
to raise any Constitutional problem."[57] To so punish, the government must
show a compelling state interest.[58] Similarly, the exercise of other
constitutional rights can be punished when a strong government need exists

---

53. United States v. Lee, 455 U.S. 252, 255 (1982).
54. *Id.* at 257.
55. *Id.*
56. *Id.* at 258–59.
57. 315 U.S. 568, 571–72 (1942) (emphasis added).
58. Brown v. Hartlage, 456 U.S. 45, 53–54 (1982); First Nat'l Bank v. Bellotti, 435 U.S.
765, 786 (1978).

to do so.[59] Even as it held that the Second Amendment right to bear arms was a right possessed by individuals and invalidated laws that too broadly banned this protection, the Supreme Court in *District of Columbia v. Heller* emphasized that laws prohibiting and punishing the possession of weapons by felons or the mentally ill and those laws that bar the carrying of weapons into schools or government buildings were still lawful.[60] In interpreting and applying *Heller* to a recent Second Amendment challenge to a federal firearms law, the U.S. Court of Appeals for the Third Circuit asserted that *Heller* allows for laws not only deemed to be non-burdensome to the right to bear arms (i.e., for groups of people deemed to have forfeited this protection) but, significantly, also for those laws that do burden that right.[61] The requirement for upholding such laws is that they be shown to have the appropriate level of government need.[62]

In yet another area of constitutional protection, the Court allowed for limitations on the right to privacy.[63] After holding that a New York statute prohibiting the sale of contraceptives to minors was unconstitutional in *Carey v. Population Services International*, the Court observed that not all intrusions into privacy rights were invalid.[64] In the Court's words, "even a burdensome regulation may be validated by a sufficiently compelling state interest."[65]

2. Can the system place a price on the constitutional right to trial?

While courts, including the Supreme Court, have taken pains to avoid acknowledging that meting out harsher penalties for trials is indeed punishment for the exercise of a constitutional right, the Supreme Court has on at least one occasion come close to both acknowledging and defending this reality. In *United States v. Jackson*, the Court considered the constitutionality of the part

---

59. Strict scrutiny is the test used by the court to determine whether the government may constitutionally infringe upon an individual's fundamental rights. This requires the government to show there is a compelling state interest for the infringement, and that the governmental act is narrowly tailored to achieving said interest. Roe v. Wade, 410 U.S. 113, 155 (1973).

60. 554 U.S. at 626–27.

61. Binderup v. AG of United States, 836 F.3d 336, 344 (3d Cir. 2016).

62. *Id.* at 346.

63. Carey v. Population Servs. Int'l, 431 U.S. 678, 684–85 (1977).

64. *Id.* at 685–86.

65. *Id.* at 686; *see also Roe*, 410 U.S. at 155.

of the Federal Kidnapping Act that provided for the sentence of death only when the defendant was found guilty by a jury.[66] In other words, the accused was not subject to capital punishment under this statute if he pled guilty or was convicted after electing a trial before a judge only.

After rejecting the government's various arguments that disputed the above meaning of the Act, the Court focused on why such a sentencing scheme was unconstitutional. In so holding, the Court concluded that the "inevitable effect of any such provision, is of course, to discourage assertion of the Fifth Amendment right not to plead guilty and to deter exercise of the Sixth Amendment right to demand a jury trial."[67] The Court did not, however, rest its decision on the existence of this effect alone and regarded as insignificant both whether this effect was intentional or collateral and whether the statute coerced or merely encouraged the defendant to forego his right to a jury trial. Instead, the Court emphasized that the government's right to "chill" the exercise of such constitutional rights depended on whether that chilling was "needless."[68] Later in the opinion, after recognizing the government's claim that the goal of the statute was to mitigate the application of the death penalty in kidnapping cases, the Court alluded to other ways such a goal could be achieved without punishing a defendant for exercising his right to a jury trial. The Court noted that, "[w]hatever the power of Congress to impose a death penalty for violation of the Federal Kidnaping Act, Congress cannot impose such a penalty in a manner that *needlessly* penalizes the assertion of a constitutional right."[69] The obvious implication to be drawn from the Court's reference on two occasions to the inability of the government to chill or penalize the exercise of a constitutional right needlessly is that such penalizing can occur if the government has a need to do so. Such an approach is consistent with the Court's holdings in the cases discussed above dealing with the right to free speech, to bear arms, privacy, and the free exercise of religion.

The task then is to discern whether the penalty meted out by the almost inevitably harsher sentence the defendant will receive because he chose to exercise his constitutional right to a trial is needless. The first logical step in this assessment is to recognize the usual cause-and-effect relationship in the decision to choose or forgo the right to trial. This requires acknowledging that the vast

---

66. 390 U.S. at 570–71 (1968).

67. *Id.* at 581; *see also Corbitt*, 439 U.S. at 218 (wherein the Court made clear, specifically in connection with plea bargaining, "that not every burden on the exercise of a constitutional right, and not every pressure or encouragement to waive such a right, is invalid.").

68. *Jackson*, 390 U.S. at 582.

69. *Id.* at 583 (emphasis added).

majority of defendants who plead guilty do so because they have been promised or have reason to believe they will receive a charge and/or sentencing reduction if they forgo their right to a trial. In other words, they believe, and almost always with good reason, that they will receive a harsher sentence if their conviction comes from a trial and not a guilty plea. Aside from exceptional circumstances, it would be the foolish defendant who pleads guilty and the incompetent defense attorney who recommends he do so without this belief.[70] Why give up the chance for an acquittal, even if slight, if the defendant derives no meaningful benefit for doing so? Once this cause-and-effect relationship is accepted, the discussion must turn to whether there is a justification, a need, for imposing this penalty on the decision of whether to choose a trial.

3. Balancing the positive and negative aspects of plea bargaining should help to determine its constitutionality

While many have leveled reasonable criticisms of the plea bargaining systems in place almost everywhere in the United States,[71] a strong argument can be made that plea bargaining, in some form, is necessary to the functioning of criminal justice in our courts.[72] The most obvious and most often mentioned need for plea bargaining relates to the limited resources available to handle the thousands of criminal cases that pass through American courts on a daily basis. The vast majority of criminal cases are disposed of without trials and most of these dispositions derive from plea bargaining. Outlawing plea bargaining and the differential sentencing inextricably linked to it would result in many more trials. Using the generally accepted figure that close to 95% of criminal cases are disposed of through plea bargaining, the system would have to accommodate up to 19 times the trials it already conducts now. Given the added time it takes to do trials, the additional manpower necessary, space lim-

---

70. John G. Douglass, Fatal Attraction? The Uneasy Courtship of *Brady* and Plea Bargaining, 50 Emory L.J. 437, 447 (2001); *see also* Albert W. Altschuler, The Defense Attorney's Role in Plea Bargaining, 84 Yale L.J. 1179, 1205 (1975).

71. *See, e.g.*, Stephen J. Schulhofer, Plea Bargaining as Disaster, 101 Yale L.J. 1979 (1992); Douglas Guidorizzi, Should We Really "Ban" Plea Bargaining?: The Core Concerns of Plea Bargaining Critics, 47 Emory L.J. 753, 767–72 (1998); Note, The Unconstitutionality of Plea Bargaining, 83 Harv. L. Rev. 1387 (1970).

72. Jeff Palmer, Abolishing Plea Bargaining: An End to the Same Old Song and Dance, 26 Am. J. Crim. L. 505, 512 (1999); *see also* Warren Burger, The State of the Judiciary–1970, 56 A.B.A. J. 929, 931 (1970).

itations, other trial expenses such as the use of expert witnesses, and the inevitable appeals that follow trials, the allocation of resources needed to try all criminal cases that are now pled out would be monumental.[73] Simply put, we could not afford to try these cases.[74]

While the resource issue dominates any discussion of the benefits of plea bargaining, other benefits of the plea bargaining system should not be ignored. Disposing of cases through pleas is more likely to bring about the desired goal of prompt justice than is the often delayed trial process, complete with appeals, possible reversals, and retrials. Additionally, the reduction in court dockets that results from this quick resolution of cases via guilty pleas allows those cases that should go to trial to be tried more expeditiously.[75] While, as discussed above, the motivation for the vast majority of defendants who plead guilty is to obtain a milder sentence, such pleas can at least offer a quicker path to rehabilitation programs for defendants wishing to take advantage of them.

Many victims understandably wish to avoid having to testify at a criminal trial. To go through what are often painful and, in certain cases, very private details of a crime in a courtroom filled with strangers can be a traumatic experience. Plea bargaining allows witnesses, especially victims, to avoid what for most is an unwanted time commitment and, for many, an indignity. Often the government's decision to offer one defendant a lenient plea assures that this defendant will testify against, or at least provide information about, others involved in criminal activity. Usually this information serves the valuable goal of implicating those higher up in the criminal chain or those who were the primary participants in a given crime. Finally, a plea of guilty sometimes allows for a more appropriate disposition of a criminal case than would a verdict of

---

73. Santobello v. New York, 404 U.S. 257, 260 (1971) ("If every criminal charge were subjected to a full-scale trial, the States and the Federal Government would need to multiply by many times the number of judges and court facilities."). See also John H. Blume & Rebecca K. Helm, The Unexonerated: Factually Innocent Defendants Who Plead Guilty, 100 Cornell L. Rev. 157, 164 (2014), in which the authors assert, "[i]t is almost universally accepted by the participants in the system that there is not enough personnel, court time, or funds to try every case, or for that matter even any significant percentage of cases."

74. In 1970, then Chief Justice Warren Burger stated that "[a] reduction from 90 per cent to 80 per cent in guilty pleas requires the assignment of twice the judicial manpower and facilities ..." and "[a] reduction to 70 per cent trebles this demand." Burger, *supra* note 72 at 931.

75. *See* Steeve Mongrain & Joanne Roberts, Plea Bargaining with Budgetary Constraints, 29 Int'l Rev. L. & Econ. 8, 10 (2009) (arguing that plea bargaining allows more resources to be devoted to cases that go to trial).

guilty or not guilty on a higher charge.[76] Take, for example, a defendant facing murder charges stemming from a fight who is claiming that he acted in self-defense. The jury's verdict of guilty of murder, because it did not accept his defense, or a verdict of not guilty of all charges, if it did, may not be as just an outcome as the manslaughter charge he was permitted to plead guilty to.

In determining whether the burden placed on the exercise of the right to trial by the use of differential sentencing is needed, courts should also pay attention to the negatives that flow from our current system. The goals of the adversary system, complete with its protections — the right to confront and cross-examine witnesses, the presumption of innocence, the requirement of proof beyond a reasonable doubt, and the right to a jury trial — are largely negated in practice by the overwhelming use of plea bargaining. As discussed above, the differential sentencing connected inextricably to plea bargaining punishes the exercise of the constitutional right to trial, which even if lawful is not desirable. Some commentators assert that with the threat of increased prison sentences for defendants who elect a trial, no plea of guilty is truly voluntary and all involve an unacceptable level of coercion. In a recent article, for example, Professor Donald Dripps compared the pressure on a criminal defendant to plead guilty when facing a long sentence of imprisonment with that of someone threatened with the whole spectrum of "enhanced interrogation" techniques for 72 hours in order to obtain information. These techniques would include "sleep deprivation," "simulated drowning," and "nonmedical rectal rehydration." Dripps's conclusion was that "the threat of forty-years imprisonment has more power to induce cooperation than seventy-two hours of torment."[77]

Disposing of so many cases so quickly invites a reduction in the time spent by attorneys in researching and preparing a case and, therefore, often results in a reduction in the quality of legal representation afforded to criminal defendants.[78] In many cases where a plea of guilty is negotiated, a search in violation of the Fourth Amendment, a statement taken in violation of the Fifth or Sixth Amendments, or an unreliable identification procedure done in vio-

---

76. Notes, Ursula Odiaga, The Ethics of Judicial Discretion in Plea Bargaining, 2 Geo. J. Legal Ethics 695, 697 (1989) (arguing that plea bargaining allows for personalized sentences which reflect the circumstances of each offender's individual case).

77. Donald A. Dripps, Guilt, Innocence, and Due Process of Plea Bargaining, 57 Wm. & Mary L. Rev. 1343–45 (2016).

78. Molly J. Walker Wilson, Defense Attorney Bias and the Rush to the Plea, 65 U. Kan. L. Rev. 271, 293–95 (2016); Rodney J. Uphoff, The Criminal Defense Lawyer as Effective Negotiator: A Systemic Approach, 2 Clinical L. Rev. 73, 78–81 (1995).

lation of due process is never litigated or even uncovered. The result of this is a reduction in the deterrent impact of the exclusionary rule on police officers for committing such violations.

Finally, although there are benefits to avoiding the testimony of victims in many trials, there are genuine concerns about avoiding the transparency of public trials in so many cases.[79]

Of course, considering and weighing the benefits derived from the system of plea bargaining against its disadvantages involves difficult, sometimes painful acknowledgments and decisions. These discussions can largely be avoided with bromides such as the one claiming that everyone wins from a plea/trial system that offers benefits to many and punishments to none. It is hardly surprising, therefore, that judges are reluctant to admit that they are punishing a defendant for his exercise of a constitutional right. To acknowledge this reality, however, contributes not just to the intellectual honesty of decisions concerning plea bargaining, but also opens the door to more tangible benefits.

---

79. Fred C. Zacharias, Justice in Plea Bargaining, 39 Wm. & Mary L. Rev. 1121, 1178–81 (1998).

Chapter III

Role of the Prosecutor

Litigation in the criminal justice system typically commences with the actions of the prosecutor and so shall our examination of the roles of each of the parties involved in plea bargaining. The influence of the prosecutor in plea bargaining begins with the decision whether to bring charges and then of equally critical importance, the decision as to what charges to bring. At some point or points during the process, the prosecutor typically makes an offer to the defendant, whereby if the defendant pleads guilty, the prosecutor will take some action that is of benefit to the defendant. In most cases, this takes the form of a reduction or dismissal of some of the charges faced by the defendant or a recommendation regarding the defendant's sentence length.[1] Unless the defendant pleads guilty to all the charges he faces without any concession or recommendation from the prosecutor (an exceedingly rare event unless motivated by some sentencing assurance from the judge), no plea can take place without the approval of the prosecutor. With such authority, the prosecutor wields enormous power over the nature of any plea agreement. This chapter will explore the motivations of prosecutors to engage in plea bargaining, the ways in which their actions during the criminal justice process impact plea agreements, and what limits, if any, exist regarding these actions.

---

1. Other benefits can include a recommendation as to where the defendant should serve any prison sentence, allowing the guilty plea to cover other outstanding charges faced by the defendant, permitting the defendant to delay the beginning of his prison sentence, or avoid prison altogether through a sentence of probation.

A. Motivations for the Prosecutor to Bargain

1. Caseload management

The basic motivation of prosecutors to attempt to settle most of their cases through guilty plea agreements rather than trials relates to the substantial resource savings such agreements produce. Trials often require enormous expenditures of time and money from all the parties to the criminal justice process. Given the high volume of criminal cases, especially in some urban areas (there are fewer cases in rural areas but also fewer prosecutors to deal with them as well), prosecutors have to settle the vast majority through guilty pleas in order to have the time to try those cases that cannot be settled for one reason or another. When I was assigned to prosecute felony cases in New York City, I had upwards of 100 files that I was responsible for at any given time. The time that would be required to take all those cases through hearings, witness interviews, researching, drafting and responding to legal motions, preparing for trial, conducting the trial itself and handling the appeal that inevitably follows a conviction at trial would have been measured in multiple years not months. Factor in the time and effort of the police officers involved in the case filling out documents, locating evidence, questioning witnesses, and testifying at various court proceedings (time perhaps better spent on the streets or investigating unsolved cases), and the government's impetus to settle most cases is clear.

2. Doing justice

While understandably this resource saving is the motivation most often cited when discussing why they settle most cases through guilty pleas, it is a mistake to lose sight of other factors that influence prosecutors to plea bargain. The ultimate goal of all good prosecutors is to see the guilty convicted and the innocent exonerated. Proceeding with a specific criminal case in an ethical manner requires the prosecutor to believe that the defendant is guilty of criminal conduct.[2] In almost all cases, possessed with this belief, prosecutors

---

2. The ABA Model Rules of Professional Conduct require the prosecutor to "refrain from prosecuting a charge that the prosecutor knows is not supported by probable cause." Rule 3.8 (a), http://www.americanbar.org/groups/professional_responsibility/publications /model_rules_of_professional_conduct.html. State and Federal rules or policies often recommend limitations on prosecutions even when probable cause is present. See, for example, the comments to the U.S. Department of Justice Principles of Federal Prosecution, 9-27.200,

feel justice is best served through some sort of criminal conviction.[3] A guilty plea from the defendant removes the risk of an acquittal at trial and most of the risks of a successful appeal,[4] thereby assuring the prosecutor of a conviction she believes is warranted. If the government's case is weak, perhaps due to credibility issues surrounding an important witness or obstacles to the admission of a key piece of evidence, for example, the prosecutor's motivation to settle the case and avoid a possible acquittal is likely to be even stronger.

The facts of certain cases might lead to an entirely different reason why the prosecutor wishes to avoid a jury verdict. There are times when the defendant's actions might technically fall within the criminal statute under which he is charged, but the prosecutor may believe the defendant for one reason or another deserves to be convicted of something less serious. While the news media regularly details especially grisly real murders and we are flooded with

---

referring to this probable cause requirement as merely a "threshold" to the prosecutor's decision to initiate a prosecution.

3. There are of course cases in which prosecutors agree to dispositions of criminal cases that delay the ultimate decision about whether a conviction of the defendant through a guilty plea will be required or that avoid an actual guilty plea altogether. Such pleas generally occur when dealing with relatively minor crimes and condition an ultimate dismissal of the charges on the defendant's fulfilling a term of the agreement. Examples of such terms include restitution to the victim, performing public service, or just not being rearrested for a certain period of time. Additionally, there are now specialized adjudicatory bodies, such as drug courts, to which some cases are referred and have their own rules for disposition of cases.

4. Different jurisdictions have different rules for when guilty pleas can be appealed. Defendants alleging that their plea was obtained in a manner that was either unknowing, involuntary, or unintelligent can always appeal their guilty plea on constitutional grounds. Unknowing or unintelligent pleas can arise from actions by the prosecutor, defense attorney, or judge regarding their communication with the defendant about the elements of the crime he is pleading guilty to, the length of his sentence, or other issues related to the plea that are regarded to be of fundamental importance. Defendants who claim their guilty plea was involuntary typically cite the manner in which the plea was obtained by the prosecutor or discussed with them by their attorney or the judge. Additionally the defendant can appeal based on a claim that the prosecutor or the judge violated a term of the plea agreement. The vast majority of guilty pleas are not appealed, and those that are have a limited chance of success.

Beyond that, sometimes a plea agreement will include a term that specifically permits the defendant to file a certain legal motion or appeal a ruling already made on a motion. For example, if the defendant is charged with possession of drugs and the search that uncovered the drugs is of questionable legality under the Fourth Amendment, he may agree to a guilty plea only if he retains the right to challenge the legality of the search. If the search is determined to be invalid, the plea is withdrawn. The prosecutor of course has to agree to that term of the bargain, but for a number of reasons she may agree to do so.

Other than those three scenarios, a defendant generally waives his appellate rights once he pleads guilty.

fictional crimes in novels and movies consisting of complex plots related to intricately planned murders, the homicides most prosecutors deal with are far less dramatic. My final years as an assistant district attorney were devoted exclusively to handling homicide cases. Not infrequently we dealt with cases we referred to as "Bronx homicides." For example, two men would be shooting craps on the street. The sore loser would pick up his beer bottle and throw it at the head of the winner. If the bottle missed its target, the winner might retrieve the bottle and throw it back at the loser. As the winner is not only a better dice thrower but also a better pitcher than the loser, this time the bottle hits the head of its target and kills the repeat loser. The "winner" might now be charged with intentional murder. He threw the bottle at the head of the loser, arguably intending to kill him. The possible claim of self-defense or justification was not available to the winner under the law, and a jury could lawfully convict the defendant of murder.

When considering how to handle such a case, I could not get out of my mind other murder cases in my files. One involved a woman who was killed to prevent her from identifying the man who raped her, another the owner of a bodega who was shot in the head during a robbery. Not to minimize the loss of life in the bottle-thrower case or any homicide, but to me that case did not warrant the same penalty as the two crimes described immediately above. If the bottle thrower case went to trial, it was possible the jury could convict of a lesser degree of homicide, but you never know what a jury will do. In such a case, a plea to a lower level of homicide, say a degree of manslaughter, is a better way to assure a just disposition of the case.

Another example of a prosecutor using plea bargaining to achieve what he regards as a just result involves a case where, for one reason or another, the defendant deserves a degree of sympathy. I prosecuted a case of a man who while driving drunk smashed into a pole, killing his wife and child who were passengers in the car. He faced serious manslaughter charges for recklessly causing the death of two people. He was clearly guilty of those charges and responsible for the deaths. As everything about him and the case indicated, he was also crushed emotionally by the accident and the family members he lost due to his own misconduct. Allowing him to plead guilty to a lesser degree of negligent homicide with a reduced prison sentence seemed to be enough punishment when combined with his own feelings of intense pain.

3. Cooperation of the defendant

At times what motivates a prosecutor to plea bargain a case involves the cooperation of the defendant in one form or another. There are two situations in which the cooperation of the defendant most often becomes an aspect of the plea negotiations. The first involves the crimes for which this defendant is charged. If the prosecutor determines that this one defendant can help convict others charged with the crime through providing testimony at the trial of the codefendants or at times just revealing information about the crime (i.e., where the gun used in the crime or the proceeds of the robbery are located), she may be disposed to offer a generous plea deal or even a dismissal of charges in exchange.[5] This often happens when the prosecutor's case is not that strong without the testimony of someone who knows all the details of the crime or when the defendant is near the bottom of the hierarchical rung of the perpetrators of the crime and can inculpate those higher up. The second situation where the cooperation of the defendant is important to the prosecutor and thus a likely bargaining factor involves information the defendant has about other crimes charged or uncharged. If the mule, the person who transports the drugs, has information about those above him in the drug importation conspiracy, that information can serve to motivate the prosecutor to reduce or even dismiss the charges against the "mule." Of course, providing that information comes with certain risks to the defendant depending on the danger posed by those higher up in the criminal enterprise and therefore is unlikely to be provided without a meaningful concession from the prosecutor. Defendants choosing to cooperate rarely do so out of the goodness of their hearts, so offering the incentive of a sentence or charge reduction through a plea bargain is usually necessary to get that cooperation.

4. Respecting the view of the victim

Finally, prosecutors should always take into consideration the wishes of the crime victim before offering a plea bargain. In some crimes, such as drug possession, where there is no specific victim, or income tax fraud, where the government or some institution is the victim, this is not a significant concern for the prosecutor. In many other crimes, such as rapes, robberies, assaults, and white-collar fraud cases, there are likely to be victims who suffered substantial

---

5. In some jurisdictions, this benefit to the cooperating defendant may not be specified but is always available as a factor included among the prosecutor's negotiating tools. In others, it is established through statute. Federal prosecutors, for example, are given the ability to petition a court to sentence a defendant to a prison term lower than even the mandatory minimum term provided for the crime to which the defendant pleads guilty if he provides "substantial assistance or cooperation in the investigation of another person who has committed an offense." 18 U.S.C. § 3553(e).

harm due to the crime and hold strong views about what should happen to the person who caused that harm.

B. The Charging Function

1. The Double Jeopardy limitation

Prosecutors have enormous power regarding when a plea bargain is arrived at, the terms of that agreement, and what happens if the terms of that agreement are not fulfilled by the defendant. This power is exercised in several ways. Initially, the prosecutor chooses from a menu of possible charges to file against the defendant. The charges he chooses to file may warrant vastly different sentences than the charges he forgoes filing. He may opt to file one charge that covers the offense or several charges for the same offense. If he opts for filing multiple charges, the sentences for those charges can run concurrently, meaning the prison time for each crime is served simultaneously, or consecutively, allowing the sentence on the second charge to be added on to that of the first charge. Because of the significance of such a determination on the length of the sentence and the normally critical factor that sentence length plays in the defendant's decision whether to accept a plea offer, it is important that we examine the law and the standards governing the decision to charge multiple offenses. In doing so, we consider first the relevant protection against certain kinds of consecutive sentences embodied in the U.S. Constitution.

The Double Jeopardy Clause of the Fifth Amendment prohibits the government from convicting and/or sentencing a person more than once for the same criminal offense. In deciding whether such a double jeopardy claim arises, courts need to consider whether two convictions and two sentences are for the "same criminal offense." Doing so is not self-evident but instead requires an understanding of the Supreme Court's decision in its foundational case on double jeopardy, *Blockburger v. United States*.[6] *Blockburger* holds that two crimes are not the same (and therefore do not involve double jeopardy concerns) even if they both result from a single transaction when each contains a required element not present in the other. Examples of two common criminal incidents make clear the distinction between permissible consecutive sentences for the same incident and those prohibited by double jeopardy. Assume the defendant is charged with having used a cell phone to hit the victim, knocking

---

6. 284 U.S. 299 (1932).

him to the floor and causing a concussion. In the mind of the prosecutor this crime warrants a charge of Assault in the First Degree and Assault in the Second Degree. In this jurisdiction, Assault in the First Degree is defined as "when an individual with intent to cause serious physical injury to another person, causes such injury to such person or another through the use of a deadly weapon or dangerous instrument." Assault in the Second Degree is "when an individual with intent to cause serious physical injury to another person, causes such injury to such person or another." The difference between the two charges involves the use of a weapon or dangerous instrument. The prosecutor, wanting to ensure a conviction, may charge both degrees of assault knowing that a jury could find the cell phone to be a dangerous instrument or not. If the jury convicts of both charges, only the first-degree conviction will stand, and the defendant can be sentenced only on that charge. That is because the two assault charges will be deemed to be one offense under *Blockburger*. While first-degree assault has an element that second degree does not (use of a deadly weapon or dangerous instrument), second degree has no element not contained in first degree and both require the same intent, causation, and injury. The law regards Assault in the Second Degree to be a lesser included offense of Assault in the First Degree. The two convictions therefore will be deemed to have merged and the defendant can be sentenced only on the first-degree assault conviction.

Now take a case where the defendant sneaks in behind a woman carrying packages into her apartment and once inside forcibly grabs the packages from her before running out. The prosecutor charges the defendant with burglary and robbery. In this state, burglary is defined as "entering a dwelling without permission with the intent to commit a crime therein," while robbery is "the forcible taking of property from another person." Once again, the prosecutor charges both crimes, but this time the defendant's conviction on both charges will stand and he can be sentenced on both, with the sentences to run either concurrently or consecutively. This is because burglary and robbery each contain a required element that the other does not (for burglary unpermitted entry, for robbery forcible taking). In such an instance, the prosecutor's decision to charge both crimes and possibly others related to the one incident if such conduct occurred (i.e., malicious destruction of property, possession of a dangerous weapon, possession of a controlled substance, assault) can result in substantially different sentencing possibilities for the defendant and therefore different positions of the parties regarding an acceptable guilty plea.

2. Prosecutorial overcharging

Such a possibility raises the issue of prosecutorial overcharging and its impact on plea bargaining. At the outset, it is important to understand the difference between overcharging that involves a crime the prosecutor cannot prove and overcharging involving a crime that can be proven but is charged at least partly to obtain an advantage in plea negotiations. The first type is clearly unethical and when done should not only result in the dismissal of said charges but also in discipline for the prosecutor. The second type, while not strictly unethical, does damage to attempts to make the plea bargaining system fair.

Many prosecutors believe that the pressures on them to plea bargain cases, whether coming from resource demands or the other factors discussed in this chapter examining the motivations of prosecutors, pushes them into plea agreements that are disproportionally lenient when compared to the seriousness of the crime committed. Assume Mary Prosecutor has interviewed the 78-year-old victim of a robbery who was pushed to the ground during the incident and suffered some injury. The defendant in the case has a criminal record, the victim identified him at a line-up, and some of her property was found in the defendant's home. Mary believes all these facts justify a conviction with a prison sentence of approximately ten years. Mary can choose to indict the defendant for Robbery in the First Degree, a forcible taking involving serious physical injury, or Robbery in the Second Degree, a forcible taking involving some injury. In addition to the scrapes and bruises caused by being pushed to the ground, the victim now suffers from more pain in her hips and knees than she did before. Whether this constitutes serious injury under the law in that state is plausible, but previous cases charging first-degree robbery invariably involve injuries more serious than those suffered by the victim here.

A number of factors beyond merely the facts of the case and the background of the defendant may play a role in Mary's decision about what to charge here. For one of many possible reasons (ranging from inconvenience to fear of retaliation), the victim has expressed genuine reluctance to come to court to testify against the defendant. This will increase Mary's motivation to settle the case through a guilty plea rather than going through motions, hearings, and a trial. Additionally, Mary knows that as is generally true of all crimes, the higher the level of offenses charged, the greater likelihood of a plea to a concomitantly more serious offense accompanied by a heavier sentence. While the facts of each case and the history of each defendant are different and those issues play a primary role in how the case is plea bargained, the original charge the defendant faces also is significant in the bargaining process. Mary knows that in this jurisdiction, most first-degree robbery cases lead to pleas to second degree and sentences ranging from five to 15 years. Defendants accept such pleas to avoid the possible 25-year sentence for a first-degree conviction. If a defendant is charged with only second-degree robbery, however, his incentive to plead to that charge is reduced substantially, and to accept such an offer it likely would have to be accompanied by a recommendation of significant sentence reduction. That is why, as Mary knows, most defendants charged with second-degree robbery plead guilty to third-degree robbery with a punishment range of one to seven years. So if Mary believes that justice requires a sentence of ten years imprisonment for this defendant, it is easy to see why she will be tempted to charge him with first-degree robbery.

Mary's decision to charge a crime-level more serious than perhaps warranted by the incident is referred to as vertical overcharging. Vertical overcharging typically involves a case when the prosecutor believes charging the higher level crime may not be warranted for one reason or another but plans to use it as a bargaining wedge. The other form of overcharging, horizontal overcharging, occurs when the prosecutor multiplies the charges against the defendant to include other conceivable offenses occurring during the criminal incident, no matter how insignificant. Here too the prosecutor is seeking an advantage in plea negotiations but also a backstop for the jurors to convict the defendant of something if the case goes to trial and they have doubts about the principal charge.

Because Mary Prosecutor has probable cause to charge the crimes she chose here, the type of vertical or horizontal overcharging in this case is not unethical, but if done primarily for strategic purposes, it can be just as damaging to the plea bargaining process. Because deciding which crimes to charge is completely within the purview of the executive branch of government, courts have very limited authority to influence these prosecutorial decisions.[7] Combine this prosecutorial authority with the broad discretion that the criminal laws afford prosecutors regarding which and what level of crimes to charge and it is easy to see the potential for successful if unfortunate overcharging.

There is a clear systemic price to be paid for the substantial authority and discretion prosecutors have over the charging decision. It interferes with the designed hierarchy and the roles that our criminal justice system assigns to the relevant parties by increasing significantly the leverage prosecutors have over plea bargaining and sentencing. In so doing it places them closer to the

---

7. That authority can be exercised primarily when the defendant is able to show that there is a lack of probable cause to support a crime for which he is charged. In such a situation the court can dismiss the charge. This happens rarely.

role of adjudicator, a role plainly set up for the courts to play. This can be seen most clearly in decisions of the prosecutor to charge crimes with mandatory minimum or recidivist sentencing consequences, decisions that may significantly restrict the judge's sentencing options. Additionally, prosecutorial overcharging threatens to diminish the role properly played by legislatures in crafting criminal statutes and setting an appropriate range of sentences for each offense based on the anticipated appropriate application of those statutes to the facts of individual cases. Finally, in some cases it will increase the inevitable disparity between the sentence offered as part of a guilty plea and that received after conviction at trial. This may make the decision to opt for a trial even more of a punishment in and of itself.

Sometimes the prosecutor uses her broad charging authority not to bring charges in a certain case or an entire sector of cases. In 2019, Baltimore State's Attorney Marilyn Mosby announced that she would no longer prosecute people arrested for marijuana possession, regardless of the amount possessed or the history of the arrestee. Mosby justified her decision based on the recent attitudinal changes regarding marijuana, the need to preserve the resources to prosecute more serious crimes, and particularly on the devastating effect such prosecutions have had in minority communities. While these justifications are reasonable, it is not hard to envision the significant impact of such a decision on the police, the people in Baltimore, and the legislatively enacted marijuana laws based on the unilateral charging decision of a prosecutor.

C. Factors Governing What Plea to Offer

As 95% of criminal cases are disposed of without trial, almost all of those through some sort of plea bargaining arrangement, the prosecutor's decision about what to offer the defendant in exchange for his guilty plea is of fundamental importance not just to the defendant but to the victim and the entire criminal justice system as well. That this decision, even if modified after negotiations, plays a critical role in the defendant's life and likely his future freedom is obvious. Perhaps less obvious is the importance of the plea offer to other parties and institutions within the criminal justice system.

While state legislatures and the United States Congress set the range for sentences for each crime, how those sentences are applied in individual cases is impacted substantially by the prosecutor's plea offer. Take, for example, laws directed against driving under the influence of alcohol. Most states have established different offenses for such behavior, that difference often depending on the amount of alcohol in the blood. In the state of New York, for example, a person can be accused of either Driving While Ability Impaired (DWAI) or Driving While Intoxicated (DWI). The state legislature defined DWAI as requiring a blood alcohol content (BAC) of between .05 and .07%. When the BAC is .08% or above, that constitutes the more serious crime of DWI. The sentencing range for DWI is predictably considerably more punitive than for DWAI. The first DWAI conviction is considered a traffic infraction and not a crime. It is punishable by a fine of between $300 and $500 dollars and up to 15 days in jail. When a driver's BAC level meets the DUI standard of .08, that is considered a crime and has possible penalties of a fine between $750 and $1500 and jail time of up to one year. The administrative penalties for DWI are also significantly more stringent than for DWAI.[8]

Whether the defendant faces the sentence prescribed by the legislature for his conduct depends in large part on the plea bargain offered by the prosecutor. It is quite common but far from inevitable that the prosecutor will offer the defendant charged with DWI a plea to DWAI, giving him the ability to avoid facing the penalties determined by the legislature to fit his criminal behavior. Based on the motivations described above, there may be policies in some of the prosecutor's offices that dictate when such plea reductions should be offered. In determining what plea should be offered, prosecutors may consider how much above the .08 BAC standard the defendant tested, his level of cooperation with the police, his criminal history, and whether his impaired driving caused an accident. Some offices may not have a specific policy but leave it up to individual prosecutors to decide what factors should determine the plea offer. In any event, it is the prosecutor's decision whether to offer the lower plea as well as whether to make a sentence recommendation. In both instances, the decision by the prosecutor is likely to play a significant role in the sentence, substantially diminishing the significance of the sentence borders created by the legislature for those offenses.

In crimes for which there are no strict office policies regarding plea offers, the three factors that typically play the largest role in determining what benefits prosecutors offer in exchange for guilty pleas are the seriousness of the crime, the strength of the case, and the background of the defendant. Other factors, such as the wishes of the crime victim, public reaction to specific crimes, potential cooperation from the defendant, and a desire to offer leniency when deemed appropriate may also contribute to what plea the prosecutor offers in specific cases. The three factors of seriousness, case strength, and defendant

---

8. *See* N.Y. Veh. & Traf. Law § 1192.

background, however, tend to play a role in almost every case, and that role is usually primary regarding the plea offered.

1. The seriousness of the case

In determining what kind of plea to offer, prosecutors usually look first at what charges the defendant faces and the seriousness of the particular crime at issue. Not all armed robberies are the same, even if all those who commit that act are charged in the jurisdiction with the same crime of robbery in the first degree. Wielding a gun or a stick during a robbery may each be considered "using a weapon or dangerous instrument" as required by the statute, but the prosecutor might reasonably believe one crime is more serious than the other. A statute may make any theft of property valued at over $10,000 grand larceny, but a one-million-dollar theft is likely to be regarded as more serious than a $20,000 theft. If the consequences of the larger theft led to people losing their life savings, that too might impact the prosecutor's view of the case. In these situations, the same charges are likely to lead to different plea offers from the prosecutor, all other things being equal. In one especially notorious case, financial advisor Bernie Madoff bilked thousands of investors of billions of dollars through the use of a Ponzi scheme. For 25 years he was able to pay some investors with the money of other investors and illegitimately enrich himself by hundreds of millions of dollars. Upon pleading guilty in 2009 to 11 federal felonies, Madoff heard the testimony of many of his investors whose lives were ruined by his crimes. He was sentenced to the maximum his plea bargain allowed — 150 years of incarceration, far more than that received by most convicted of those crimes.[9]

At times, the sentencing possibilities contained in the prosecutor's guilty plea offer are limited by laws that require mandatory minimum sentences for certain crimes. Such sentences exist in both federal and state statutes. For example, there are mandatory terms of imprisonment for the use of a gun during the commission of a federal drug offense.[10] If the prosecutor offers a plea to such a charge, she knows that if the plea is accepted the judge will have to sentence the defendant to at least what those minimums require. To avoid the minimum sentence thus making the offer more likely to be accepted by the

---

9. Grant McCool & Martha Graybow, Madoff Gets 150 Years for Massive Investment Fraud, Reuters (June 28, 2009), https://www.reuters.com/article/us-madoff/madoff-gets-150-years-for-massive-investment-fraud-idUSTRE55P6O520090629.

10. 18 U.S.C. §924(c).

defendant, the plea offer will have to be to a different crime, perhaps just drug possession.

2. The strength of the case

While anyone claiming to know with certainty the result of a future jury trial is foolish, attorneys with experience in specific jurisdictions can often make educated guesses as to the outcomes. These guesses are based in large part on the strength of the cases for both the prosecution and the defense as measured by a number of factors. How impactful and credible will the witnesses for each side be? How clear is it that the demonstrated conduct of the defendant will make out the charges he faces? Is there physical or scientific evidence supporting the charges? Are there legal impediments regarding the admissibility of key pieces of evidence, and can those impediments be overcome?

Perhaps the victim of the robbery did not get a good look at the perpetrator owing to a number of factors, a problem that became apparent with her shaky and uncertain identification of the defendant at the lineup. The police officer may have seen the suspect of a jewelry store burglary right outside the store when the crime took place, but the defendant was not observed inside the store nor did he have any stolen property on him. The murder case against the defendant was many years old resulting in the disappearance of some witnesses and the faded memories of others. The key witness in the case now is the inmate who shares a cell with the defendant on another matter to whom the defendant bragged about his involvement in the old murder. Because of his own criminal background and the sentence reduction promised to him by the prosecutor in exchange for his testimony, the credibility of that witness before a jury will be substantially compromised. If the critical evidence against a defendant comes from his own confession, but the statement was obtained by the actions of officers that raise significant issues under the Fifth Amendment[11] or other constitutional protection,[12] the jury might never get to hear that confession. Does the prosecution's case rest on eyewitness testimony with no fingerprint or DNA evidence to support it?

Any or all these concerns and many others could weaken the government's case considerably and persuade the prosecutor to offer greater concessions

---

11. Miranda v. Arizona, 384 U.S. 436 (1966).

12. Such claims can arise under the Sixth Amendment as well. *See* Massiah v. United States, 377 U.S. 201 (1964). The statement may also be suppressed under the Fourth Amendment, for example, if it is the product of an illegal seizure of the defendant. *See* Dunaway v. New York, 442 U.S. 200 (1979).

during his plea negotiations with the defendant. While the seriousness of the crime forms the basis for what range of concessions to offer the defendant, these concerns and their potential impact on the likelihood of a conviction at trial could become the dominant factor as the prosecutor negotiates a possible guilty plea.

If the concern raises questions about the defendant's actual guilt as opposed to a purely legal impediment (i.e., the admissibility of contraband clearly possessed by the defendant but challenged as the product of an illegal search), another potential problem arises. In some cases where there are questions that relate to the guilt of the defendant, the weakness of the evidence corresponds to the likelihood that the defendant is not guilty of the crime. This weakness in the prosecutor's case and the accompanying lower likelihood of a conviction at trial will often lead to greater concessions in the plea offer. As the charge or sentence concession from the prosecutor becomes greater, the corresponding difference between the penalty contained in the plea offer and that which the defendant would be exposed to if convicted at trial becomes greater as well. This means the incentive for the defendant to accept the generous plea offer and avoid the risk of a far heavier sentence if convicted at trial is strong. With this greater incentive to avoid trial, there is a real danger that those wrongly charged with a crime may plead guilty. The idea that innocent people may plead guilty is one of the reasonable criticisms offered by opponents of plea bargaining. Of course, innocent people are convicted at trials as well, so such criticism of plea bargaining must be considered in that context.

The chapter on defense attorneys (Chapter IV) will explore in depth the conundrum posed by defendants who are actually innocent or at least claim to their attorneys they did not commit the crime, yet still wish to plead guilty. It is enough to recognize here that despite the clichés and noble sounding sentiments expressed by some courts about ensuring that innocent people should never plead guilty, the unfortunate truth is that at times it makes sense for them to do so. Imagine being charged with a serious crime you did not commit and facing a maximum of 25 years in prison if convicted. The prosecutor, aware that her chief witness has told different stories about the crime thus seriously weakening the government's case against you, is offering a plea with little or no prison time. Although you may believe the chance of your being convicted at trial is doubtful, is that a risk you want to take with the prospect of serving years in prison for the price of being wrong?[13]

---

13. To see 31 examples of innocent defendants who pled guilty, see When the Innocent Plead Guilty, Innocence Project (Jan. 26, 2009), https://innocenceproject.org/when-the-innocent-plead-guilty/.

3. The background of the defendant

Except in cases requiring specific sentences,[14] usually limited to mandatory life imprisonment for certain types of homicides, the prior criminal history of the defendant is almost always a critical factor in sentencing and thus in plea offers made by prosecutors.[15] Whatever theory or theories of punishment dominate the prosecutor's thinking as to what sentence the defendant should receive, criminal history plays a significant role in framing the plea offer. As discussed in the chapter on punishment for exercising the right to trial (Chapter II), those theories are retribution, deterrence, rehabilitation, and incapacitation. Arguably, a defendant who has a long criminal record deserves a harsher sentence (a retributionist's response), has shown he needs a harsher sentence to be incentivized not to commit future crimes (the concern of a deterrence advocate), is less likely and will take longer to correct whatever condition caused him the be an offender (the view of those whose sentencing approach looks to rehabilitation), and has shown he is more of a danger and therefore needs to be separated from the rest of society (incapacitation).

The use of the defendant's prior criminal history can be more than just a weighty consideration in the prosecution's decision about what plea to offer. The defendant's criminal record can prove to be a weapon in the prosecutor's arsenal in attempting to get the defendant to accept the plea offer. This is best seen through a consideration of recidivist statutes, common in jurisdictions throughout the country. Sometimes referred to as three-strikes laws when the statute requires three felony convictions to activate the heightened sentencing provisions, these laws allow or require substantial prison time based on the defendant's criminal history that go above that which the crime normally allows. The prosecutor's use of such statutes to influence the defendant to accept a plea offer can be seen quite clearly in the Supreme Court's decision in *Bordenkircher v. Hayes.*[16]

Charged in Kentucky with uttering a forged instrument involving $88.30, Hayes faced a penalty of two to ten years in prison if convicted. The prosecutor

---

14. Not to be confused with typical mandatory minimum sentences that, although containing a minimum sentence beneath which the court cannot go, usually allow for a range of sentences above the minimum.

15. Additionally, certain crimes, usually minor ones, are sometimes subject to a flat policy regarding the plea offers made by prosecutors. Possession of small amounts of marijuana are typical of low-level crimes where prosecutors often have a set policy regarding plea offers, uninfluenced by the defendant's prior record.

16. 434 U.S. 357 (1978).

offered to recommend a sentence of five years imprisonment in exchange for Hayes' guilty plea. Given the fact that Hayes had two previous felony convictions, the prosecutor apparently thought this to be a fair plea, especially considering Kentucky's Habitual Criminal Act requiring life imprisonment for those convicted of three felonies. To persuade Hayes of the wisdom of accepting the plea offer, the prosecutor informed Hayes that if the offer was rejected, he would re-indict Hayes under this recidivist statute. In response to the offer, either Hayes or his lawyer apparently made between one and three tragically bad assumptions that led to his rejection of the offer. The first assumption might have been that the prosecutor was bluffing and would not go through the trouble of re-indicting him and then trying him as a habitual felon. The prosecutor was not and he did. Hayes' second assumption was probably that he would be acquitted at trial and face no sentence. In fact he was convicted of the principal forgery charge by a jury and sentenced to life imprisonment. Hayes' third faulty assumption might have been that if the case got that far, a court would ultimately rule that the prosecutor's action in re-indicting him after the plea offer was rejected constituted improper prosecutorial vindictiveness and violated due process. The ruling by the Supreme Court laid waste to that assumption as well. The Court reasoned that what the prosecutor did was all part of the give-and-take of plea negotiations. In other words, caveat emptor — let the buyer beware. The law thus allows this, but the question remains as to whether such prosecutorial behavior is good for our criminal justice process. Posturing, negotiating, and the "you choose you lose" reasoning aside, Hayes received a sentence of life imprisonment for an $88.30 forgery. Should not such harsh sentences be reserved for those who commit very serious offenses, usually characterized by extreme violence?

4. The wishes of the crime victim

Unlike the United Kingdom or France where criminal prosecutions in certain instances can be brought by private parties (referred to as private prosecutions in the U.K. and citations directe in France), in the U.S. it is only the government in some entity that can prosecute a criminal case. That is why criminal cases in the U.S. have titles such as People vs. Defendant, State vs. Defendant, or United States vs. Defendant. In American civil cases, the title is usually some form of Plaintiff v. Defendant, but in criminal cases it is never Victim v. Defendant. The significance of this for the prosecution of a criminal case goes well beyond nomenclature. It is the prosecutor and not the victim who decides whether to bring charges, what those charges will be, and how the case will be handled throughout its prosecution. Among the most significant decisions made by the prosecutor rather than the victim is what offer to make the defendant in exchange for his guilty plea and how the negotiations related to that offer will proceed.

Still, it is the insensitive and unwise prosecutor who does not consult in one manner or another with the victim before offering a plea deal or agreeing to one after negotiations with the defense and possibly the judge. While the government is the party bringing the prosecution, in most criminal cases there is a victim who suffered harm as a result of the crime. At times, the harm to the victim is relatively minimal and he or she has no strong feelings about the final disposition of the case. At other times, where the victim suffered some sort of property damage, their concern may be only that any plea bargain include restitution for the expenses that were incurred because of the criminal act. There are times, such as drug possession cases, where there is no victim other than the government or the public in general. But there are crimes in which the victim suffered great harm and is deeply invested in having the case resolved in a way that recognizes and reflects his or her feelings. Victims of violent crimes, such as rape, assault, or armed robbery, may have lasting scars, emotional as well as physical, that they want addressed through what they believe is an appropriate disposition of their criminal case. The families of murder victims often believe that the taking of their loved one's life deserves the most serious punishment allowed under the law. People who have lost their life savings through various white-collar crimes (think, for example, of those committed by Bernie Madoff) are justifiably angry and often want those who took advantage of them to be punished severely. As a matter of simple justice, prosecutors owe it to crime victims to listen to the views of these victims and consider them as a factor in how the case will be handled.

Not only is it a matter of being sensitive to the wishes of the victim because it is the right thing to do, but it is also poor prosecutorial strategy to ignore the wishes and feelings of victims. Victims who are ignored often make poor or angry witnesses at trial. The kind of cooperation between witness and attorney that is critical for direct examinations to be most effective is likely to be lost when the witness is a victim unhappy with how she was treated by the prosecutor. In fact, the victim who is very upset with the prosecutor may choose not to cooperate with the prosecutor at any phase of the prosecution. Given that the victim is often a key witness for the government, this obviously reduces the chance of obtaining a successful conviction. Finally, angry victims are often not reluctant to make their feelings known to others. This includes friends, family, and the media at times. Aside from making prosecutors look bad, such publicity or even word-of-mouth communications can have a negative impact on future crime victims. For example, hearing how a particular prosecutor's office mistreated a crime victim might make future victims or witnesses reluctant to come forward or fully participate in the criminal justice process.

While it is important for the prosecutor to listen to and consider the views of the victim for these reasons, the ultimate decisions regarding how to conduct a criminal case rest with the prosecutor. As a matter of law, this is because the government and not the victim is the named party in any criminal case. There are, however, important policy reasons that support ultimate control of the case by the prosecutor. That the views and feelings of a crime victim should be taken into consideration is different than allowing such feelings to control the outcome of the case. Sentences in criminal cases are traditionally based on concerns about justice and accepted justifications for punishment, such as the proportionality of crime to punishment, deterring the commission of future crimes, the potential for the defendant to be rehabilitated, and the need to incapacitate to him in especially serious cases. The views of the victim can play a role in these concerns, but many other important factors go into such determinations as well. The anger the victim feels towards his or her predator may be justified, but the plea offer must take into consideration another essential party in the prosecution of a criminal case. That party is the ultimate consumer of the criminal justice system — the public at large.

Broadly speaking, the system and its consumers are concerned with justice in the many forms that justice can take. As indicated previously, criminal sentences have been meted out traditionally with four primary goals in mind. Retribution, when applied correctly, is designed to create a fair proportion between the seriousness of the crime and the harshness of the punishment. Deterrence aims to create a punishment that serves as an effective disincentive to prevent the defendant or others from committing similar crimes in the future. A sentence based on rehabilitation principles is designed to correspond to what it will take for the conditions that caused the defendant to commit the crime to be corrected or substantially diminished.[17] The final punishment goal of incapacitation, generally reserved for the most dangerous of criminals, is to separate them from society and thus prevent these individuals from committing terrible crimes in the

---

17. Related somewhat to rehabilitation is a relatively new approach focused on restorative justice. In restorative justice, the sentencing is deferred or transferred entirely to a group in the community, including at times the crime victim, who meet with the defendant on several occasions. The defendant listens to the reactions caused by his criminal behavior and hopefully develops an understanding of what his behavior caused. The goal then is to repair any damage caused by the crime and to work with the defendant on developing strategies for avoiding his reoffending.

future. There is much debate among legislators, judges, attorneys, and commentators about how, when, and to what degree these goals should be applied in sentencing. What is clear, however, is that sentences are almost always based on one or more of these punishment goals. Satisfaction of these goals in some form is what consumers of the criminal justice system demand and what every prosecutor must take into consideration when making a plea offer.

In considering these punishment goals, the plea offer the prosecutor makes to the defendant may upset the victim. Victims might believe the offer is too lenient and does not reflect the harm which they suffered as a result of the crime. Any responsible prosecutor will consider that harm before making a plea offer but should also weigh in other factors such as the strength of the case, the background of the defendant, and his potential cooperation, as discussed above. Other victims for various reasons encourage prosecutors to treat the defendant with more leniency in making a guilty plea offer. The prosecutor owes it to the victim to explain very clearly why a particular plea offer was made or agreed to. The victim still may not agree with the offer, but the wise and sensitive prosecutor does all he or she can to foster understanding if not agreement.

D. Issues Related to the Timing of the Plea Offer

One important strategic concern faced by both prosecutors and defense attorneys that tends to get overlooked by commentators involves the timing of the plea offer and any time limit imposed by the prosecutor for acceptance of the plea. The prosecutor's determination of just when to make a firm plea offer depends on a number of factors. One of those factors relates to the prosecutor's discovery requirements. States have different rules regarding discovery. Some require the prosecutor to make available to the defense a list of witnesses and a description, if not an examination, of tangible and other evidence at a fairly early point in the litigation process. Other jurisdictions postpone this requirement almost until the trial is commenced. Some prosecutors have adopted a policy of open file discovery, allowing the defense attorney access to almost all the information they have about the case early in the prosecution. Others provide discovery only regarding what state law requires and only when state law requires it.[18]

---

18. See and compare generally Federal Rules of Crim Procedure Rule 16, California Penal Code § 1054.7, and Minnesota Rules of Criminal Procedure 9.01.

All jurisdictions must provide any information of an exculpatory nature, that which tends to exonerate the defendant of the crimes with which he is charged. Based on the Supreme Court's decision in *Brady v. Maryland*,[19] failure to provide such information to the defendant is a violation of constitutional magnitude and could result in a reversal of any conviction as well as disciplinary action against the prosecutor. Examples of exculpatory evidence are the names of witnesses who suggested someone other than the defendant committed the crime, scientific tests identifying another person as the perpetrator, and a lineup or photo array in which a witness expressed doubt about the defendant being the offender or in which he selected another person. Additionally, information related to the credibility of a certain witness, such as an agreement with the government for lenient treatment of the witness in his own criminal prosecution in exchange for his testimony against the defendant, must be provided to the defense. What is less clear (as reflected in a division among state and federal courts) is just how long before trial must such exculpatory material be turned over to the defense and how the requirements of Brady are implemented.

There may be an advantage to the prosecutor in working out a guilty plea in the case before he is required to inform the defense of information that might make the government's case and therefore the prosecutor's bargaining position weaker. Beyond that, early discovery might allow the defense attorney to speak with government witnesses to give her a better assessment of how effective their testimony would be at trial. Knowledge of scientific test results the prosecutor plans to use allows the defense attorney to consult with her own experts about whether such testimony can be effectively minimized. On the other hand, if the information in the prosecutor's file demonstrates the overwhelming strength of the government's case, revealing it to the defense might increase the likelihood that the plea offer will be accepted. In either situation, timing the plea offer with discovery issues in mind may be of strategic importance to the prosecutor.

There are other concerns for prosecutors that could affect the timing of their plea offers that are rarely mentioned in judicial opinions but can matter a great deal in the real world. The prosecution of a criminal case often requires a victim or a witness to make a significant time commitment in order for the case to proceed. For example, it is not uncommon for a witness to be subjected to being interviewed initially by the police, having to participate in the drafting of a witness statement, appearing at identification procedures, testifying at var-

---

19. 377 U.S. 83 (1963).

ious preliminary hearings and in the grand jury, and spending time with the prosecutor to prepare for trial. The prosecutor may time his plea offer and the date required for acceptance to avoid some of these witness appearances.

Legal motions made by the defense can weaken or even result in the dismissal of certain cases. If, consistent with his ethical obligations, the prosecutor seeks to avoid these motions for strategic purposes or merely because he does not wish to put in the time and effort to respond to them, he may insist on the defendant accepting a plea offer by a certain time. As discussed in the chapter on defense attorneys, this timing can force the attorney into a difficult decision regarding whether to recommend the plea offer to her client before the time is right to do so.

E. Dealing with the Judge

Judges play a large role in the professional lives of prosecutors. They make important decisions in all criminal cases and invariably those decisions affect the prosecutor's likelihood of success in a given case. Understandably then, prosecutors want to stay on the good side of judges where that is possible. That desire not to irritate the judge is unlikely to affect the prosecutor's legal argument regarding the admissibility of evidence or his manner in presenting his case before a jury to make it as convincing as possible. In those situations, judges expect and therefore generally do not hold it against prosecutors that they will pursue the best strategic approach for winning their case, assuming that approach is not inappropriate. The dynamics are different in plea bargaining. When the judge suggests to the prosecutor that he modify his plea offer to make it more acceptable to the defense and therefore resolve the case without a trial, the prosecutor might feel some pressure to accede to the judge's wishes. Sometimes those suggestions are communicated in forceful ways and may even be accompanied by indications that if the case goes forward without a plea, the prosecutor's likelihood of a conviction may not be great. "Of course you can refuse to lower your plea offer as I suggest, but although I have not heard the motion yet, it seems to me that the search warrant here is of questionable validity." Hearing this from the person about to decide that motion might persuade the prosecutor to accept the half-a-loaf plea-deal suggestion from the judge.

As we have seen, plea bargaining affords the prosecutor vast discretion, and many judges expect the prosecutor to use that discretion to make "reasonable" accommodations to settle a case. What is reasonable to the judge of course may not be reasonable to the prosecutor, which at times, as in the example above, leaves the prosecutor in an uncomfortable position. Some prosecutors will not want the judge to view them as obstructionists to the efficient running of their courtrooms, which in the mind of some judges means disposing of as many cases as possible. This is especially true if the prosecutor appears before the same judge often. In smaller judicial systems, such as exist in many rural areas, the prosecutors appear before the same few judges almost all the time. But even as a prosecutor in New York City, my cases were assigned to a particular courtroom for the most part, and therefore I appeared before the same judge or set of judges quite frequently.

Possessed with substantial authority over the plea bargaining process and broad discretion regarding their decisions within the process, the manner in which prosecutors handle plea negotiations is of critical importance from its beginning to its end.

Chapter IV

Role of the Defense Attorney

It in no way minimizes the crucial parts played by the prosecutor and the judge in the plea bargaining process to suggest that no person in the process has a more important role than the defense attorney. The attorney has two critical functions in plea bargaining. The first relates to the bargaining process itself. That is, the attorney must negotiate effectively in her client's best interest with the prosecutor and later the judge. Second, the attorney must counsel her client about the benefits and disadvantages of accepting the plea and offer advice on what she regards as the wisest approach. Each of these functions requires a different skill set, but both are fraught with potential problems.

As with Chapter III on the role of the prosecutor, this section will begin by exploring the motivations of the defense attorney in seeking a plea bargain on behalf of his client. Next will be a discussion of how those motivations play a role in the way a defense attorney conducts negotiations with the prosecutor and the judge. Here we will examine the good and bad ways in which attorneys act both in conducting the negotiations and in ultimately formulating the agreement that includes the defendant's guilty plea. Of critical importance is the degree and nature of the communication between attorney and client at the various phases of the process. Do the two discuss in advance of negotiations what approach the attorney should take with the prosecutor? As the negotiations proceed, at times a somewhat drawn-out process that can take months, does the attorney consult with her client on the progress of the bargaining? Finally, how does the attorney communicate the offer or offers from the prosecutor, and especially in what way does she provide her opinion on whether and why the plea offer should be accepted or rejected? There is no stage during the entire representation of the client in which the attorney's counseling skills need to be as effective as they do when advising a client about what the plea entails and whether it should be accepted. Because the stakes are so high at this time, the pressures on both client and attorney ratchet up substantially, and understandably tension and sometimes dissonance often characterize this particular interaction between the two.

This chapter will examine the real motivations and conduct of the defense attorney to the process. This means going beyond the examples of such conduct that appear in the small percentage of guilty pleas challenged on appeal to examine the nature of the everyday issues and problems that the defense attorney confronts before a plea bargain is agreed to by all parties. Additionally, it means deconstructing the clichés and euphemisms that sometimes characterize judicial opinions dealing with the conduct of the attorney during plea bargaining.

A. Motivations for the Attorney to Bargain

1. Get the best outcome for the client

The most obvious motivation for the criminal defense attorney to engage in plea negotiations is that the ultimate disposition (charge and/or sentence) resulting from a guilty plea will almost always be better for her client than what would follow a conviction at trial. All participants in the criminal justice system know this and tend to proceed with plea bargaining in accordance with this reality. Ask any defense attorney what is his or her primary incentive for engaging in plea bargaining and the above reason will invariably be the response. As lawyers have a fiduciary relationship with their client, their responsibility is to act in the best interests of those they represent. In almost all instances, it is in the client's best interest for the attorney to at least negotiate the best plea offer possible should the defendant opt to avoid a trial. As plea bargaining is an intensely human endeavor for all involved, however, it would be a mistake to ignore the factors apart from the above that might motivate an attorney to plea bargain a case.

2. Caseload management and financial issues

In most jurisdictions, a clear majority of criminal defendants are represented by some sort of public defender or a private attorney assigned to the case and compensated by the government. It has been estimated that overall in this country, approximately three-fourths of criminal cases are handled by publicly compensated attorneys.[1] It is no secret that most public defenders carry a very heavy caseload. For example, in Missouri in 2017, 320 state public defenders handled 80,000 cases, which comes out to more than 240 per lawyer, a staggering amount.[2] Such an overwhelming burden compromises the ability of these attorneys to provide the quality of representation required by the Sixth Amendment's right to competent counsel. Understandably then, public defenders at some point often triage their cases, attempting to identify those which are most likely to go to trial and those most likely to be resolved through a guilty plea. To do the best for their clients during plea negotiations, the defense attorney should do an investigation of the law, the background and needs of his client, and the facts of the case. As all attorneys know, however, the kind of preparation that is necessary to conduct a criminal trial is exponentially greater. Classifying those cases as trial likely or not allows public defenders to allocate time and resources in a manner that is appropriate to the needs of the client and to handle their caseload as efficiently and effectively as practicable.

As noted in the previous chapter, prosecutors often carry more cases than is ideal as well. At times, therefore, one factor in determining the level of the plea involves which attorney has the heavier caseload and is therefore more anxious for a plea bargain. An attorney may consciously factor caseload pressures into his decisions during plea bargaining, or this type of case management may just affect him subconsciously. Either way, it would be foolish to discount this very human motivational factor in considering how an attorney bargains a case.

Although private attorneys normally also have a strong personal motivation to settle a case without a trial, what underrides their motivation in this area unsurprisingly tends to be financial. Criminal defense attorneys structure their fees in different ways. Some set a flat fee for their representation of a criminal case. It may be higher for certain cases than others, but the defendant is told at the beginning what the cost of the entire legal representation will be. Sometimes attorneys set the fee contingent on whether the case is disposed of through a trial or some quicker method such as a guilty plea. Other attorneys charge by the hour—the more time they spend on a case, the higher the fee. Of course, there too the preparation and conduct of a trial will require the attorney to spend many hours.

Under most of these fee structures, an attorney will make more money off an individual case if it goes to trial. Yet barring the highly exceptional wealthy,

---

1. https://www.bjs.gov/content/pub/pdf/dccc.pdf

2. https://www.pbs.org/newshour/show/missouri-public-defenders-are-overloaded-with-hundreds-of-cases-while-defendants-wait-in-jail

white-collar defendant or major drug dealer, it is almost always in the financial interest of the private attorney to turn the case over quickly and move on to other cases. What one of the leading experts on American plea bargaining, Albert Altschuler, wrote in 1975 is still very much true:

> There are two basic ways to achieve financial success in the practice of criminal law. One is to develop, over an extended period of time, a reputation as an outstanding trial lawyer. In that way, one can attract as clients the occasional wealthy people who become enmeshed in the criminal law. If, however, one lacks the ability or the energy to succeed in this way or if one is in a greater hurry, there is a second path to personal wealth — handling a large volume of cases for less-than-spectacular fees. The way to handle a large volume of cases is, of course, not to try them but to plead them.[3]

When I prosecuted cases, there were always the same two or three lawyers hanging around the courthouse trying to pick up cases from defendants as they walked into the building or after they were arraigned in court if they did not have an attorney. Invariably, these attorneys would plea bargain their cases as soon as possible, often doing no investigation of the case or the client beyond interviewing them. The somewhat unfair but not entirely inaccurate stereotype of these lawyers with shiny suits waiting to pounce on potential clients in this manner is undoubtedly less a problem today, but sadly such attorneys still exist. Prosecutors of course realize these attorneys are looking to turn over cases as quickly as possible and that knowledge can be a factor in what level of plea they offer.

3. Psychological and emotional factors

In addition to these concrete caseload and financial factors motivating attorneys to plea bargain, there are also psychological and emotional factors that play a role in incentivizing attorneys to avoid trials. For any attorney, the trial of a case requires a substantial commitment of time and energy. Beyond that, the trial can be an intense intellectual and emotional experience for the attorney. When the stakes at trial center on whether the person sitting next to you and is entirely dependent upon you is going to lose his freedom for a significant period of time, the intensity of the experience increases exponentially for many attorneys. Beyond just the normal feelings that legal advocates in our

---

3. The Defense Attorney's Role in Plea Bargaining, 84 Yale L.J. 1179, 1182 (1975).

highly adversarial judicial system have of not wanting to lose the ultimate test of their advocacy skills, attorneys are also constantly aware of the price to be paid by their client for such a loss. Related to this is the lack of self-confidence (at times warranted, unfortunately) some attorneys have in their own skills as a trial lawyer. As all attorneys know, the ability of defense counsel to utilize the variety of skills necessary to try a criminal case most effectively is often crucial to the outcome of the trial.

4. Attorney's relationship to the prosecutor and the judge

Additional motivations encouraging some attorneys to bargain cases involve their relationship with the other parties in the criminal justice process. In many courtrooms throughout the country, the overwhelming number of criminal cases are handled by that county's public defenders, and many of the remaining cases by a relatively small group of criminal defense lawyers. The result is that local prosecutors and criminal defense attorneys often become quite familiar with each other. Based on their personality, their views of how best to represent their clients, and perhaps other reasons, the relationship of defense attorneys with prosecutors ranges from highly cooperative to completely obstructionist. Most involved in the criminal justice system believe that in most cases neither of these extremes is the best approach for attorneys to take.

One example of extreme "cooperation" by the defense attorney can be found in the 1954 Illinois case of *People v. Heirens*.[4] Heirens was a deeply disturbed 17-year-old who believed it was his alter ego who was sexually attacking and murdering women in the Chicago area. The primary evidence against him consisted of a confession obtained by methods that even back then would have led to a suppression of the statement. Instead of challenging the confession that possibly would have led to Heirens' freedom, the defense counsel instead worked out a plea bargain that led to a sentence of life imprisonment. Before his sentence was pronounced, the prosecutor, after acknowledging the cooperation of defense counsel said, "The small likelihood of a successful murder prosecution of William Heirens early prompted the State's Attorney's office to seek out and obtain the co-operative help of defense counsel and, through them, that of their client. * * * Without the aid of the defense we would to this day have no answer for the death of Josephine Ross."[5] From this and other in-

---

4. 122 N.E.2d 231 (Ill. 1954).
5. *Id.* at 236.

dications within the opinion, it appears that at least one motive of the defense attorneys was ensuring that while Heirens should not face the death penalty, he was too dangerous to be set free. Accurate though this assessment might have been, it is a clear violation of the ethical requirement for attorneys to represent their client zealously. Even if for reasons that apparently would benefit the public, an attorney cannot sell out the interests of his clients as these attorneys did.

While such extreme conduct on the part of defense attorneys is rare, there are some attorneys whose conduct is affected by their concern for how rejecting too many plea offers from the prosecutor will affect their reputations. If regarded by prosecutors as unreasonable, defense attorneys may feel that this reputation could make prosecutors more likely to play hardball on matters such as discovery, witness availability, and requests for postponements. Additionally, they may worry about the attitude of prosecutors regarding the treatment of their future clients. Such beliefs can play a conscious or unconscious role in tilting defense attorneys to accept and recommend to their clients plea offers that may not be optimal for the defendant.

On the other hand, there are some attorneys who view the criminal justice system as inherently evil or at least fundamentally unfair for all criminal defendants. Some of them regard all prosecutors, judges, and everyone else in the system as an enemy to be interacted with only when necessary. Regardless of a defense attorney's views about the system, it is unfortunate if those views are detrimental to the interests of their clients. Many plea offers help criminal defendants avoid the near certainty of harsher sentences should they be convicted at trial. If the evidence seems to point strongly to the likelihood of a conviction, it is the duty of every attorney not only to engage in plea negotiations but to inform and explain any potential deal to his client. Additionally, he must offer advice on whether to accept the plea offer based on what he believes to be in the client's best interest. The attorney should not allow his views of the criminal justice system to interfere with this obligation. Still, as guilty pleas are agreed to in 95% of cases, it is likely that this is not a significant problem, especially weighed against attorneys who feel the need to be unduly cooperative.

Additionally, attorneys are at times concerned about their relationship to the judge in the case. This is especially true with respect to judges who take a more active role in the plea bargaining process. The role of judges in plea bargaining will be explored in depth in Chapter V, but suffice it to say here that state judges (the role of federal judges in the bargaining process is severely limited by Federal Rule of Criminal Procedure 11), with their own motivations to settle cases through a plea, often assume a significant role in the bargaining. Picture this scenario that occurs with great frequency in state courts. A prosecutor makes a plea offer that a judge, in addition to the defense, must accept for the plea agreement to take effect. The judge indicates either that she finds the original offer acceptable and will incorporate the bargain in her sentence or successfully persuades the prosecutor to modify the offer to make it more appealing to the defendant. Now if the defense attorney rejects the plea, he is essentially saying no the judge as well as the prosecutor. Of course, it is the defendant and not the attorney who is actually rejecting the plea offer, but that distinction tends to lose much of its force with a judge who suspects the attorney might have counseled his client to reject it. Judges are human too, and defense attorneys might fear that this rejection of a plea accepted or at times affirmatively advocated by the judge may have an adverse effect on this judge's decisions somewhere down the line. That concern too may creep into the attorney's advice to his client about whether to accept the plea.

I want to be clear here in what I am saying and especially about what I am not saying regarding the motivations of defense attorneys to engage in and ultimately settle cases through plea bargaining. I have no doubt that in the overwhelming number of cases where attorneys recommend acceptance of a plea offer to their clients, it is done in the perceived best interests of those clients. What this means is that the attorney has assessed the strength of the government's case, considered possible legal motions challenging the prosecutor's evidence among other things, and evaluated his ability to offer a successful defense case. Only after concluding that his client will likely be convicted at trial and factoring in his reasonable assumption that any post-trial sentence will be harsher than the plea offer does the attorney recommend acceptance of the plea to his client. It bears repeating, however, that plea bargaining is among the most human of processes for all parties involved. Therefore, disregarding the possibility of other motivations that may influence how a defense attorney plea bargains a case may offer an incomplete picture of the process. Whether consciously or unconsciously, the kinds of financial, workload, and psychological factors that impact many of our decisions in life can certainly affect the attorney's actions during plea bargaining.

B. Constitutional Standard of Competent Representation

1. What is the standard?

In conducting their dealings with the prosecutor, the judge, and their client, there are many factors that defense attorneys must take into consideration with respect to plea bargaining. Unfortunately, some of these factors seem to be at odds with one another. The first area the attorney needs to be aware of involves the legal issues that relate to the representation of her client during plea bargaining.

As in every area of legal representation, the attorney is ethically required to be a zealous advocate for her client. In plea bargaining, this usually means working out an agreement that minimizes as much as possible the charge and/or sentence the defendant is exposed to as a result of his plea. Often this relates to whether and to what extent the defendant faces incarceration, but it can involve other matters, such as fines, restitution to the victim, or the conditions of probation.

Beyond this ethical responsibility is the Sixth Amendment's guarantee of the right to the assistance of counsel for criminal defendants. As the Supreme Court made clear in 1966, "[I]f the right to counsel guaranteed by the Constitution is to serve its purpose, defendants cannot be left to the mercies of incompetent counsel."[6] Attorneys, therefore, are charged with representing their clients in a competent manner. Unfortunately, the standard of competence to which defense attorneys are bound is viewed by many people as being embarrassingly low. Based on the Supreme Court's opinion in *Strickland v. Washington*, whether such representation is determined to be competent depends first on an assessment of whether the attorney's conduct of the case was performed with "objective reasonableness."[7] This means comparing the conduct to the manner in which other attorneys perform in similar situations and evaluating the conduct within the context of all aspects of the particular case, including the information possessed by the attorney at the time the conduct occurred. Additionally, if the attorney based her decisions and actions on strategic considerations, even if those considerations turned out to be largely misplaced, there would be insufficient grounds for a claim under the Sixth Amendment of incompetent representation. Years ago, I testified as an expert witness in a case in which the defendant was seeking to overturn his conviction based on the errors committed by his original attorney both in the filing of pre-trial motions to suppress evidence and the attorney's deficient performance during the trial. While many of these errors were significant and clearly harmful to the defense case, I had to acknowledge on cross-examination by the prosecutor that at least some of the errors could have been committed for strategic considerations, even though these considerations were weak. Unsur-

---

6. McMann v. Richardson, 397 U.S. 759, 771 (1966).
7. 466 U.S. 668, 688 (1984).

prisingly, the court ultimately used the strategic considerations justification as the reason to deny the Sixth Amendment claim. It is not the purpose of this book to go into depth about this standard, but it is safe to say that judicial opinions are rife with embarrassing examples of awful decisions and conduct by attorneys that have been deemed to pass the constitutional muster of objectively reasonable representation under the *Strickland* standard.

Making the attorney-competence standard even easier to meet is the second obligation defendants must satisfy under *Strickland* in order to prove a Sixth Amendment violation. No matter how defective counsel's conduct was, if the defendant cannot show he was prejudiced by that conduct, there is no constitutional violation. This has come to mean that the defendant must show the outcome of the case would have been substantially different but for the attorney's defective representation. Such cause-and-effect proof is not easy to demonstrate. In one notorious example of this, a panel of the United States Court of Appeals let stand the conviction and death sentence of a man whose counsel fell asleep at several points during the trial, sometimes for as long as 15 minutes, because it could not be proven that those times were critical to the verdict and constituted prejudice under *Strickland*.[8] While the decision was later overturned on further appeal,[9] it is not atypical of cases in which the prejudice requirement has been utilized to defeat Sixth Amendments challenges.

The *Strickland* standard was made applicable to plea bargaining in the Supreme Court's 1985 decision in *Hill v. Lockhart*.[10] In applying the first prong of *Strickland*'s test for determining incompetence of counsel, the Court adopted the requirement that the defendant demonstrate that the legal representation regarding the bargaining and client counseling functions fell beneath what is regarded as objective reasonableness for attorneys in similar situations. The defense lawyer had incorrectly stated how long under the plea agreement Hill would have to serve in prison before he became eligible for parole. The Court said it did not have to determine if that error constituted incompetence because Hill failed to satisfy the prejudice prong. The Court's conclusion as to prejudice was based on the failure of Hill to claim and prove that but for his lawyer's incorrect advice about the parole period, he would have rejected the plea offer and insisted on going to trial. Additionally, the Court noted that Hill had no "special circumstances" that would suggest that the term of his eligibility for parole was of particular significance to Hill in his decision to plead guilty and forego a trial.[11]

---

8. Burdine v. Johnson, 231 F.3d 950 (5th Cir. 2000).
9. 262 F.3d. 336 (5th Cir. 2001).
10. 474 U.S. 52 (1985).
11. *Id.* at 60.

2. The difficulty facing the defendant in trying to show the attorney's conduct during the plea bargaining process fell below the Sixth Amendment's requirement for competent representation

In cases dealing with pleas accepted by the defendant, therefore, prejudice can usually be shown only if the defendant can prove the hypothetical that but for the attorney's error, he would have rejected the plea and opted for a trial. As you can imagine, proving such a hypothetical is not easy. In fact, because so much of what occurs before a guilty plea is accepted takes place off the record and is subject to often unprovable assertions about exactly what was said or done, both *Strickland* prongs are more difficult to meet in plea cases than those that result in trial convictions. While in cases that go to trial there may be some significant off-the-record attorney-client interactions as well as the defense attorney's private meetings with witnesses and others, still the record of the trial and earlier court proceedings form a strong basis for assessing the attorney's conduct. We can see what motions were filed and not filed, how ably they were prepared and argued, the attorney's performance at pre-trial hearings, and most importantly how the attorney conducted the trial. Did the attorney cross-examine the government's witnesses effectively, did he call the right witnesses and elicit their testimony in a coherent and convincing manner, did he use the rules of evidence effectively to have admitted or excluded key testimony or exhibits, did he deliver a crisp opening statement that addressed the key defense issues in the case, and was his summation organized and persuasive?

Applying the *Strickland* standard to such issues regarding cases that went to trial can lead to reasonable disagreements within the courts as to whether the attorney's performance met the somewhat subjective competence standard (the first *Strickland* requirement), but at least the courts have a firm body of evidence with which to form such an opinion. While the prejudice determination is hypothetical when looking both at cases that went to trial (*Strickland*) and those involving plea bargaining (*Hill*), proving prejudice in the plea cases is more difficult because the supporting evidence is both more unprovable and the ultimate determination more questionable.

Plea agreements are not official until entered into in open court before the judge after an allocution including what rights the defendant is surrendering because of his guilty plea and a recitation of the basic facts of the crime. The defendant must either offer that factual account or agree to it when offered by another party. The judge must accept the plea before the agreement is binding. Although acceptance of the plea occurs in court, actual formation of the plea bargain invariably occurs entirely off the record through discussions between the prosecutor and defense attorney. At certain times, such as when the defense attorney is seeking a sentence commitment, the judge is included in some of these off-the-record conversations. If a later claim of inadequate representation by the defendant stems from something that the defense attorney allegedly heard from the prosecutor or even the judge during one of those discussions, proving what was said is not easy.

What the defense attorney was told by the prosecutor or judge can be critical to the outcome of the defendant's Sixth Amendment claim. For example, did the prosecutor reveal to the defense attorney exculpatory evidence that the attorney did not follow up on before recommending acceptance of the plea to her client? In negotiating for the best plea, did the defense attorney inform the prosecutor of information regarding the defendant's background or of issues which raised questions about the victim's credibility or the seriousness of the offense? Informing the prosecutor of any of this information might have generated a more lenient offer. The precise wording of conversations between the defense attorney and the prosecutor regarding such matters could be critical in determining whether the attorney's representation fell below the standard of reasonableness required by *Strickland* and *Hill*. Because these discussions could have taken place months or even years before the defendant's Sixth Amendment claim is adjudicated and almost always were conducted off the record, accurate representations of these discussions can fall victim to memory lapses and differences in interpretation and meaning.

Many claims of inadequate legal representation involving plea bargains stem from conversations between attorney and client. Obviously, all of these are off the record as the requirement of confidentiality regarding such conversations demands. When the defendant claims a Sixth Amendment violation based on these conversations, he most likely waives that confidentiality, and those conversations, when relevant, will be revealed. Aside from the memory issues alluded to above, there is a different dynamic at play here. When a defendant, now represented by a different lawyer than the one who represented him when he pled guilty, claims his former attorney's conduct demonstrated a level of incompetence so egregious that it violates the Sixth Amendment, that former attorney is in an especially uncomfortable position. The DNA of a criminal defense attorney, formed by his training and experience, confirmed by constitutional and ethical requirements, leads him always to do what is in his client's best interest. Now, however, his former client's best interest seems to be in direct conflict with his own. To support the defendant's claim, there is a good chance the former attorney will have to admit to saying something that was erroneous ("you can't get more than six years if you take this plea," when he can and does get 10), not saying something he should have ("but this was a bad search so I think we can get the evidence suppressed and beat this case"), or in some other meaningful way failed in his counseling duties. Imagine how difficult it is for the attorney to acknowledge his own alleged incompetence. How much damage does he do to his professional reputation and future career because of this acknowledgment? Beyond that, what harm does he do to his ego and to his self-confidence? While I don't think most attorneys in this situation would intentionally lie about their communications with their clients, recalling events and conversations is a highly subjective process, and it is not unreasonable to assume that these significant professional and personal concerns influence just how the attorney recalls a specific conversation from a time in the past.

Faced with a choice between the claim made by the defendant, whose self-interest is also obvious, and the former attorney, the court considering the Sixth Amendment claim is likely to believe the former attorney unless the defendant can bring forth other supporting evidence of his claim. In a recent case decided by an appellate court in Alaska, for example, the court chose to accept the testimony of the defense attorney regarding whether he explained sufficiently the nature of the charges and possible sentence the defendant faced if he rejected a plea offer and was convicted at trial. The court made this choice despite the fact that the defendant testified in detail about the conversation, whereas the attorney said he did not remember the conversation but typically informs his clients of those matters.[12] In these situations, the former defense attorney customarily offers an affidavit or even testifies in support of the prosecution's attempt to have the defendant's Sixth Amendment claim denied.

The federal district court in Vermont in 2010 dealt with a case in which a defendant went through the representation of five attorneys during the course of his prosecution. Among the defendant's many claims was that one of the attorneys coerced him into accepting a plea bargain. Although in comments to the court, the attorney had referred to needing time to "leverage" or "pressure" his client to plead guilty, the court ultimately accepted the testimony of that attorney that he employed no coercion in counseling his client about the guilty plea.[13]

---

12. Vann v. State, No. A-13093, No. 6873, 2020 Alas. App. LEXIS 37 (June 3, 2020).
13. United States v. Moses, No. 05 Cr. 133, 2010 WL 3521724 (D. Vt. Sept. 7, 2010).

3. Examples of attorney incompetence

a. Failure to inform client of plea offer

In an important holding, the Supreme Court made clear that in addition to being violative of American Bar Association standards for criminal defense attorneys,[14] the failure of an attorney to inform his client of a plea offer made by the government constituted inadequate representation and met *Strickland*'s first prong of incompetence. The Court in *Missouri v. Frye*[15] acknowledged that defendants have no constitutional right to receive a plea offer from the prosecution, but once a formal offer is made during negotiations, the attorney must communicate the offer to his client. This part of the *Frye* holding was clear enough, but far less clear was how defendants in such situations needed to satisfy the *Strickland/Hill* prejudice prong. Remember that in *Hill*, when the Court adapted the prejudice prong from *Strickland* to guilty plea cases, it was dealing with a plea that was accepted after incorrect advice from the defense counsel. In *Frye*, the question was how does the defendant show prejudice when he was never informed of a plea offer and subsequently was convicted at trial? In answering that question, the *Frye* Court held that the defendant must show that the plea offer was indeed made by the prosecution but never communicated to the defendant, the probability that he would have accepted the offer had he been so informed, that the prosecutor would not have withdrawn the offer before it was accepted in court, that the judge would have accepted the plea deal, and finally, that the deal would have been more favorable to the defendant than what he ended up with after being convicted at trial.

While the difficulty for a defendant to prove this series of hypotheticals is obvious, looking at one particularly notorious defendant's attempt to do so demonstrates this quite clearly. In 1995, John Merzbacher, a former teacher at a Catholic middle school in Maryland, was convicted of rape and other crimes he perpetrated 20 years earlier on a female student. The judge who sentenced Merzbacher to four life terms of imprisonment called this crime and the alleged attacks on 13 other students he was originally charged with as acts "beyond the comprehension of rational people." Fifteen years later, a federal district court judge accepted Merzbacher's contention that during plea negotiations in 1995, the prosecution told his lawyer that if Merzbacher pled guilty it would recommend a sentence of ten years in prison but that Merzbacher

---

14. ABA Standards for Criminal Justice, Pleas of Guilty 14–3.2(a) (3d ed. 1999).
15. 566 U.S. 134 (2012).

was never informed of this offer.[16] This satisfies the first prong of *Strickland/ Hill* that the attorney's conduct fell below the standard of objective reasonableness.

What about the prejudice prong? While Merzbacher's testimony that he would have accepted the offer was understandably characterized as self-serving, the federal district court nevertheless accepted that given all the circumstances, this was a good offer for Merzbacher that he would likely have accepted. In reversing this conclusion, a federal appeals court held that among other things, Merzbacher's consistent protestations of innocence tended to refute the claim that he would have accepted the offer.[17] Many defendants protest their innocence, especially when, as in Merzbacher's case, conviction comes from a contested trial and therefore guilt is not acknowledged in a guilty plea. Many change their mind about their guilt when offered a favorable guilty plea bargain. So Merzbacher's claim of innocence hardly shows he would not have accepted a plea that would have covered numerous serious charges. The state trial judge in charge of Merzbacher's case when the plea offer was made, although retired when this motion was heard, testified that he would have reluctantly accepted the offer, seemingly satisfying another requirement for defendants to show prejudice under *Frye*. The appellate court, though, found that as the structure of the ten-year guilty-plea offer was not fully formed, it is plausible that the prosecutor would have withdrawn the plea or the trial judge would not have accepted it in final form.

Unsurprisingly, not many tears were shed for the decision to keep John Merzbacher in prison. Among other things, his victims claimed that Merzbacher held a gun to their heads threatening to kill them if they revealed his horrific crimes. But his case does illustrate that while there was no certainty about either the findings of the federal district court or the opposing findings of the appellate court concerning the acceptance of the plea offer, it is exceedingly difficult for defendants to satisfy the numerous hypothetical determinations required by the *Hill* prejudice prong in cases alleging non-disclosure of plea offers to clients by their counsel.

b. Giving incorrect advice regarding fundamental matters related to the plea bargain itself

There are two types of errors made by defense counsel during their consultations with their clients about whether to accept a plea bargain that courts

---

16. Merzbacher v. Shearin, 732 F. Supp. 2d 527 (D. Md. 2010).
17. Merzbacher v. Shearin, 706 F.3d 356 (4th Cir. 2013).

have consistently regarded as essential to the guilty plea itself, and therefore likely to meet the first *Strickland/Hill* prong for demonstrating incompetent representation. The first relates to the defendant's understanding of the specific charge or charges to which he will be pleading guilty. The second involves the possible sentence the defendant could or will receive as the result of his plea.

Fifty years ago, the Supreme Court held that for a waiver of the right to trial to be valid, the defendant's guilty plea must be knowing, intelligent, and voluntary.[18] That the defendant understands he committed some crime due to an act he admits having perpetrated is insufficient to demonstrate that his guilty plea to a specific charge meets this knowledge requirement. Instead, the defendant must understand and with limited exception admit that his conduct met the elements of the specific crime or crimes to which he is pleading guilty. In *Henderson v. Morgan*,[19] the defendant admitted to stabbing his victim several times, causing her death. What he did not admit and was not specifically mentioned during his plea allocution was that he intended to kill her. As this kind of specific intent was a required element of the second degree murder charge to which he pled guilty, such an acknowledgment by the defendant is necessary to establish his guilt for that particular offense. Even though a prospective jury might have been able to infer from the number and nature of the stab wounds that Morgan intended to kill his victim, that was deemed insufficient to show that Morgan was aware his guilty plea meant he intended to kill his victim. The Court noted that aside from there being no acknowledgment of this by Morgan when he pled guilty in court, there was no indication that his attorney gave him this necessary advice about the intent element being required for his plea to be valid.

While the attorney's error in the *Morgan* case involved not informing the defendant of the elements of the crime to which he was pleading guilty, other attorneys give the defendant more overtly mistaken advice about the nature of the relevant offense. For example, an attorney incorrectly advised a client to reject a plea offer because if the case went to trial, the fact that he shot the victim in the midsection could not show intent to kill as required by the murder charge. The Supreme Court in *Lafler v. Cooper*[20] affirmed the decision of lower federal courts that such advice by the attorney met the first prong of *Strickland*'s standard for incompetence.

---

18. Brady v. United States, 397 U.S. 742, 748 (1970).
19. 426 U.S. 637 (1976).
20. 566 U.S. 156 (2012).

Many appeals arising from a plea agreement based on incompetent advice offered by counsel relate to the attorney's explanation of sentence possibilities under the plea offer, or if the defendant rejects the offer, the sentence he may receive if convicted at trial. Such appeals often fall victim to the defendant's inability to satisfy the prejudice prong of *Hill*. Although defendants may be able to show that their attorney misunderstood, miscalculated, or miscommunicated the length of a potential plea based or post-trial sentence, the defendant's claim of a Sixth Amendment violation often proves unsuccessful due to his failure to demonstrate that the mistake was the causative factor in his decision to accept or reject a plea bargain. At times, courts will not bother to determine whether the attorney did convey incorrect sentencing information to the defendant, rejecting the defendant's claim based on his failure to satisfy the prejudice prong. In *Dillehay v. State of Indiana*,[21] defense counsel advised Dillehay that if she rejected the guilty plea offer from the state and was convicted at trial, she would face two mandatory 20-year sentences that would have to run consecutively, meaning 40 years in prison. Dillehay claimed that faced with this possibility, she chose to plead guilty and accept the 20-year sentence that accompanied her guilty plea. It turned out that counsel's advice was incorrect in that if convicted at trial of both counts, the sentences could run concurrently and *Dillehay* could be released in 20 years. In rejecting Dillehay's request to vacate her guilty plea, the court said, "we are not persuaded by Dillehay's retrospective belief that she would have risked the maximum sentence had she known the minimum was twenty rather than forty years."[22]

There are of course some cases involving mistaken sentencing advice by the attorney in which the defendant can show prejudice as well. In *Harris v. United States*, for example, the defendant had a choice between two guilty plea offers.[23] She made the wrong choice due to her lawyer's mistaken advice. He was unaware that under federal law, she could be sentenced not just for the crime she pled guilty to but additionally for conduct "relevant" to that crime. As a result, her sentence was 151 months of incarceration as opposed to the 120-month sentence she would have received had she accepted the other plea offer. In this case, the defendant's acceptance of the other guilty plea acknowledged her willingness to admit her crime in exchange for a sentence reduction and thus showed that but for her attorney's error, Harris would have chosen the other path. When, as in most such cases, the rejection of the plea offer leads to con-

---

21. 672 N.E.2d 956 (Ind. App. Ct. 1996).

22. *Id.* at 960.

23. 701 F. Supp. 2d 1084 (S.D. Iowa 2010).

viction at trial, it is more difficult to prove the hypothetical prejudice prong that but for the attorney's error, the plea would have been accepted.

c. Failure to advise the client about "collateral" consequences of plea

One question left unsettled until relatively recently was whether incorrect advice by an attorney regarding significant matters not directly related to the proposed plea agreement could constitute Sixth Amendment incompetence. More specifically, did failure to advise a client about the immigration consequences of a plea agreement satisfy the first *Strickland* prong of incompetent representation? In its 2010 decision in *Padilla v. Kentucky*,[24] the Supreme Court interpreted the Sixth Amendment to require criminal defense attorneys to inform their clients of the immigration consequences of any plea where those consequences are succinct and clear. When the consequences are not clear, the attorney still has to let the defendant know there may be such consequences before recommending acceptance of the plea to her client. This decision is important for the many criminal defendants, such as Padilla himself, for whom a conviction can lead to deportation. Equally important was the Court's rejection of a standard used by many courts in determining whether the attorney's failure to advise a client about a relevant consequence of his guilty plea rendered the plea invalid. Courts had previously often distinguished such consequences that were deemed material to the plea itself, and therefore encompassed *Strickland's* "below objective reasonableness" prong (such as matters related to the length of imprisonment), from those regarded as collateral which did not (such as losing a license of some sort). In rejecting this approach, the *Padilla* Court focused instead on looking at the significance of the consequence to the defendant and the likelihood that such a consequence would flow from his guilty plea.

Although most defense attorneys favored the Court's decision in *Padilla*, the opinion raised questions about how to apply the standard for advising clients of the immigration consequences of their conviction and created real professional burdens for them. In his concurring opinion in *Padilla*, Justice Alito pointed out that an understanding of what is succinct and clear regarding immigration consequences for criminal convictions is far from succinct and clear itself. Referring to this standard as a "vague, halfway test," Alito predicted the result would be "much confusion and needless litigation."[25] The extra bur-

---

24. 559 U.S. 356 (2010).
25. *Id.* at 375 (Alito, J., concurring).

den on attorneys relates to the specialized discipline that immigration law has become. While always somewhat of a specialized area of law practiced customarily by attorneys with particularized knowledge and experience in immigration law, the area was later to become particularly complex with the Trump administration's focus on restricting immigration and limiting the protections for immigrants already in the country. In the days before the decision in *Padilla*, very few criminal defense attorneys had any more than a basic understanding of the nuances of immigration law. Similarly, in a judicial system where most criminal defendants are represented by public defenders or private attorneys whose practices include a high volume of criminal cases, immigration lawyers are usually not that experienced in representing those accused of crimes. Stated simply, post-*Padilla*, criminal lawyers now have to become at least somewhat versed in immigration law.

C. Advising the Client Whether to Accept the Plea Offered

Among the most important single tasks performed by the defense attorney in our criminal justice system is advising the client whether to accept an offer from the prosecutor (and possibly the judge as well) and thus to waive his constitutional right to a trial. This counseling responsibility is crucial because advising a client to accept a plea means surrendering his opportunity to walk away with an acquittal and the somewhat limited consequences for his arrest that accompany an acquittal[26] and instead agree to accept what usually is a permanent criminal conviction[27] that often involves a prison sentence as well

---

26. There are real consequences for the defendant even when charges against him are dismissed or he is acquitted at trial. For example, there are various law enforcement databases which may now include his name, depending on the crimes with which he was charged. The record of prior arrests is generally available to courts and prosecutors should the defendant be arrested for a subsequent crime. These prior arrests, even though not ending up in convictions, can play a significant role in bail determinations, plea bargaining offers, and ultimately in his sentence should the defendant be convicted of the subsequent crime. Additionally, there are employment, license, and other civil applications that ask about arrests as well as convictions.

27. Laws in many jurisdictions now allow for some convictions to be expunged. *See, e.g.*, Md. Code Crim. Proc. § 10-105. Other jurisdictions that do not provide for expungement do permit a sealing of the record which has some of the same effects. *See, e.g.*, N.Y. Crim. Proc. Law § 160.59.

as other negative consequences.[28] On the other hand, advising the client to reject a plea offer will almost always result in the defendant's receiving a harsher sentence should he be convicted at trial than that contained in the plea offer. Plainly put, in many cases this means being deprived of one's freedom for what is a substantially longer period of time. The stakes here are high indeed.

While the importance of this counseling role performed by the defense attorney is clear, its systemic significance is magnified because such counseling occurs in one form or another in virtually all criminal cases. In some cases, usually especially serious ones, no offer is made by the prosecutor. But those cases are rare. The motivations for all parties to settle a case without a trial, as discussed in this and other chapters, is strong, and the data regarding how many cases are resolved through plea bargaining is compelling. So in almost every case, the defense attorney needs to offer critical advice on whether her client should accept a deal in exchange for surrendering his right to trial. Understandably, there is pressure on the attorney to advise her client to make the wisest decision and almost as importantly to communicate that advice in a manner that best serves her client. Let us examine what goes into both of those vital counseling responsibilities.

1. Preparation for counseling the client about the plea offer

In deciding whether to recommend acceptance of a plea offer, the attorney takes into consideration a number of factors. Most of these are the same concerns evaluated by the prosecutor in deciding what plea offer to make. Obviously, the seriousness of the charges and the potential sentencing possibilities are the first things the attorney will look at. The next consideration is usually the likelihood of prevailing at trial. This takes into account the quality of the witnesses for the prosecution and the defense, assessing both their credibility and the significance of their testimony in proving or disproving the charges. A government witness may testify to direct knowledge of the crime, for example, by actually seeing the incident or being told about it by the defendant himself. Such testimony on its face is obviously very damaging to the defense, but if the witness was offered a favorable deal regarding his own criminal liability in order to testify, jurors may question his believability and the testimony

---

28. These consequences can relate to future employment, immigration status, voting rights, custody matters, and professional licenses, as well as the possibility that the conviction may have an impact on future criminal charges the defendant may face.

could lose much of its significance. If there is a witness who can provide an alibi claiming he was with the defendant at a different location from the crime when it was committed, such evidence can be powerful for the defense. But if that witness has prior criminal convictions, the prosecutor is usually able to bring out those convictions and thus raise questions about the credibility of the witness and his testimony. The victim may be completely credible, but there might be real issues concerning his ability to identify the perpetrator or recall important details of the crime. In addition to evaluating witnesses for each side, the defense attorney must weigh the likely success of any motions she might file or other legal impediments that would make it difficult for the government to obtain a conviction. If after considering all factors that relate to the likelihood of the government's obtaining a guilty verdict at trial the defense attorney believes that the chances of an acquittal are slim, such an assessment will motivate the attorney to recommend acceptance of the best offer he can wrangle from the prosecutor.

2. Issues related to time and timing

One impediment the attorney may face in doing the important work described above to flesh out the chances of an acquittal at trial before recommending acceptance or rejection of a guilty plea offer relates to issues of time and timing. As discussed earlier in this chapter, defense attorneys, both public and private, have limitations on how much time they can spend on each case. When the attorney is convinced that the case will end up being resolved through a guilty plea, human nature and reasonable time-allocation priorities will likely cause the attorney to spend less time on those cases than on ones likely to be tried and surely for those about to be tried. Without researching important legal issues or speaking directly with her own potential witnesses or those government witnesses made available through discovery, an attorney is less likely to gain an accurate sense of potential success at trial.

Worse still for the attorney is that he may have additional time pressure in acquiring all the information he needs to determine the wisdom of recommending a guilty plea to his client. The attorney may be at the whim of the prosecutor with respect to the timing of the plea agreement. Prosecutors often want to dispose of cases as quickly as feasible, not just to save themselves time and effort, but to avoid inconveniencing witnesses or in some cases putting them through traumatic court proceedings. Victims of serious crimes, such as rape, may have expressed to the prosecutor their reluctance to have to revisit in front of strangers the horrific experience they suffered through. Responding to that concern, prosecutors may offer defendants more generous deals if they plead guilty before a preliminary hearing or when the victim's testimony is taken in the grand jury. Should the plea not be accepted by then, the prosecutor may later offer a less generous plea deal or none at all. In order to do more work on the case, the attorney can always seek a postponement from the judge as to the date scheduled for the plea to be accepted. Even if the judge grants the postponement, however, nothing usually prevents the prosecutor from withdrawing the offer or conditioning the offer on it being accepted on the originally scheduled date.

3. Getting to know the client

In addition to gauging the strength of the case against her client, the attorney should also get to know the client before deciding whether to recommend acceptance of a plea offer. The attorney should never lose sight of the fact that it is the defendant and not the attorney who bears the consequences of any plea decision, and therefore it is the defendant and not the attorney who must believe the decision made is the best one possible. While this point seems obvious, in reality in can be difficult for an attorney to bear that in mind when the client is resistant to accepting a plea offer that she regards to be beneficial. Convinced that the evidence against her client is overwhelming and the likelihood of his getting convicted and receiving a sentence harsher than contained in the plea offer is almost inevitable, she knows that all objective indicia point to the wisdom of accepting the plea. But very few decisions are more subjective and more difficult than the one faced by a criminal defendant in deciding to plead guilty and thus giving up his chance of walking free. Although less frequent, the same counseling difficulty arises in situations when the defendant wishes to plead guilty for one reason or another, whereas the attorney is convinced there is an excellent chance for an acquittal at trial and recommends against acceptance of the plea.

Any good defense attorney, as early as possible, should gain knowledge of just who her client is, the people whom he trusts and matter to him, his experiences in life and with the criminal justice system, and his hopes and plans for the future. Knowing these things at an early stage allows the attorney to tailor her negotiations with the prosecutor to matters that are most significant to her client and then later to counsel her client regarding acceptance of the plea offer in a more meaningful way. Some clients may wish to stay out of jail at any cost, meaning in some cases they are willing to cooperate with the government by providing information in this case or others. That primary goal of not facing incarceration may also mean the client does not care about what particular charge he pleads guilty to or whether he needs to pay a fine or restitution if it keeps him out of jail. Other defendants may care a great deal about the actual charge they plead guilty to because of the collateral consequences of such a plea (i.e., deportation or loss of professional license) or because the nature of the charge he pleads to can bring other problems. It is well known, for example, that child abusers are often considered at the bottom of the social hierarchy in prisons. This can result in prison assaults on anyone the inmates know has committed such a crime. Better in such a circumstance for the defendant to plead guilty to a more innocuous sounding offense, such as assault, if the prosecutor agrees to that. Some defendants may be most concerned about spending the period of their imprisonment at a facility close enough for friends and family to visit them. While the Department of Corrections in most jurisdictions controls this assignment, a recommendation from the prosecutor or particularly from the court may have some influence on this decision. Still other defendants may wish to delay the start of their incarceration because of some approaching event such as the birth of a child or just to get their affairs in order. To negotiate a plea offer and later counsel a client on whether to accept that offer without knowing such concerns is poor lawyering.

4. Methods for the attorney to counsel the client about the plea offer

The attorney has negotiated a plea offer from the prosecutor which she feels is the best deal the defendant will receive in exchange for waiving his right to trial. The attorney may believe that even this deal should be rejected by her client because he has a good chance of beating the case through either legal motions or by an acquittal at trial. Alternatively, the attorney may think that if the defendant rejects this offer, a better offer will come at a later point of the judicial process. As discussed above, the attorney has the legal obligation to present the offer to the defendant regardless of how she values it. On the other hand, the attorney might have concluded that given the unlikelihood of prevailing at trial and the heavier sentence that would flow from a trial conviction, the plea offer should be accepted by her client. In either case, the attorney must give considerable thought to just HOW to present both the plea offer and her recommendation to her client.

In these situations, where the attorney's view of whether the prosecutor's plea offer should be accepted initially differs from that of her client, she needs to consider how affirmative she should be in attempting to persuade the defendant of her position. The counseling approaches regarding the recommendation to accept or reject a guilty plea offer range considerably from attorney to attorney. There are some who present the plea offer, discuss the consequences of both acceptance and rejection, and then basically tell the defendant it is up to him to decide whether he wishes to plead guilty. Perhaps they follow this up by asking if the defendant has any questions but make no actual recommendation unless pressed by their client to do so, and even then, some attorneys refuse to do so. Those attorneys may be motivated by an understanding that due to the differences between attorney and client regarding vulnerability and powers of persuasion, it is important to ensure that the client makes his own choice rather than just accepting what the attorney thinks is the best path forward.

In one such case, *Boria v. Keane*,[29] a plea was overturned based on the incompetence of a lawyer who admitted to not making a recommendation to his client regarding whether he should accept a plea offer in part because the attorney felt clients should always make that decision for themselves.[30] In holding that a lawyer's failure to make a recommendation of acceptance or rejection of a plea offer constituted incompetent representation, the decision in *Boria* was clearly exceptional. Far more common are cases like *Purdy v. United States*, in which the court reasoned that while counsel's advice should include a discussion of the strengths and weaknesses of the case, "[T]here is no per se rule that defense counsel must always expressly advise the defendant whether to take a plea offer."[31]

At the other end of the spectrum of how affirmative an attorney should be when counseling a client whether to accept a plea offer are those attorneys who will use any method at their disposal to persuade the client to follow their advice. Consider the typical situation where defense attorneys might adopt this approach. The prosecutor has offered her client a plea with a maximum sentence recommendation of one year in prison. Either the judge has already committed to that maximum or the attorney is confident that, as in most cases, the judge's sentence will not exceed that recommendation. In assessing the strength of the case, she is convinced that a conviction at trial is highly likely. Given the defendant's criminal record and the fact that the sentence following a trial conviction is almost always higher, often substantially higher, than the plea offer, the attorney is convinced her client should accept the plea. For reasons discussed earlier in this chapter, the defendant is extremely reluctant to accept the plea offer. The attorney knows it is ultimately the client's decision whether to accept the plea offer, but that realization tends to get lost for the

---

29. 99 F.3d 492 (2d Cir. 1996).

30. For a discussion of the reasoning in this exceptional case, see Steven Zeidman, To Plead or Not to Plead: Effective Assistance and Client-Centered Counseling, 39 B.C. L. Rev. 841, 847–49 (1998).

31. 208 F.3d 41, 48 (2d Cir. 2000).

attorney who sees her goal as minimizing the negative consequences the client will suffer at the end of the criminal adjudication process. How forceful should the attorney be in persuading her client to avoid making a decision she believes will be disastrous for the person she is sworn to protect?

In considering the methods defense attorneys use to convey and recommend a guilty plea offer to their clients, we need to distinguish between what attorneys can do and what they should do. Unless the attorney fails to disclose a plea offer, misstates an element of the law to which the client will be pleading, or makes a significant error in communicating an essential part of the bargain such as the sentencing possibilities, the counseling method of the attorney will rarely lead to the plea being invalidated.[32] A striking example of this can be seen in the 1991 Illinois murder case of *Williams v. Chrans*.[33] Williams claimed that his guilty plea (here the guilty plea advocated by the lawyers was not pursuant to an offer from the prosecutor) was coerced and testified that one of the four attorneys who represented him "came to visit me. He continued to press me to enter a guilty plea. I did not want to do that. He repeatedly told me that I was hurting my family by holding out, that the only way to spare them was to plead and that I would die if I did not plead. Finally, against my will, I agreed to enter a guilty plea."[34] Perhaps even more striking was the testimony of one of his lawyers about the approach taken to get Williams to plead guilty:

> As a response to our client's position, the four of us as well as [the psychologist] attempted to pursuade [*sic*] the defendant that a plea of not guilty would be a mistake. These conversations were not discussions of trial strategy, nor were they reminiscent of the numerous occasions in which I pursuaded [*sic*] a client to plead guilty to accept the plea bargain being offered by the State. In this case the psychological pressure and the sophisticated tactics used with Hernando Williams to convince him to adopt our approach were unlike any other conversations I ever had with any other client. Also, it goes without saying, that in this case there were no plea bargaining offers from the State.
>
> All of the psychiatric and psychological information which had been gathered and developed by [the doctors] was used by me and my associates to compel Mr. Williams to accept our point of view.

---

32. Even if one or more of those mistakes are deemed sufficient to demonstrate incompetent representation by the attorney, the plea will not be invalidated unless the defendant can meet the prejudice prong of *Strickland/Hill* and show that the attorney's error was the causative factor in his accepting or rejecting the plea.

33. 945 F.2d 926 (7th Cir. 1991).

34. *Id.* at 931.

This constituted a unique form of coercion. We took advantage of our client, maximizing the use of the information we had gathered for a purpose other than which it was intended. Our strategy was developed to accommodate us and not our client. There is no question that during this period (which lasted over a year) we did not act in accordance with our client's wishes. Rather, we used every means available to force him to change his plea.[35]

In rejecting Williams' claim that the attorneys coerced him into accepting the plea, the court held that, "'advice—even strong urging' by counsel does not invalidate a guilty plea."[36] Most defendants' claims of coercion by their attorneys are less dramatic than what happened here and far less likely to include such a confirmatory acknowledgment from the attorney, making it unsurprising that so few such claims are successful.

Then there are the cases in which the attorney recommends acceptance of a plea by attempting to assuage the defendant's concerns about the uncertainty of the sentence possibilities left open by the plea agreement. In the Oklahoma capital murder prosecution of Bobby Joe Fields, the defendant was advised by his lawyer that a guilty plea would almost assuredly allow him to escape the death penalty. She was apparently convinced of this by conversations with the judge in which, among other things, he told the lawyer that "if the facts are as you say they are, I will very, very, very seriously consider giving him life or life without parole."[37] Apparently the three "verys" convinced the lawyer, who then persuaded her client to take a blind plea to capital murder, meaning that the death sentence was still on the table after the plea. In trying to demonstrate for her client the unlikelihood of his being sentenced to death after his guilty plea, the attorney drew a six-inch line and then sectioned off one-half an inch which she claimed represented his chance of receiving the death penalty. Unfortunately for Fields, the attorney was wrong, and after a hearing, the judge sentenced him to death. Fields' claims that the attorney was incompetent and that she coerced him into the plea were rejected by the court. Although the attorney acknowledged "she pulled out all the stops"[38] to secure his agreement to the deal, neither she nor the judge ever guaranteed that Fields would be spared the death penalty.

In seeking to reverse a conviction based on claims of attorney coerciveness or incompetence regarding counseling about a guilty plea offer, a defendant

---

35. *Id.* at 932.
36. *Id.* at 933.
37. Fields v. Gibson, 277 F.3d 1203, 1210 (10th Cir. 2002).
38. *Id.*

is faced with several obstacles to overcome, some of which played a major role in the *Williams, Fields,* and *Purdy* decisions. There is a presumption that the representation by the attorney was not incompetent — a presumption it falls on the defendant to overcome. Most such cases will lead to a factual dispute or at least a difference in interpretations of a conversation between attorney and client about how the client was counseled. As there is no record of these private conversations, most reviewing courts understandably will accept the attorney's version of what was communicated absent some concrete reason not to. Even if there is an agreed-to version of the communications in which pressure from the attorney is evident, the two-prong requirement to show incompetence under *Strickland/Hill* is a difficult hurdle for a defendant to overcome. Additionally, courts often observe that there are a wide variety of acceptable ways in which an attorney can counsel her client about whether or not to accept a plea offer. During the plea allocution in court, the defendant would have been asked in some manner whether anyone coerced him into accepting the plea deal. Obviously he said "no" or the plea would not have been accepted, and this denial is often used to defeat his later claim of coercion. Finally, as the Supreme Court famously declared in 2012, "criminal justice today is for the most part a system of pleas, not a system of trials."[39] The system relies upon and therefore encourages guilty pleas. Even more strongly it resists surrendering a guilty plea once obtained, as the plea is viewed as having finalized the resolution of a criminal case. One more case the system needs no longer to worry about. Given all these obstacles, it is not surprising that relatively few guilty pleas are deemed to have been improperly obtained.

On relatively rare occasions, the allegation of the defendant that his attorney coerced him into a guilty plea decision will be accepted by the court and lead to a reexamination or invalidation of a plea agreement. In the case of *In Re Vargas,*[40] the defendant alleged that his attorney presented him "with an ultimatum — take the deal or have a sham trial in which she would present no evidence on my behalf and would stand mute."[41] Largely because the court found this attorney had exhibited so many deficiencies in her representation of the defendant, it credited the accuracy of this outrageous statement and understandably found it to be improperly coercive. At times an attorney will threaten to withdraw from continuing to represent the defendant if his client refuses to accept the recommended guilty plea. In *Downton v. Perini,*[42] such coercive

---

39. Lafler v. Cooper, 566 U.S.156, 170 (2012).
40. 100 Cal. Rptr. 2d 265 (Ct. App. 2000).
41. *Id.* at 277.
42. 511 F. Supp. 258 (N.D. Ohio 1981).

behavior by the attorney was deemed to make the guilty plea involuntary although the court was quick to note that such plea invalidations are rare because "this case presents a unique factual circumstance: the attorney acknowledged making the statement intending that it change the defendant's mind."[43] In most cases, attorneys are less likely to damage their reputations by making such acknowledgments.

Judicial opinions describe the required standard that attorneys **must** live up to when counseling clients whether to accept a guilty plea offer. Beyond that standard, though, is what lawyers owe their clients as a matter of their professional duty regarding how they **should** conduct those counseling sessions. They should endeavor to be accurate, careful, and caring during these critical discussions with their client. Attorneys should begin the session by explaining in depth the bargain that has been offered and taking care to clarify any ambiguities or uncertainties regarding the charge or sentence that may be present in the proposed agreement. Next, they should assess the case as accurately as possible, specifically gauging and discussing with the client the likelihood of conviction at trial should the plea be rejected and the range of possible and likely sentences that would follow such a conviction. Attorneys should discuss with the client the possible collateral consequences that may flow from his guilty plea. Finally, they should familiarize their clients with the procedure that will take place in court before the guilty plea can be formally accepted by the judge. At some point, the attorney should ask the client if he has any questions about these matters. Then comes the hard part.

Attorneys should share with the client their thoughts on the wisdom of accepting or rejecting the plea offer. As they do so, the attorney should always be mindful that as the defendant is the one who will bear the consequences of this decision, it is his or her decision to make. Hopefully by this time, the attorney has gotten to know her client, learned what the client's primary concerns are, and created some sort of hierarchy regarding those concerns that will enable the attorney to assist her client in making the choice that is best for him. The attorney has at least some experience in and knowledge of the criminal justice system that allows her to offer an educated opinion about whether the plea should be accepted. To deprive the defendant of that experience, knowledge, and hopefully wisdom in making a decision of such critical importance is an abandonment of the fiduciary duty an attorney owes to a client.

In providing that recommendation, the attorney has to be careful not to use her position of trust and authority to manipulate or compel her client into

---

43. *Id.* at 266.

choosing the option he really does not wish to choose. That is true where even, as in the *Williams* case, the attorney believes that accepting his advice will save his client's life. The most common example of this kind of attorney bullying is probably where the attorney, based largely on her assessment of the likelihood of conviction at trial, is convinced that accepting the plea offer is in the best interest of her client. Attorneys in such situations are highly tempted to use strong words such as "you are going to go away for a long time if you reject this plea" to get the defendant to accept the plea. Another method to persuade the client is to offer analogies in the form of mathematical assessments or hypothetical comparisons designed to demonstrate the likelihood that that attorney's assessment of the decision is highly likely to be the correct one. Mindful that he cannot guarantee that the defendant will be convicted at trial, the attorney may say your chance of being acquitted is about one in a hundred. In *Fields*, the attorney drew a line and sectioned off a very small portion to demonstrate the unlikelihood he would receive the death penalty if he accepted the blind plea she was advocating. In another case, the attorney told a client that his chances of receiving a sentence above the two years of incarceration recommended by the prosecutor was the same as being hit by a car when the client left his office.[44] The good news for the defendant was that he was not in fact hit by a car. The bad news was that the judge sentenced him to ten years in prison and his attempt to overturn the plea on the basis of his attorney's misleading advice was unsuccessful. The dilemma for the attorney then is to convey why she is making the recommendation she is without compulsion, manipulation, or overstatement.

With this in mind I suggest avoiding the following methods of persuasion. While an experienced criminal attorney can make a reasonable assessment of the likelihood of a trial verdict in most situations, there are way too many variables that come into play before and during the trial for the attorney to be able to offer any kind of mathematical percentage of the likelihood of that verdict. Offering a percentage or something similar is unwise because the number has no basis in fact and because the very nature of offering percentages may have an overly powerful impact on the defendant by conveying a degree of mathematical accuracy that does not exist. To the vulnerable defendant, comparing his chances of success at trial to being hit by lightning, making two consecutive basketball shots from half court, or winning the lottery communicates virtual certainty. The lawyer may think to himself that he is leaving the door open to his assessment being incorrect, but the client is not likely to share that nuanced

---

44. Huffman v. State, 499 S.W. 2d 565 (Mo. Ct. App. 1973).

interpretation of his words. The best approach, I believe, is to use general words that describe what in the end is only the attorney's opinion and then to thoroughly explain the basis for that opinion. "I think it would be wise to accept this plea because as we have discussed, the government's case against you is strong, our legal motions have been denied and I do not see a successful appeal of them. Your case depends on the testimony of one witness, who as I explained is likely to have his prior convictions elicited by the prosecutor which may cause a jury to disregard your alibi. The guilty plea offer guarantees you no more than five years in prison and we can argue for less. While I don't know what the judge will do, I can tell you in the past she has sentenced below the maximum on guilty pleas such as this. Similarly, I can't say what your sentence will be if you are convicted at trial, but given your record, the seriousness of the charges, and the typical post-trial sentence for such charges, it is highly likely to be substantially more than five years." A difficult moment for the attorney can arise if the defendant, who understandably seeks certainty, requests more precision in the attorney's assessments. When combined with the attorney's belief that accepting her recommendation is in the best interest of her client, the temptation is strong to use the kind of comparisons and assertive techniques of persuasion that she has so far successfully avoided. She should continue to avoid them. "I'm sorry but I don't want to make something sound certain that is not certain. I can offer you my best assessment as I have done and try to answer any questions you have."

One method of pressuring a resistant client into accepting a guilty plea is for the attorney to convince members of his family of the wisdom of accepting the plea and then recruit them to work on the defendant. In one notorious example of such a tactic, we can see both the lengths to which some attorneys are willing to go to persuade their client to accept their judgment about the plea offer and the difficulty defendants have of convincing a court that this pressure made their guilty plea coercive. In the New York capital murder case of *United States ex rel. Brown v. La Vallee*,[45] Brown's attorneys tried to persuade him to accept the prosecutor's offer of a guilty plea to second degree murder and thus avoid the possibility of a death sentence. Based on the strong case against Brown, the attorneys believed and a court later agreed the plea offer was clearly in Brown's best interest. Brown, however, was convinced he would be acquitted at trial based on his claim of self-defense and rejected his attorneys' repeated arguments that this defense would prove unsuccessful. Despite months of trying to convince Brown of the benefit of a guilty plea, they

---

45. 424 F.2d 457 (2d Cir. 1970).

were unsuccessful and finally decided that they needed reinforcements. The attorneys then spoke to Brown's mother, convinced her of the wisdom of her son's accepting the plea and brought her in from Texas to persuade her son. The court record then reveals the following about their conversation:

> The confrontation was stormy and emotional. At the hearing below, Mrs. Parker recalled the conversation:
>
> Well, I asked him if he would plead guilty, and he said no. I said, "Well, don't you care anything about me or consider my feelings or your brothers or sisters?" And we talked all like that for a little while, and he begin to kind of look like he had a soft feeling for me. And I realized that maybe he was changing his mind.
>
> Q. Do you recall saying anything to him?
>
> Well I brought out the fact that it would be awfully hard on the family to come here and have to claim a body that had been electrocuted, for a mother to have to do something like that.
>
> Brown recalled:
>
> My mother started to talk to me. She told me that she had talked to the lawyers about the case, that they had told her that I was going to the electric chair if I didn't plead guilty.
>
> I tried to explain to my mother that I didn't believe that the jury was going to find me guilty of murder, that I wanted a jury trial, and that she didn't have anything to worry about.
>
> However, she had already talked to the lawyers and her mind was made up on that point, that I was going to the electric chair, and she explained to me about the other members of the family, my two brothers and a sister, that were younger than I, and she said "You should at least think about them."
>
> She kept pleading with me to plead guilty and I kept telling her that I was not going to do it. She finally became hysterical and very upset, and I said "All right, try to be calm. I'll plead guilty. You won't have nothing to worry about."
>
> And at that point she informed the lawyers that I had changed my mind.[46]

In agreeing with the trial judge's decision denying Brown the right to invalidate his guilty plea because it was coercive, the U.S. Court of Appeals focused on

---

46. *Id.* at 459–60.

the wisdom of accepting the guilty plea offer as agreed to apparently by everyone in the case except Brown. It then decided:

> To say that Brown's will was overborne is an unrealistic assessment of his situation. If his will is defined as a predetermination to contest his guilt, certainly this was overcome: the proposition is self-evident, for almost every claim that a plea was coerced involves an initial determination not to plead guilty. Indeed, almost every guilty plea is preceded by a plea of not guilty. When, however, Brown's will is assayed at the time he had reached a reasoned assessment of all the factors militating for and against a plea, it is apparent that his decision was a free and rational choice.[47]

In other words, no matter the tactics used to get Brown to accept the plea offer, because acceptance was the wise thing for him to do, it was clearly a rational decision and not coerced.

While I think the Brown case was wrongly decided, I want to be clear about the apparent intent of the attorneys in their actions with their client. It seems that they were trying to save their client's life by getting him to accept a plea that would do just that. They viewed with apparent accuracy the weakness of his defense and the likelihood of his conviction at trial with the strong possibility of a death sentence following the verdict. In other words, the plea offer made sense. It is therefore understandable why they tried every tactic at their disposal to get their client to see the wisdom of accepting the plea. But attorneys should know where to draw the line and never lose sight of the fact that the decision of whether to accept a plea offer is for the client to make, free of coercion. Additionally, allowing or even encouraging their clients to consult with family members they trust before making the critical decision of whether to accept a guilty plea offer is a valid approach for attorneys to take. But once again, as in the *Brown* case, too much is too much, and the attorney must ensure that the ultimate decision is that of the client alone.

5. The special problem created by the client's claim of innocence

It is then a critically important responsibility for the defense attorney to consider whether and how to recommend acceptance or rejection of a guilty plea offer to her client. As described above, this should be based on an assess-

---

47. *Id.* at 461.

ment of the likelihood of success at trial, an educated guess as to the difference between the sentence offered in the plea deal and the nearly certain heavier sentence her client will receive if convicted at trial, and finally, her knowledge of her client's interests and concerns. While such an assessment can be difficult, the goal is clear — the best likely outcome for her client in terms of the offense and the sentence. This, of course, is the overall goal in representing a criminal defendant that all attorneys assume and with which they are familiar.

In at least one scenario, however, that goal is not so clear. When a client continues to insist that he is not guilty of the crime to which he is being asked to plead guilty, an ethical as well as a strategic dilemma for the attorney arises at two points in the process. First, when discussing the plea bargain with the client, should the attorney recommend a plea of guilty to a person who claims innocence? Second, at the moment during the allocution when the defendant is asked in court whether he is in fact guilty of the crime he is pleading to, he must in almost every case answer in the affirmative for the plea bargain to take effect. Here the ethical question for the attorney is, if she does recommend acceptance of the plea, what should she advise the client regarding how to answer that question? Before we explore how attorneys deal with these problems, we should take note of why clients tell their attorneys they are innocent and then consider the two types of pleas that may somewhat reduce these moral dilemmas for the attorney.

A client may tell his lawyer that he is innocent of a crime because he suspects the lawyer will work harder for him in such a case. While we hope that lawyers will do their utmost for every client, it is not unreasonable for a defendant to believe that lawyers feel more responsibility when representing those they believe to be innocent. Then there are those defendants who are too embarrassed to admit their guilt, even to their own lawyer (and sometimes even to themselves). Involvement in crimes such as child molestation or embezzlement from friends or family would be examples of the types of crimes that might be too emotionally painful for some defendants to admit. Some defendants may mistakenly regard their conduct as non-criminal, perhaps because "he (the victim) deserved what happened to him." Finally, some defendants say they are innocent because they actually are innocent.

The two exceptions to the requirement that the defendant must acknowledge his guilt in order to accept a plea bargain (to be discussed in depth in Chapter VII on types of pleas) are what are referred to as Alford and no lo contendere pleas. An Alford plea permits a defendant to plead guilty and accept the deal offered to him while still denying his guilt for the crime. No lo contendere pleas are those in which the defendant neither admits nor denies his guilt. No lo contendere pleas are often taken to avoid certain negative consequences in civil suits that flow from traditional guilty pleas. In both types of pleas, the defendant can receive the same sentence as in a traditional guilty plea. It is important to recognize that while these types of pleas can offer partial solace to defense attorneys by allowing their clients to avoid having to say in court that they committed a crime they claim to be innocent of, these pleas are relatively rare. One study published in 2009 reported that only 6% of guilty pleas were taken via Alford pleas.[48] While no such study for no lo contendere pleas was found, their number is likely far less.

There are several reasons why these types of pleas are so rarely taken. For one thing, many defendants care far less about acknowledging their guilt than about what charge or sentencing considerations they will receive for doing so. As both of these alternative pleas permit the same punishments as traditional convictions for the same charges, the benefit of seeking one of these alternative pleas is often viewed as negligible and therefore the incentive for maintaining innocence is diminished. But specifically as to those who maintain their innocence, the numbers of such pleas are still likely to be relatively rare. Both the prosecutor and the judge must go along with the defendant's request to plead guilty via an Alford or no lo contendere plea. Some judges will not accept such pleas as a matter of principle, believing that anyone who claims innocence should not be convicted of a crime without a trial—regardless of the defendant's preference. Even judges who do accept Alford or no lo contendere pleas may accept them only rarely even when requested to do so. Prosecutors, who might believe they are speaking for the victim, are often reluctant to let the defendant derive some benefit from a plea agreement without first acknowledging his participation in the crime. While it is the prosecutor and not the victim who makes the decision about plea bargaining offers, most prosecutors appropriately take the victim's feelings and opinions into account before doing so. Some victims may indicate that they can get closure from the crime only after the defendant's admission to it and thus argue for prosecutors to accept only traditional guilty pleas.

Faced with the strategic and moral problems that arise from clients who maintain their innocence, defense attorneys confront these problems in a variety of ways. Some attorneys attempt to avoid these problems altogether by deliberately not asking their client if he committed the crime. To avoid the defendant's volunteering this information, many attorneys who pursue this strategy will tell their clients upfront that they do not wish to know if the client is

---

48. Alan Feuer, Alford Pleas: A Violation of Rights or Psychological Salve?, Seattle Times (originally published in N.Y. Times, Nov. 23, 2017), https://www.seattletimes.com/nation-world/alford-pleas-a-violation-of-rights-or-psychological-salve/.

guilty. The information about the crime they seek from their client is often limited to learning what the prosecutor knows and planning for whatever defenses that can be raised. By not inquiring as to the defendant's guilt, these attorneys can counsel acceptance of a plea based solely on whether they think the deal is a good one regarding charge and sentencing considerations and not on the ethical questions raised by recommending a guilty plea to someone who maintains his innocence. Additionally, there are ethical issues related to the trial itself that limit a defense attorney's strategic options if the defendant informs the attorney that he is in fact guilty of the crime.[49] Understanding the ethical and strategic benefits that can be gained from not asking a client if he committed the crime, it is still safe to say that most defense attorneys choose not to follow this approach. These attorneys feel that without getting all the information they can from their client about the crime, they are severely limited both in their trial strategy and in how to negotiate and counsel during plea bargaining.

Situations involving the special concerns that emerge for attorneys whose clients claim innocence typically arise in the following scenario. Through negotiations with the prosecutor, the defense attorney has secured a plea offer that the attorney regards as highly beneficial to the defendant. The government has strong evidence and is likely to obtain a conviction at trial. From his knowledge of the judge's sentencing pattern and the typical sentences in this jurisdiction for these crimes, the attorney has concluded that the sentence offered as part of a guilty plea will result in the defendant's spending significantly less time in prison than were he to be convicted at trial. The attorney then recommends acceptance of the plea offer to his client. The defendant makes clear his innocence of the charges to his attorney, but because he is convinced by her of its benefits, he is still willing to accept the guilty plea offer.[50]

At this stage, what is the responsibility of the attorney? Should she tell her client that as an innocent man, he should not plead guilty? If the client

---

49. For example, an attorney is ethically bound not to perpetrate a fraud upon the court. If the defendant has told his attorney that he is guilty of the crime, that could severely limit the defense attorney's ability to elicit testimony from the defendant or other supporting witnesses at trial. *See* Nix v. Whiteside, 475 U.S. 157 (1986).

50. While the defendant might have proclaimed his innocence to his attorney earlier, it is likely she still would have engaged in negotiations with the prosecutor designed to obtain the best offer from the prosecutor. It is not unusual for clients to tell their attorneys they are innocent for some of the reasons discussed above in the text and then acknowledge their guilt to their attorney at some point later in the process. In the event this occurs and the case against the defendant is strong, the attorney will want to ensure that she has secured the best possible outcome for her client by participating in plea negotiations.

still wishes to plead guilty, what does she advise her client about how to answer the question posed to him in court at the plea allocution inquiring if he is in fact guilty of the crime? Some years ago, a federal district court offered what it believed was a clear-cut answer to the first question. In *United States v. Rogers*,[51] the defendant told his lawyer he was innocent of the crimes for which he was charged, and he asserted that innocence at various stages of the judicial process. However, faced with a trial apparently dependent on a jury's weighing the credibility of a government agent against "a convicted felon and narcotics addict," the defense attorney recommended acceptance of the guilty plea offer made by the prosecutor. In reviewing this advice by the attorney, the court here acknowledged that it was "reasonable" for the attorney to think the best path for Rogers was to plead guilty.[52] Still the court invalidated the plea, holding that it was wrong for counsel to recommend a guilty plea to a client who maintains his innocence even if the plea appears beneficial to the client. As to counsel's apparent view that even if innocent, the defendant would likely be convicted at trial, the court asserted that, "such a view is not only cynical but unwarranted. Innocent men in the past have been convicted; but such instances have been so rare and our judicial system has so many safeguards that no lawyer worthy of his profession justifiably may assume that an innocent person will be convicted."[53] Easy for the court to say.

In 2019, the North Carolina Court of Appeals reviewed this question from a different perspective. In *State v. Chandler*,[54] the defendant was charged with a first-degree sex offense and taking indecent liberties with a child. His attorney reached an agreement with the prosecutor whereby Chandler would plead guilty to the indecent liberties charge only and face a maximum sentence of 59 months incarceration. Chandler indicated both in writing and before the court that he wished to accept this plea bargain and that he was in fact guilty of the charge. However, when pressed on the question of his guilt by the judge, Chandler said he was pleading guilty to avoid further trauma for his granddaughter, not because he was guilty of the crime. Despite Chandler's continued desire to plead guilty, the judge would not accept the plea and launched into a statement about how as a lawyer he would never let a client plead guilty unless he admitted his guilt unequivocally and how he maintains that require-

---

51. 289 F. Supp. 726 (D. Conn. 1968).
52. *Id.* at 729.
53. *Id.* at 729–30.
54. 827 S.E.2d 113 (N.C. Ct. App. 2019).

ment as a judge.[55] Chandler was then forced to go to trial and was convicted of both charges. He was sentenced to a period of incarceration of from 208 months to 320 months. The court of appeals denied Chandler's claim that he should have been allowed to plead guilty. Chandler then will have from 12 to 21 years of extra prison to time to be grateful to the trial judge for "protecting" him from his guilty plea. This is an example of the paternalism that runs rampant in plea bargaining decisions.

Since *Rogers* was decided, the work of various innocence projects and others has demonstrated through scientific evidence and other means that many people have been convicted at trials for crimes they did not commit. No one can give anywhere near a precise estimate of criminal cases in which innocent people have been convicted, so it is unsurprising that the percentage is said to vary from less than 1%[56] to upwards of 6%.[57] Regardless of the actual number, it means thousands of people have been wrongly convicted of crimes and that defense attorneys must keep this in mind as they consider whether to recommend a guilty plea to a client who maintains his innocence. The problem for attorneys goes deeper, however, because for reasons discussed earlier, a defendant may tell his lawyer he is innocent even if he is not. So the actual dilemma faced by attorneys relates to clients who tell their lawyer they are innocent regardless of whether the defendants' actual innocence is ever determined. It is safe to say this number considerably exceeds the cases of actual innocence.

There are several ways in which attorneys can deal with claims of innocence by their clients in addressing guilty plea offers from the prosecution. They can adhere to the reasoning of the *Rogers* case and counsel their client not to plead guilty, going even further and withdrawing from the case if the defendant insists upon pleading guilty. Another approach is for the attorney to conduct a thorough assessment of the witnesses and evidence to be presented by both the defense and the prosecution before making a plea recommendation. If, after that assessment, the attorney concludes that despite the defendant's assertion of innocence he is in fact guilty of the crimes charged, the attorney might recommend acceptance of the guilty plea. If the defendant then admits

55. *Id.* at 115.

56. Paul Cassell, How Often Are Innocent Persons Convicted?, reason.com/The Volokh Conspiracy (Nov. 1, 2018), https://reason.com/2018/11/01/how-often-are-innocent-persons-convicted/.

57. Michele W. Berger, Wrongful Convictions Reported for 6 Percent of Crimes, Penn Today (May 8, 2018), https://penntoday.upenn.edu/news/first-estimate-wrongful-convictions-general-prison-population.

his guilt, the problem is resolved. This position is an implicit acceptance of the difference between a client who claims he is innocent and one who appears to be actually innocent. Finally, the attorney may decide that his client's best interest is served by honoring the client's expressed primary interest of not going to prison or minimizing the time he must serve. In such a case the attorney might decide to proceed with the plea agreement regardless of the defendant's innocence claim. It becomes necessary then to explore how an attorney operating under this final approach actually proceeds regarding the plea agreement.

Recall that there are two separate points in time that the attorney recommending a plea of guilty to a client who maintains innocence must be concerned with. The first is the actual recommendation to the client. In this situation, the client will undoubtedly ask his lawyer how he can plead guilty if he is innocent. Here the attorney must think of how to protect herself as well as her client. She should be aware that if the defendant later challenges his guilty plea for whatever reason and her knowledge of the defendant's claim of innocence at the time she recommended acceptance of the plea comes out, the attorney may face sanctions as well as damage to her reputation. One way of handling this potential problem is to see if the prosecutor and judge would be open to an Alford plea, allowing the defendant to maintain his innocence while pleading guilty. Assuming for reasons discussed earlier that path is not open to the attorney, she might explain to the defendant the situation quite clearly and allow him to make the decision. "I believe this is a very good deal for you given the likelihood of your being convicted at trial and the much heavier sentence you will probably receive after trial than what you are being offered now. But if you tell the judge you did not commit the crime, the plea will not be accepted and you will have to go to trial. So I want you to think very carefully if you are innocent before you tell me whether you want to accept this plea." Statements such as this from attorney to client are far from a perfect solution both ethically and in terms of counseling approaches generally. Still, this statement to the defendant walks the line between the sanctimonious pronouncements of courts about not having an innocent man plead guilty even if it is in his best interest to do so and crossing a line that can get the attorney into trouble.[58]

Having dealt with this sticky counseling situation, the next time the attorney will feel his throat constrict will be during the allocution in court when the de-

---

58. *See, e.g.,* Wisconsin Supreme Court Rules of Professional Conduct 20:1.2 (d) ("A lawyer shall not counsel a client to engage, or assist a client, in conduct that the lawyer knows is criminal or fraudulent, but a lawyer may discuss the legal consequences of any proposed course of conduct with a client and may counsel or assist a client to make a good faith effort to determine the validity, scope, meaning, or application of the law").

fendant is asked if he committed the crime to which he is pleading guilty. It is a clear ethical violation for an attorney to perpetrate a fraud upon the court. Even if the attorney took the counseling approach suggested immediately above before having the client make the choice, that nuance may be lost on a reviewing court or a bar association attorney grievance commission. If the defendant later challenges the plea, then "I told my lawyer I didn't commit the crime, but he told me to tell the court I did anyway" not only sounds bad but can have significant professional consequences for the attorney. Still, the attorney should always endeavor to do what is in his client's best interest within the bounds of law and ethics. If the client agrees that his best interest is served by accepting the plea and understands that he will have to acknowledge his guilt in court for that plea to be accepted, the choice must be his. The attorney should explain the client's options carefully and then memorialize in notes (protected by confidentiality and never to be revealed unless the attorney is later accused by the client of perpetuating a fraud on the court) that when asked to think carefully about his guilt, the client agreed that he was guilty.

Chapter V

Role of the Judge

The third party who plays a critical role in plea bargaining is the judge. Cases and commentators often institutionalize this party by referring to him or her as "the court." As it is a person and not a structure who determines if and for how long someone's freedom should be deprived in a criminal case, we shall call the judge, "the judge." We begin our examination of the role judges play in plea bargaining by looking at their motivations to settle cases without trials. Only then can we understand fully how the judge impacts plea bargaining at several critical junctures of the process. We can see the role the judge plays in the plea bargaining process at three points in the prosecution of a criminal case. The first point occurs during negotiations designed to arrive at a plea agreement, the second when the judge conducts the allocution formally accepting the guilty plea in court, and the final time is at sentencing.

A. Motivations for the Judge to Bargain

1. Pressures on the judge

As with the prosecutor, the judge has a large stake in seeing that the criminal justice system operates with relative efficiency. Judges, then, feel the same caseload pressure as prosecutors. In a highly influential law review article written in 1976, Albert Altschuler explored the nature of this particular motivation by interviewing judges who disposed of many cases in their courts through guilty-plea agreements and criminal defense attorneys who worked with the judges. One New York City attorney said that in order to minimize trials, "most trial judges look for guilty pleas the way that salesmen look for orders."[1] Altschuler relates a conversation between two Illinois judges, one from Chicago and the other from a rural area in the state, in which the rural judge discussed his opposition to actively participating in plea bargaining. He asked the Chicago judge how he could justify the more active role the latter took in a process that should be handled primarily by prosecutors and defense attorneys. This led to the following colloquy between them:

> Without replying directly, the Chicago judge asked his downstate counterpart, "How many cases will you have on your docket when you return to the bench on Monday?" "Four or five," said the downstate judge. "How about you?" "One hundred seventy five," said the Chicago judge, "and that is the answer to your question."[2]

Given the increased percentage of cases disposed of through plea bargaining since 1976, this causative factor for judges to encourage such bargaining is likely to have grown stronger.

Additionally, trial judges inevitably have to answer to administrative judges, who in turn have to answer to their superiors up the judicial chain and to politicians to account for any substantial delays in handling criminal cases. The politicians have to respond to complaints from constituents coming at them in various ways. Victims want to know why they have to wait so long for justice in their cases. The families of defendants want to know why their relative spent months or even years in jail before getting the opportunity to prove his innocence. The public wants to know why politicians are spending so much of their hard earned tax dollars on the criminal justice system, expenses incurred in part by delays in finalizing cases. While plea bargaining cannot solve these problems, they would be more severe if significantly more cases went to trial.

As both a prosecutor and defense attorney, I recall quite clearly the pressure that came from judges to settle as many cases as possible. Two of the primary ways in which judges were evaluated was by how many cases they disposed of and how many days their courtroom was deemed to be busy. Absent a trial or hearing, it was a case disposed of through a guilty plea that kept most courts "busy" each day and satisfied the administrative judge.[3]

---

1. Albert Altschuler, The Trial Judge's Role in Plea Bargaining, Part 1, 76 Colum. L. Rev. 1059, 1099 (1976).

2. *Id.* at 1100.

3. For a fairly recent study of judges that explores their various motivations for wishing to dispose of criminal cases as quickly as possible, see Nancy King and Ronald Wright, The

2. Plea bargaining reduces the stress surrounding sentencing

While allocation of time and resources is the most prominent motivation for judges to plea bargain cases, others exist as well. Among the heaviest of emotional burdens placed upon judges is the decision of whether to send a person to prison and for how long. Child custody and sentencing matters are reportedly the two decisions that judges struggle with the most.[4] It is not to diminish the importance of the many other kinds of decisions judges make to recognize the critical nature of determining with whom to place a child or the deprivation of a criminal defendant's freedom. One lawyer experienced in the criminal courts said, "[v]irtually every judge will tell you that sentencing is the most solemn and difficult decision they must make."[5] Because many judges struggle with deciding sentences in criminal cases, plea deals in which the prosecutor and the defense have agreed on a sentence, a sentencing range, or at least a maximum sentence make the judge's job easier, or at least less emotionally troubling. While the judge has the right to reject a plea agreement or accept it only if the other parties agree that her sentencing hand won't be bound by the conditions proposed by the parties, many judges welcome guidance from the attorneys who are likely to know more about the case than will the judge. Additionally, if the case and/or sentence is notorious or controversial, any agreement between the attorneys can provide the judge with a degree of cover from public criticism.

Invisible Revolution in Plea Bargaining: Managerial Judging and Judicial Participation in Negotiations, 95 Tex. L. Rev. 325 (2016).

4. As one federal district court judge wrote, "If the hundreds of American judges who sit on criminal cases were polled as to what was the most trying facet of their jobs, the vast majority would almost certainly answer 'Sentencing.' In no other judicial function is the judge more alone; no other act of his carries greater potentialities for good or evil than the determination of how society will treat its transgressors." Judge Irving R. Kaufman, Sentencing: The Judge's Problem, The Atlantic (Jan. 1960), https://www.theatlantic.com /past/docs/unbound/flashbks/death/kaufman.htm.

Regarding custody decisions, see Thomas J. Reidy, Richard M. Silver, & Alan Carlson, Child Custody Decisions: A Survey of Judges, 23 Fam. L.Q. 75 (Spring 1989), https://www.jstor.org/stable/25739798?seq=1.

5. Joel Cohen, When Judges Struggle with Sentencing, Law.com/N.Y.L.J. (December 14, 2018), https://www.law.com/newyorklawjournal/2018/12/14/when-judges-struggle-with-sentencing/.

3. Minimizing the likelihood of an appeal

As plea bargains are essentially agreements between the parties, it is hardly surprising that only a very small percentage of them are challenged through appeals. When the sentence is left open to some degree at the time of the plea and the defendant is later disappointed in the sentence meted out, he may challenge the plea agreement. The defendant could also suffer from buyer's remorse, based perhaps on what friends and relatives are telling him about how he could have beaten the case by prevailing at trial. Such disappointment or buyer's remorse alone will not allow the defendant out of a plea that has been finalized in court. If, however, there is some issue regarding the manner in which the plea was agreed upon, its formal acceptance in court, how it was implemented, or the nature of the plea itself (directed usually at its knowing or voluntary nature), a successful appeal from the plea is possible. In a system whose survival is often seen to depend on plea bargaining, comparatively few of these challenges are successful.

Convictions obtained after trials, on the other hand, are almost always the subject of appeals, often several appeals. The judge's many decisions throughout the criminal justice process are among the issues addressed on appeal. These include decisions on pre-trial matters (such as the constitutionality of searches, confessions, and identification procedures), evidentiary rulings made during trial, and finally, the judge's sentence. Judges generally do not like having their rulings reversed by an appellate court. As one experienced litigation attorney put it:

> I don't think there's any distinction to be made between how a trial court or an intermediate court of appeals judge would react to a reversal: judges are like most people in that they don't enjoy being told publicly that they are wrong. Lawyers as a profession—and all major court judges are former practicing lawyers—don't tend to handle being wrong well. And being people in a position of power and authority, it's fair to wager that judges don't hear they're wrong very often, at least not compared to most people. All of this is to say that being publicly told by one's peers that you made a mistake has to sting at least a little bit.[6]

One effective way for a judge to significantly minimize the chance of being corrected by an appellate court is to dispose of the case through a plea bargain.

---

6. Quoting Ty Doyle, Esq., https://www.quora.com/Do-judges-get-mad-when-their-decisions-are-reversed-on-appeal-Or-do-appellate-judges-get-mad-when-they-are-reversed-again-by-a-higher-court.

B. Judicial Involvement in Plea Negotiations

Most civil cases include pre-trial conferences. In these conferences, the attorney for each party and the judge get together to resolve whatever issues can be decided at that point in the litigation process. Most attorneys and judges will tell you that another important purpose of the pre-trial conference is to attempt to arrive at a settlement of the case, thus avoiding the time, expense and uncertainty of a trial. During these settlement discussions, judges are often active participants in making suggestions, sharing their opinions on the strength of each side's case and offering what they believe to be a fair way to settle the case. Although judges cannot compel the attorneys to settle the case, some judges are particularly aggressive in pressing the attorneys to accept a settlement proposal. While such an aggressive role by the judge can be quite concerning, no one is going to prison in a civil case because the judge pressured them or their attorney to accept a deal. In criminal cases, plea bargains often result in prison time and constitutional issues can arise based on the conduct of the judge during negotiations; thus, the role of the judge in settling a case without a trial is even more controversial.

It is not surprising that there have been many cases and comments dealing with the nature of the role assumed by the judge in plea bargaining. If arriving at a plea agreement is a positive for the participants in a criminal case (as suggested by the overwhelming number of cases disposed of through such agreements) and the participation of the judge can facilitate or make more likely such a deal, is not having the judge participate in plea negotiations a good thing? Well, maybe. This section will look at the benefits and disadvantages of judicial participation in plea negotiations, examining the rules and judicial opinions regarding such participation and the different ways in which judges participate.

1. Can the judge become involved?

At one end of the spectrum regarding judicial involvement in plea bargaining is the position federal judges must assume. The rules that govern all federal criminal prosecutions prohibit judges from participating in the negotiations surrounding a possible guilty plea. Federal Rule of Criminal Procedure 11(c)1 reads in part, "An attorney for the government and the defendant's attorney, or the defendant when proceeding pro se, may discuss and reach a plea agreement. The court **must not** participate in these discussions."(emphasis added). Still, because the federal judge may reject a plea agreement between the parties, the judge could reject all agreements until she gets the one she

thinks appropriate and thereby become involved in the negotiations in fact if
not in form. Those who practice in the federal courts say this almost never
happens, as judges want to honor the purpose of the statute and because they
do not wish to impede plea agreements except in the rarest of cases.

In federal courts, then, it is usually only the prosecutor and defense attorney
who engage in guilty plea negotiations — negotiations which, as demonstrated
by the statistics, are successful in about 19 of every 20 cases. These agreements
may leave sentencing totally within the judge's discretion, restricted only by
the minimum and maximum sentence for the charges to which the defendant
pled guilty and other requirements of the law, such as the consequences of
prior convictions and mandatory minimum sentences. Other plea agreements
limit the judge's discretion by specifying the range of sentences that can be
imposed, while still others dictate a specific sentence. If the judge accepts the
plea agreement, he is bound by those terms.

At the other end of the spectrum is the approach taken by some judges in
state courts. In varying ways and with varying degrees of assertiveness, some
judges participate quite directly in the plea negotiations, in order to reach a
deal acceptable to both parties. As a state prosecutor in New York City, I
worked with many judges who welcomed the opportunity to influence plea
negotiations. As a public defense attorney in Syracuse, New York, I worked
with one judge whose participation in plea negotiations was especially direct.
This judge would schedule meetings with the prosecutor and me to discuss
the progress of plea negotiations in all of our cases and offer his opinion about
what an appropriate settlement of the case would entail. The judge was always
reasonable and never attempted to force his opinion on either of us. Possibly
as a result, many cases were disposed of at those meetings. There are many instances, however, where judges have affirmatively pushed plea deals on one or
both parties, pressuring acceptance. Between this aggressive approach and the
non-involvement of federal judges and some of their state counterparts, there
are many ways in which judges play a role in plea bargaining. It is necessary,
therefore, to explore the advantages and disadvantages of judicial involvement
during the negotiations aimed at arriving at a guilty plea agreement.

2. When does judicial advocacy become judicial coercion?

If the law takes a relative default position on judicial involvement in plea
bargaining, it is that judges should minimize their participation in plea negotiations as much as possible. In addition to the absolute ban on participation

in plea bargaining imposed on federal judges, the American Bar Association recommends against judicial participation as well.[7] Approximately one-third of states bar judicial participation in plea bargaining either by statute, procedural rule, or case law, and many others discourage the practice.[8] Additionally, appellate decisions have generally frowned upon judicial participation in plea bargaining and invalidated pleas if that involvement was deemed excessive. There are several reasons for this. The reason most frequently offered for why judges should not participate in plea negotiations relates to their fundamental role in the judicial process and in criminal cases in particular. The judge's role is often compared to that of a referee, one who makes decisions based on rules (or interpretation of those rules) where possible and on fairness and common sense where no specific rule is applicable. What is crucial about the way in which a judge conducts herself is that however one views her functions, she must always remain neutral. Cynics might reasonably respond that judges are human beings, and decisions made by humans are rarely completely free of the biases and predispositions that affect all of us.[9] Still it is fair to say that almost all judges strive to decide issues with all the neutrality they can muster and that the judicial system expects and depends on such neutral decision-making from them. If a judge becomes an advocate for a plea offer, she is taking a position on the critical matter of the ultimate disposition of the case. When pushing a prosecutor to make a certain plea offer or accept one made by the defendant or by the judge herself, she is abandoning her neutrality. If the subject of the judge's pressure is the defendant or his attorney, the situation is even more problematic.

Consider how a situation involving judicial pressure on a defendant to accept a plea offer often develops.[10] The prosecutor has made a plea offer to the defense with a recommendation for a range of possible sentences. There are several ways in which the judge can respond to that offer to enhance the likelihood that a plea will be agreed upon by the parties. The judge can, for example, try to persuade the prosecutor to modify the offer to make it more at-

---

7. ABA, Standards for Criminal Justice: Pleas of Guilty (3d ed. 1999) [hereinafter ABA Standards 3d ed.].

8. Rishi Raj Batra, Judicial Participation in Plea Bargaining, A Dispute Resolution Perspective, 76 Ohio St. L.J. 565, 573–77 (2015).

9. This is one reason why, where possible, this book avoids institutionalizing judges as many judicial opinions do by referring to individual judges as "the court."

10. This situation reflects what can occur in many state courts where judges are not bound by the federal rule barring their participation in plea negotiations. Despite the attention often given to federal cases, state cases make up the overwhelming number of criminal prosecutions handled annually.

tractive to the defense, he can accept the sentencing range agreed to by the parties, or, more specifically, he can pledge that the sentence will be at the bottom of the range. Once the judge has made whatever suggestions or modifications to the proposed plea offer he thinks appropriate, he will most likely believe the deal is a good one for both sides. Some judges, based on their view about the extent of involvement they believe courts should take to foster plea bargains, may encourage or even pressure one or both sides to accept the proposed deal. As we will see, judges exert this pressure in a number of ways.

Now consider how this type of judicial pressure night be seen through the eyes of a criminal defendant. Assume, as in many instances, the defendant is reluctant to accept the offer to plead guilty, more than likely because he believes he has a decent chance of prevailing at trial. This belief could be based on a reasonable assessment of the law and facts of his case coming from his attorney, or perhaps on no good reason whatsoever. Regardless, as it is his life, the decision whether to accept the offer is his and his alone. Seeing the judge advocate for acceptance of the offer raises concerns in the mind of the defendant regarding how the judge will react if he rejects the deal. While a defendant might worry about the reaction of the prosecutor should the defendant reject the deal, the prosecutor is already not a neutral party in our adversary system. More importantly, the power of the prosecutor over the case differs significantly from that of the judge. While the prosecutor can make recommendations,[11] the crucial decisions during and after the trial on issues such as the admissibility of evidence and the sentencing fall to the judge. Even if the judge can make those decisions free of any negative feelings she may have towards the defendant for rejecting a plea offer she has advocated, the perception of the defendant might be that the judge is now aligned against him.[12]

If this pressure from the judge unduly influences the defendant's decision to accept the plea, that can be seen as judicial coercion. All pleas of guilty must be voluntary,[13] therefore undue pressure from a judge can lead to the invalidation of the plea at a later date. In assessing the impact of such pressure, it is important not to lose sight of the power the judge has over the life of the criminal defendant and the extremely vulnerable position in which the defendant

---

11. Prosecutors can make some unilateral decisions largely free of judicial control that punish defendants for rejecting plea offers in some instances. See the discussion of *Bordenkircher v. Hayes* in Chapter III. Role of the Prosecutor.

12. The negative view that most defendants are likely to already have of the criminal justice system and the role of the judge in that system undoubtedly contributes to this perception.

13. Boykin v. Alabama, 395 U.S. 238, 242–43 (1969), requires all pleas of guilty to be knowing, intelligent, and voluntary.

finds himself. In our criminal justice system, the defense attorney is entrusted with protecting the rights of the accused in many situations, and she can be a barrier to some kinds of additional coercion that may arise during the plea bargaining process. Additionally, appellate courts often invalidate guilty pleas where there is clear judicial coercion.

As one federal court put it:

> The unequal positions of the judge and the accused, one with the power to commit to prison and other deeply concerned to avoid prison, at once raise a question of fundamental fairness. When a judge becomes a participant in plea bargaining he brings to bear the full force and majesty of his office. His awesome power to impose a substantially longer or even maximum sentence in excess of that proposed is present whether referred to or not. A defendant needs no reminder that if he rejects the proposal, stands upon his right to trial, and is convicted, he faces a significantly longer sentence.... Intentionally or otherwise, and no matter how well motivated the judge may be, the accused is subjected to a subtle but powerful influence.[14]

As discussed in Chapter II, the mere fact that a sentence after conviction at trial is longer than the sentence contained in a plea offer, even if that offered sentence was agreed to by the judge, does not invalidate the post-trial sentence. To so invalidate would upend most post-trial sentences as they are invariably longer than the sentence offered as part of the proposed plea deal. At the risk of restating the obvious, were it otherwise, it would take an incompetent attorney and a foolish defendant to surrender the right to trial without receiving any benefit for doing so. As we have seen, appellate courts are extremely reluctant to hold that this difference between the sentence offered in the plea deal and the one imposed after a trial conviction constitutes judicial punishment or vindictiveness for exercising the right to trial. Where the trial judge is deemed to have participated excessively or improperly in the bargaining process, however, the assessment of post-trial vindictiveness changes. In such a situation, appellate courts generally are more amenable to considering this sentencing disparity among other factors in determining whether the guilty plea was achieved in part through judicial coercion. One appellate court enumerated these factors as follows:

(1) whether the trial judge initiated the plea discussions with the defendant ... ; (2) whether the trial judge, through his or her com-

---

14. United States ex rel. Elksnis v. Gilligan, 256 F. Supp. 244, 254 (S.D.N.Y. 1966).

ments on the record, appears to have departed from his or her role as an impartial arbiter by either urging the defendant to accept a plea, or by implying or stating that the sentence imposed would hinge on future procedural choices, such as exercising the right to trial; (3) the disparity between the plea offer and the ultimate sentence imposed; and (4) the lack of any facts on the record that explain the reason for the increased sentence other than that the defendant exercised his or her right to a trial or hearing.[15]

As this approach has developed, appellate courts often will look to see if the trial judge unduly attempted to encourage the defendant to accept a plea-bargained sentence. Such a finding is likely to lead the court to consider whether the considerably harsher sentence imposed after trial has any explanation other than judicial vindictiveness in response to the defendant's rejection of the plea. The implicit assumption here is that the judge's involvement in the plea negotiations made her an advocate for the deal, and therefore the defendant's negative response to the offer will be seen as a rejection of the judge's position in the case. If the post-trial sentence handed out by the judge is significantly longer than that contained in the plea offer rejected by the defendant, that sentence, absent a different justification, is often regarded as improperly vindictive.

In one case, the defendant described the judicial pressure on him to plead guilty as follows:

> I had no intentions of pleading guilty, but by my being young and inexperienced, being ignorant of the law, you invited me into [your] chambers, you influenced me and pressured me into giving a guilty plea....
>
> Your Honor, since I originally turned down a plea bargain in the hallway, I can honestly say if you wouldn't have taken me in your chambers, I wouldn't have never pled guilty. Myself being in a powerful judge's chambers, you eroded my ability to make a decision of my own.[16]

The judge involved in the case did not expressly deny the defendant's account, and unsurprisingly, the appellate court found this plea to be involuntary.

---

15. Wilson v. State, 845 So. 2d 142, 156 (Fla. 2003).
16. State v. Williams, 666 N.W.2d 58, 62 (Wis. Ct. App. 2003).

3. Comments by the judge during the bargaining regarding the likely sentence if the defendant rejects the plea and is convicted at trial

The more difficult issue to resolve regarding improper judicial participation in the bargaining process relates to comments made by the judge comparing in some way the sentence offered as part of the guilty plea to the sentence expected if the defendant is convicted at trial. As discussed in Chapter II on punishment for exercising the right to trial, courts offer several justifications for why post-trial sentences are allowed to be invariably harsher than those offered to the same defendant as part of a plea bargain. This differential sentencing (the difference between the sentence offered as part of a plea deal and that imposed after conviction at trial) occurs in the overwhelming number of criminal cases, and the increase in the post-trial sentence is rarely the subject of a successful attack by defendants. Defense attorneys of course know of the sentencing penalty to be imposed on defendants who are convicted after trial and factor that into discussions with their clients about whether to accept the plea offer. What the courts hold on a fairly consistent basis is that while judges may sentence the defendant who is convicted at trial more severely than the defendant who pleads guilty, they may not actually tell or even suggest to the defendant that the decision to choose a trial is a factor in the sentence.[17] There are two instances in the process where such a lapse into transparency and honesty by the judge can lead to the invalidation of a post-trial sentence. The first is during the negotiations when the judge, most likely to encourage a guilty plea, conveys either directly or indirectly to the defendant that there will be a harsher sentence should he reject the plea deal and be convicted after opting for a trial. The second occurs after trial when the judge is explaining the basis for her sentence and suggests the decision to decline the plea offer is a factor in the sentence.

One example of the first scenario is the case of *United States v. Stockwell*.[18] In *Stockwell*, the judge agreed to the three-year prison sentence arrived at by the attorneys if the defendant pled guilty. The judge then told Stockwell that if he rejected the plea and was convicted at trial, his sentence range would be

---

17. During the plea allocution, the judge does tell the defendant the possible sentences he faces if convicted at trial of the various charges. That those sentences are almost always more severe than the sentence possibilities included in the plea bargain poses by itself no problem regarding the voluntariness of the plea.

18. 472 F.2d 1186 (9th Cir. 1973).

from five to seven years. Stockwell rejected the plea and was convicted of a charge that carried a maximum prison term of 15 years and other counts that carried additional prison time. The judge honored what he told Stockwell before the plea was rejected and sentenced him to seven years. The court of appeals invalidated the sentence because "courts must not use the sentencing power as a carrot and stick to clear congested calendars, and they must not create an appearance of such a practice."[19] In this case, the record failed to show that "the court sentenced the defendant solely upon the facts of his case and his personal history, and not as punishment for his refusal to plead guilty."[20]

Of course, Stockwell received more prison time for choosing to go to trial and rejecting the plea offer as does virtually every defendant who opts for trial over a plea offer. In fact, the additional time he received is nowhere near as large as many differential sentences that have not been regarded by courts as punitive. What is different in this case was that the judge provided the defendant with information about the sentence range he was likely to face if convicted at trial, thus allowing Stockwell to make a more informed choice about whether to accept the plea offer. It was the very fact that the judge provided him with this information that the court of appeals regarded as improper. The obvious message to the trial judge is that you can sentence the defendant to more prison time if he rejects a plea and is convicted at trial. Just don't signal you are going to do so by mentioning it to him before he decides on the plea offer. In other words, the defendant's ignorance is legal bliss.

In the *Stockwell* case, the appellate court was concerned that the judge's comments regarding the likely sentence to be imposed if the defendant was convicted at trial had the potential to coerce the defendant to accept the plea bargain. This is the reason offered by most courts for why judges should not inform defendants who are considering a guilty plea what their sentence range is likely to be if they reject the plea and are convicted at trial. As Stockwell rejected the plea, the actual problem according to the appellate court was that the judge's words combined with Stockwell's post-trial sentence demonstrated the judge punished him for exercising his right to a trial. While perhaps true to a degree, the appellate court ignored the fact that the judge's words made the plea considerably more knowing as well. The judge, undoubtedly aware of the facts of the case and the defendant's prior record at the time of the plea discussions, had a sense of what he thought the appropriate sentence should

---

19. *Id.* at 1187.
20. *Id.*

be if the defendant was convicted at trial. The judge's informing the defendant of what he already knew he would do is where the problem arose. Unfortunately, the constitutional requirement that pleas of guilty must be knowing, intelligent, and voluntary is silent regarding what to do when a conflict arises among those requirements. Making the plea more knowing might also make it less voluntary in certain instances.

Let us be clear about what were not the bases for invalidating the guilty plea in *Stockwell* and are not likely to be causes in any other case. First, that the judge had a post-trial sentence already in mind is not unusual and when not expressed to the defendant will not invalidate the plea.[21] Second, as discussed previously, the additional prison time imposed on the defendant after the trial conviction compared to that offered in the plea deal happens almost all the time and is rarely regarded as improper, especially where, as here, that difference is not excessive. Third, that the judge offered no valid reason for the difference in the two sentences would not have invalidated the plea either except for his informing Stockwell at the time of the plea agreement about the likely post-trial sentence. Judges often offer reasons for why they chose a certain sentence to impose, but usually those same reasons were largely known to the judge at the time he agreed to the plea-based sentence and do nothing to explain the difference in the sentences.

Looking at other important decisions we make in life illustrates the value of providing a criminal defendant with more rather than less information before he makes the critical decision of whether to plead guilty and surrender his right to trial. Imagine, for example, being told that you had a possibly life-threatening tumor. After exploring the various medical issues with you, the doctor suggests you seriously consider a complicated surgery to have the growth removed. You will naturally inquire as to your chances for survival if you have the surgery. Let's say the doctor tells you your chances of survival are 50% with the operation. Can you make an intelligent decision based on

---

21. As a matter of sentencing policy, it is often wise for a judge to wait until he or she hears more details about the crime during the trial and receives a pre-sentence report after conviction that adds material on the defendant's background among other pertinent items. Still, it is clear from statistics on the number of cases disposed of through guilty pleas that judges arrive at a sentence or at least a sentencing range in the overwhelming number of cases without trials. They do so by learning the facts of a case from the attorneys and defendant as well as reviewing the documents available to the judge at the time of the plea. When they feel they have inadequate information upon which to base a sentence at the time of the guilty plea, judges generally have the ability to order a presentence report to provide them with those details before sentencing.

that information alone? I hope so, because when you ask the obvious next question, "What are my chances if I do not have the surgery?" the doctor politely demurs. He chooses not to tell you that your chances of survival without the surgery are only about 25% or even that they are less than if you have the surgery because he does not wish to coerce you into having the surgery. Time to find another doctor.

The plea bargaining equivalent of the above medical hypothetical is far less hypothetical because it happens frequently in American criminal courts. The prosecution and defense have agreed to a sentence or sentencing range that should be part of the defendant's guilty plea. Judges in both state and federal courts have the right to either accept and thereby be bound by the sentencing agreement or refuse to be so bound. If the judge refuses to so commit, the defendant may seek to renegotiate the deal with the prosecutor, eschew such negotiations and opt for trial, or accept the plea bargain with the prosecutor's sentencing recommendation but without the judge's commitment. In situations where the prosecutor and defense have agreed to a sentence as part of a plea deal, the defense attorney will invariably seek the judge's commitment to a sentence that is equivalent to or no greater than that agreed to by the parties. The defendant can bargain for a favorable sentence recommendation from the prosecutor, and judges and don't normally exceed that recommendation, but what defendant would not want some degree of certainty from the individual who metes out the sentence?

Assume now that the judge has accepted the five-year sentence that the prosecutor and defense attorney have agreed to as part of the guilty plea. The defendant is now faced with the most important choice he will have to make throughout the criminal justice process. Will he choose to plead guilty, thus assuring himself of a certain sentence, or seek an acquittal at trial, knowing that if convicted there he faces a significantly harsher sentence? His attorney has likely told the defendant that a trial conviction will undoubtedly lead to more prison time than five years but can only guess as to how much more. If you were in the defendant's position, could you make a fully informed choice about whether to accept the plea without knowing what was behind Door B as well as Door A? Five years if you plead guilty, but we are not telling you what you will get if you are convicted at trial because we don't want to coerce you into accepting the plea. Even if the judge avoids specifics as to the post-trial sentence and merely suggests it will be longer than the one provided for in the plea offer, that is likely to invalidate the plea as well.

This almost universal prohibition on providing the defendant with any information regarding what his sentence might be if he rejects a plea bargain and is convicted at trial beyond informing him what sentence the charged crimes allow, however, is paternalistic in nature and in most cases harms the party it is designed to protect. As with plea bargaining, it is true that being told of the greater likelihood of negative consequences in forgoing surgery might persuade or even pressure you into making a certain decision. Still, would you want to make such a critical decision in your life without having access to that information? The intelligent patient might wish to get a second opinion before choosing the surgery, just as the accused in a criminal case will seek the opinion of his counsel and perhaps his family before making his critical decision about whether to accept a plea-based sentence that a judge will mete out in lieu of the defendant's going to trial. The primary pressure that results in 95% of criminal defendants accepting guilty pleas comes from the nature of the criminal justice system itself and the near inevitability of a greater sentence after a trial conviction. It is the fact of that greater sentence, not the revelation of it to the defendant, that constitutes the fundamental coercion. This particular type of coercion is one the criminal justice system is willing to accept as necessary. Revealing this near certainty about differential sentencing to the defendant, however, will not be tolerated.

The 2014 case of *Lindsay and Davis v. United States*,[22] decided by the District of Columbia Court of Appeals, offers an example of what happens when a judge informs the defendant about a sentence range he knows he will employ if there is a conviction at trial. During plea negotiations, the judge made the following statement:

> I want to make sure that everybody's clear on this, and this would apply to all three defendants. All three of you are charged with a count of Simple Assault, as to the complaining witness here, and if there is a rejection of the plea offer and, therefore, no deferred sentencing agreement, and your clients go to trial on the Simple Assault and you're convicted on that count, there really isn't a question of whether there will be jail time because there will be. The question is how much jail time I will impose, and each one of you is exposed to ... 180 days in jail.[23]

After Davis' conviction at trial, the judge sentenced him to spend 45 days in jail to be served on consecutive weekends. The judge told Davis he was being sentenced to jail time because "you beat up on the mother of your child," and because "[your attorney] has been in my courtroom enough times to know that and I'm sure he counseled you on that and the reason for that is that anytime there is an offense to the person, that is more offensive than an offense

---

22. 84 A.3d 50 (D.C. 2014).
23. *Id.* at 51.

to property."[24] The court held that the judge's words during plea negotiations, specifically telling the defendant he would go to jail if convicted at trial, demonstrated that the ultimate sentence was an improper penalty for the defendant's rejection of the plea deal.

During the plea negotiations, the judge knew he would sentence the defendant to jail time if he was convicted at trial. As the defendant rejected the offer of a deferred sentence with the strong possibility of no jail time, this should have been obvious to the defendant and his attorney even had the judge not stated it. After Davis' conviction at trial, the judge did what he said he would do. Furthermore, it is fair to say that the sentence was less than severe, as well as considerably less harsh than the maximum that the judge could have imposed. The judge's words accompanying the post-trial sentence expressed indisputably proper sentencing factors. Where the judge went wrong, according to the appellate court, was informing the defendant during plea negotiations of the general framework of the intended sentence should he be convicted at trial. That the judge would have approved the plea deal with no jail time included was not a problem. That he decided before the trial that Davis would go to jail if convicted at trial also posed no problem (unless the judge had expressed that intent to the defendant). The ultimate sentence of jail time and the reasons stated for it at the time of sentencing were also perfectly proper. The problem according to the court here was that providing Davis with a fully informed choice at the time of the plea offer constituted improper coercion.

This invalidation of a sentence is typical of what happens when judges during plea negotiations tell or even hint at the post-trial sentence. Contrast that with consideration of the vast number of sentences affirmed by appellate courts in which trial judges have clearly punished defendants for rejecting plea deals, as indicated by the significant difference between the post-trial sentence and the agreed upon guilty-plea sentence. Such a consideration makes it clear current law considers the problem to be what judges say far more than what they do. In the 2005 California case of *People v. Guevara*,[25] for example, the defendant was charged with having sexually molested his daughter repeatedly over several years and having sexually assaulted his wife as well. The prosecution offered and the judge indicated he would accept a guilty plea to two of the counts with a total sentence of nine years' incarceration to cover all the charges. After the judge explained to him the difference in potential sentences he could receive from the plea deal as opposed to the sentence possibilities after a trial conviction

---

24. *Id.* at 52.
25. A101011, A105127, 2005 WL 2995338 (Cal. Ct. App. Nov. 9, 2005).

on the existing charges (such an explanation is permissible), Guevara opted for a trial. The jury convicted him on 17 counts and the judge sentenced Guevara to 96 years in prison. Unsurprisingly, the defendant appealed, arguing that imposing a prison term more than ten times that which was deemed sufficient by the judge as part of the plea offer was punishment for exercising his right to trial. The court's rejection of the defendant's argument and especially its reasons for doing so are as typical as they are revealing.

One justification offered by courts as to why differential sentencing, even when as substantial as in the *Guevara* case, is not a trial penalty is that new information arose during the trial that warranted a harsher sentence. Chapter II discusses why this justification is flawed most of the time, and we can see an example of that in *Guevara*. In response to the defendant's claim that nothing was revealed to the judge at trial that he was not aware of when the judge accepted the nine-year sentence in the plea bargain, the court responded that, "Defendant's daughter testified to repeated rapes and molestations over a long period of time. The court also heard evidence of the repeated rapes of defendant's wife. Although the trial court may have been aware of the general contours of these crimes prior to trial, the detailed narration of them legitimately entered into the sentence imposed." In other words, the judge knew already about the sexual assaults, but hearing about the details angered him, a conclusion certainly not contradicted by the judge's words at the time of the sentence, "[t]he thrust of what the court is doing is sentencing the defendant to a life of misery because that is what he sentenced his daughter to: A life of misery." While the judge's reaction to hearing the details of the crime at trial from the victims might be an understandable human response and even justification for the 96-year sentence, it in no way justifies the additional 87 years' imprisonment for a crime and a defendant the judge knew about when accepting the nine-year sentence as part of the plea bargain. The other possible justification offered by the court for accepting the far lighter sentence as part of the plea was because it "assume(d) that the nine-year sentence recognized in some way that by pleading guilty defendant was remorseful and willing to accept responsibility for his wrongdoing."[26] This of course is the classic justification for differential sentencing and the one that makes it difficult for anyone who has ever practiced in a criminal court to keep a straight face. Defendants plead guilty because they (and usually their attorneys) believe it is in their best interest to do so, and if they feel remorse, that rarely has anything to do with their decision to plead. Even if you have never set foot in a criminal courtroom,

---

26. *Id.*

would your understanding of human behavior lead you to believe that had Guevara accepted the nine-year sentence rather than the possibility of spending the rest of his life in prison, that his decision was the product of remorse rather than self-preservation? Prosecutors often reduce charges and/or sentences in exchange for a guilty plea, and judges accept them not because they somehow detect remorse on the part of the defendant but for the systemic and other benefits we examined when looking at their motivations for plea bargaining. But even if the appellate court was somehow unaware of this reality, does it believe that the defendant's remorse as exhibited by a guilty plea could have warranted the enormous difference in sentences exhibited here? Or to phrase the issue differently, does the defendant deserve a sentence nine times longer than that offered in exchange for a guilty plea because he failed to show re-morse? If so, that failure to show remorse dwarfs the traditional justifications for sentencing related to the seriousness of the offense and the background of the defendant as they relate to the difference between the sentence offered dur-ing plea negotiations and that meted out after trial.

Now in our medical hypothetical, would it help you to decide whether to have the surgery if the doctor discussed with you the outcomes in similar cases where patients chose one option or the other? If a judge merely tells a defendant about the sentences that were imposed in cases similar to his after the defen-dants were convicted at trial, that too is likely to be viewed as coercion. As one federal appellate court expressed this in 2014 when invalidating a plea agree-ment, "our main concern is with the district court's repeated description of similarly situated defendants and the consequences that befell them when they did not accept plea offers."[27]

In our medical hypothetical, if the doctor did not provide the patient with specifics about the comparative recovery rates with and without surgery, the patient would want to know at the very least which option is more likely to lead to recovery. In criminal cases, not only are judges barred from informing defendants of the likely sentence should they be convicted at trial, but judges are not permitted to suggest even that the post-trial sentence will be greater than that contained within the plea offer. An opinion rendered by the Supreme Court of Georgia made this point quite emphatically and then offered examples of pleas being invalidated due to the variety of ways in which judges commu-nicated this realty to defendants.[28] On one hand, this limitation matters less

---

27. United States v. Hemphill, 748 F.3d 666, 673 (5th Cir. 2014).
28. Winfrey v. State, 816 S.E.2d 613 (Ga 2018):
   Let us be plain: if a trial judge communicates — either explicitly or implicitly —
   to a criminal defendant that his sentence *will* be harsher if he rejects a plea deal

than the comparative limitation in the medical hypothetical. Without being told which medical option has a better chance for success, the patient may have no information about the best outcomes before making his critical decision. In criminal cases, any competent defense attorney will inform his client that the sentence or sentencing range contained in the plea bargain is less than what the defendant faces and will almost inevitably receive if convicted at trial. On the other hand, that pleas are invalidated merely because the judge conveyed this obvious reality to the defendant exposes how such an approach to judicial participation exalts form over substance.

Again, this is not to suggest that the judge's role in plea bargaining, particularly when discussing with the defendant and/or his counsel the likely sentencing range if he is convicted at trial, cannot become unduly coercive. As with the hypothetical surgeon discussed above, such coercion can come from the manner in which the judge communicates the expected likely post-trial sentence range. Just as the surgeon can browbeat a patient into surgery by overdramatizing the benefits of the operation or using terrifying language to warn of the dangers of rejecting the surgery, judges can use threatening language and other coercive means to pressure a defendant into accepting a plea. Take a look at the language used by one judge in Maryland to convey his opinion about the wisdom of accepting a guilty plea (Clarke is the prosecutor, Friedman the defense attorney):

> (The prosecutor) is recommending 50 years. I told your attorney. I don't know anything about this case. I don't know you from Adam, I really don't. But if you wanted to plead guilty, I was willing, even though the State is screaming and kicking for 50 years, I was willing to go around it today in 15 minutes. I would give you a total of 30

---

and is found guilty at trial, then Rule 33.5 (A) has been violated and the plea may be found involuntary. See, e.g., McDaniel v. State, 271 Ga. 552, 553, 522 S.E.2d 648 (1999) (a "trial court's stated inclination as to sentence" may "skew the defendant's decision-making") (emphasis added); Cherry v. State, 240 Ga. App. 41, 43, 522 S.E.2d 540 (1999) (impermissible participation in plea negotiations although trial judge did not "expressly state that [defendant's] sentence would be harsher if he did not plead guilty" because the judge did comment that the recommended sentence was "too lenient" and "suggest[ed] that a decision by the defendants to proceed to trial would be unwise") (emphasis supplied). In other words, "[c]omments by the trial judge that reinforce the unmistakable reality that a defendant who rejects a plea offer and instead opts to go to trial will likely face a greater sentence" are impermissible. Gibson v. State, 281 Ga. App. 607, 609, 636 S.E.2d 767 (2006) (emphasis supplied). *Id.* at 616.

years. That is what I told Mr. Friedman, and Ms. Clarke got angry. She walked out the door. I know you are not a party to anything. Listen to me. You tell me the man is incompetent for what he did for you. You are facing two life terms plus 50 years. He got me to offer you not over 30 years and you are telling me that this man is incompetent? Is that what you are telling me? Listen to me because I want an answer right now. I am not fooling around now. I swear to God that is true. You can ask anyone down here. I have never presided over a jury trial. I have never had a jury come back not guilty. If this jury comes back guilty, depending on what the pre-sentence report is, I could give you a total of two life sentences plus 50 years. I want you to know that. I am going to give you two minutes to talk to Mr. Friedman. If you want him as your lawyer, fine. If you don't want him as your lawyer, I will exclude him and you try the case without your lawyer or you can have him as your lawyer. But in two minutes that 30 year offer I am going to withdraw forever. Do you understand me, yes or no? Do you understand me?[29]

This plea was vacated due to the "intimidating and coercive" manner in which the judge discussed the plea offer with the defendant.[30]

4. Comments by the judge at sentencing

The second time in the criminal case in which the judge's comments can suggest the defendant was punished for exercising his right to a trial occurs after a trial conviction when the judge imposes the sentence. In these cases the potential problem is the judge's indication that the greater sentence (more severe than that contained in the guilty plea offer) he is about to impose is somehow related to the defendant's decision to reject the plea offer. Once again, it is not the fact of sentencing the defendant more harshly because he opted for a trial that determines the outcome of these cases. It is how the judge articulates his sentencing decision that matters. Compare, for example, two typical cases dealing with allegations by the defendant that the judge's comments when imposing sentence demonstrated punishment for turning down a plea offer and opting for a trial. In *State v. Sandefer*,[31] the defendant claimed he was so punished because of the judge's words at the time of sentencing which were as follows:

---

29. Barnes v. State, 523 A.2d 635, 636–67 (Md. App. 1987).
30. *Id.* at 643.
31. 900 P.2d 1132 (Wash. Ct. App. 1995).

I frequently ... in sentencing within the standard range give a defendant a more lenient sentence if the defendant has entered a plea of guilty. And the predominant reason I do that, not because I'm trying to be nice to a defendant, but I know that defendants who do enter pleas of guilty, in cases of this nature, it saves the parent and the child a lot of grief, in that they don't have to go through this experience, this heart rendering experience in the courtroom in having a poor little girl testify in front of a whole bunch of strangers about what happened to her.

Mr. Sandefer, if you entered a plea of guilty, I very possibly would have given you a more lenient sentence towards the lower end of the range, because of saving the victim being victimized by going through this court process. You didn't, and I'm not going to give you that break.[32]

In *Commonwealth v. Bethea*,[33] the judge's words at sentencing were:

Well Gerald, it's a great shame, but you are going to learn in life that you have a responsibility for your actions, and it is not only your interests that have to be taken into account but it is the interest of the community. This was, as I say, an aggravated crime. As far as I'm concerned, even though it is your first offense I think substantial punishment must be inflicted here. If you had pled guilty, perhaps you were involved, there is no question in my mind, but had you pled guilty it might have shown me the right side of your attitude about this, but you pled not guilty, fought it all the way, and the jury found you guilty, and I'm going to sentence you at this time.[34]

In *Sandefer*, the court determined that the judge's words did not demonstrate the defendant was punished for choosing a trial but merely showed the judge withheld a plea bargain benefit,[35] whereas in *Bethea*, the court found such punishment did occur. Yet in each case, there is no question that the judge's words make clear the defendant's choice to go to trial resulted in a heavier sentence.

On rare occasions, and usually in concurring or dissenting opinions, appellate judges will acknowledge that this distinction between punishment and

---

32. *Id.* at 1133.

33. 379 A.2d 102 (Pa. 1977).

34. *Id.* at 105.

35. 900 P.2d at 1135. One can view as appropriate the trial judge's stated reason for meting out a harsher post-trial sentence, but that still constitutes punishment for Sandefer's decision to opt for a trial.

benefit based on the judge's words is somewhat illusory. In the *Bethea* case, the concurring judge expressed this perfectly:

> Although the majority does not reach the issue, it makes no sense to suggest that a refusal to plead guilty and stand trial may not be considered as a factor in sentencing a defendant, but a guilty plea could be considered by a sentencing judge as a mitigating factor in a proper case. The chilling effect is the same in either situation; an accused who believes he can get a lighter sentence by pleading guilty will eschew his right to a trial by jury and enter a guilty plea. Moreover, it seems incongruous to suggest that a judge may not penalize an accused for not pleading guilty, but can reward the accused for pleading guilty. The ABA Standards ... not only defy logic but also place an impermissible chill on the exercise of the right to trial by jury.[36]

5. Other arguments against judicial participation

In addition to the potential coercive impact of the judge's participation in plea negotiations, defendants have raised other arguments against the judge involving herself at that stage of the criminal justice process. The defendant always has the right to challenge his guilty plea if he alleges that the plea was not knowing, intelligent, or voluntary. In many instances, that will be decided, at least initially, by the same judge who took the plea. This potential judicial bias in favor of maintaining the guilty plea that the judge accepted can arise even if the defendant clams that it was his lawyer or the prosecutor who was the cause of the error in the process that led to an agreement. When the defendant asserts that it was the judge whose conduct during the negotiations caused the plea to be involuntary or unknowing and therefore a violation of the constitution, the ability of the judge to decide the challenge impartially is even more in doubt. Imagine the judge who encouraged a plea bargain having to decide if his own conduct on the bench was so defective that it resulted in an error of constitutional magnitude.

The final argument raised by those opposed to judicial participation in plea bargaining relates to the concern that such involvement will encroach on the important functions of other institutions within the criminal justice process. While the focus has been on how judicial involvement affects the defendant, it can impact the prosecutor as well. Being pressured by the judge into making or accepting an offer that the prosecutor may be resistant to diminishes the

---

36. 379 A.2d at 107 (Manderino, J., concurring).

proper institutional role of the prosecutor as the person who decides what charges to pursue against the defendant and how to conduct that pursuit. Additionally, by advocating or even agreeing to a sentence during plea negotiations, the judge usually deprives all parties of the benefit of a presentence report.[37] These reports, often prepared by probation officers, provide details of the crime, the views of the victim and witness concerning the crime, and potential sentence and often deep background material on the defendant. They can help the judge in framing an appropriate sentence.

C. The Role of the Judge in Accepting the Plea (the Allocution)

Once a plea bargain has been agreed to by the parties and the judge has informally accepted the deal, it falls upon the judge to formally accept the defendant's guilty plea in court and on the record. Before accepting the plea, the judge is required to conduct a colloquy with the defendant to ensure that the plea is both voluntary and knowing. That colloquy, specifically the defendant's statement to the court, is known as the allocution. Slight variations exist between and among federal and state courts regarding some of the specifics of this colloquy, but all jurisdictions have rules enumerating those matters the judge must discuss and what assurances he must receive from the defendant before the plea may be accepted.[38]

All allocutions will require an acknowledgment by the defendant of the rights he is giving up as part of his guilty plea, such as the rights to a jury trial and to confront witnesses. Additionally, it will include a summary of the facts constituting the crime to which the defendant is pleading guilty. Sometimes the recitation comes from the prosecutor, sometimes the judge, and at other times by the defendant or his attorney. At the very least, however (with the exception of certain special pleas discussed in other areas of the book), the defendant must admit that he committed those acts that constitute the crime or

---

37. Judges usually can request presentence reports to be prepared in cases disposed of through plea bargaining as well as after trial. Because of the time commitment preparing such a report takes on already overworked probation officers, judges are generally reluctant to take this step unless they sense something significant they are unsure of may become clear through the report.

38. Compare, for example, FRCP 11(b), ABA Criminal Justice Standard 14-1.4, and New York State Guilty Plea Colloquy (https://www.nycourts.gov/judges/cji/8-Colloquies /Plea%20of%20Guilty.pdf).

crimes to which he is pleading guilty. Finally, there is a discussion about what if any agreement was entered into between the parties. This agreement virtually always includes the prosecutor, the defendant, and often the judge as well. For example, the judge may agree to the exact sentence recommended by the parties, a limit on the possible sentence she metes out (e.g., no more than ten years' incarceration), or other possible matters sought by the defendant or prosecutor (i.e., a recommendation regarding the details of the defendant's probation conditions).

1. The history of dishonesty during the allocution

I first was exposed to the plea bargaining system and the allocution process decades ago as a prosecutor in New York City. At that time, the defendant was required to agree that no promises were made to him as part of his decision to plead guilty. I suppose there are gentler words that could characterize this acknowledgment by the defendant, but the word "lie" would be the most accurate. It was a lie because in almost all plea bargains then as now, the defendant pleads guilty *because* of the promises made to him. While these promises take various forms, sometimes coming from the prosecutor (e.g., a recommendation of no more than eight years or dropping the Assault 1 charge if he pleads to Assault 2) or the judge (e.g., agreeing to dismiss the Assault 1 charge or a sentence of no more than five years), there was rarely a plea of guilty made without some promise to induce it, as anyone with a basic understanding of human nature would realize and expect.

What made this lie noteworthy was that the prosecutor, defense attorney, and the judge knew of it. Not only were they co-conspirators in the creation of the lie, but the guilty plea would not go forward without the defendant making this statement known by all parties to be false. In other words, the lie was not merely accepted—it was required. It was amusing on those occasions when the defendant, apparently insufficiently prepared by his attorney or forgetting his cues, lapsed into the truth and said he had been promised a reduced sentence for pleading guilty. This invariably led to semi-panic among the lawyers and judge in order to ensure that the guilty plea was acceptable. The defense attorney could be seen whispering forcefully to the defendant explaining the disastrous consequences of his telling the truth—the plea would not be accepted, and he faced a heavier sentence if convicted at trial. The prosecutor and judge might take turns making sanctimonious statements for the record about how they would never make promises merely to get the defendant to surrender his right to a trial or at a minimum that the plea would not be accepted absent what they silently knew to be the defendant's false statement.

After this dance was done, the defendant would see the error of his ways and say that of course no promises were made to induce his guilty plea.

In order to understand why otherwise ethical lawyers participated in such a sham, one needs to understand the way in which plea bargaining was and still to some degree is regarded by the courts and the public. From its beginnings, plea bargaining was viewed as the dirty underbelly of the criminal justice system. It was something that was done but not spoken about. The pejorative expression "copping a plea" was born to describe criminals getting off easy by pleading guilty and saving the government from having to try them. Plea bargaining was seen as the criminal justice system's deal with the devil, perhaps necessary but nonetheless unsavory. While there are all sorts of reasons why prosecutors agree to plea bargains (see Chapter III on prosecutors), the victims and the public often viewed the bargains as being too lenient for those who committed serious crimes.

These negative views of plea bargaining were fostered by a process that was done largely off the record and in private. It would be an enormous understatement to say that plea bargaining lacked transparency for most of the 20th century. Criminal trials are and were then conducted in open court with a record of the proceedings kept and maintained. While the allocution and acceptance by the court for a guilty plea is also conducted in open court on the record, the actual deal-making is almost always done by the prosecutor and defense attorney and sometimes the judge in private with no record being kept. This secrecy raised all sorts of doubts among the public about how the deal was arranged and what went into the plea agreement. Further, the failure to reveal the promises that were made at the time the plea was accepted by the court extended the period of secrecy regarding those promises.

Fortunately, this particular type of chicanery has largely been eliminated by requirements in courts both federal and state that promises made to the defendant be placed on the record at the time the plea is accepted by the court. Human behavior is such that undoubtedly there are some promises still kept secret among the parties, and cases arise concerning whether and to what extent an off-the-record comment by a judge or a prosecutor should be considered part of the plea bargain. But defendants are asked as part of the allocution whether any promises beyond those acknowledged already were made, and they are almost always held to their negative response to that question. Given changes in the rules making most off-the-record promises unenforceable and the strong belief by most lawyers and judges that promises made to induce the guilty plea should be put on the record, it is clear that the no promises sham has been mostly eliminated.

Today the intellectual dishonesty surrounding the institution of plea bargaining goes to the foundation of nearly every one of the thousands of plea bargains that take place in our criminal justice system every day. That the defendant receives a benefit for his trial-avoidance plea of guilty is beyond dispute. The dishonesty arises from the ardent resistance to the concomitant notion that this also results in punishment for those defendants who reject a plea bargain and are then convicted at trial. The chapter on punishment for exercising the right to trial explored the nature of this disingenuousness, the damage it does, and why it exists today.

2. The judge must ensure the guilty plea is knowing and voluntary

As part of the allocution, the judge must ensure that the defendant's guilty plea is knowing. This requirement for the protection of defendant's rights has several aspects. First, the defendant must be told the specifics of the charge(s) to which he is pleading guilty and must acknowledge he understands the elements of the crime and is admitting to such conduct.[39] When pleading guilty to passing a counterfeit bill, for example, it is not enough for a defendant to be asked by the judge and then admit that he in fact passed the counterfeit bill. To constitute that crime, the defendant needed to know the bill he passed was counterfeit and to admit to that knowledge. The leading Supreme Court case on this subject is *Henderson v. Morgan*.[40] Morgan, a 19-year-old man described as having substandard intelligence, was charged in New York with Murder in the First Degree for having killed his landlady. Pursuant to a plea agreement with the prosecutor, Morgan pled guilty to the reduced charge of Murder in the Second Degree. During the allocution accompanying the formal acceptance of the plea in court, Morgan admitted to killing his landlady and knowing that the guilty plea included such an admission. The law to which he pled guilty, however, required that the defendant intended to kill the victim and Morgan was never specifically asked by the judge nor admitted to the element of intent to kill. The Court held that while no ritual allocution is necessary, a defendant's plea is knowing only if he admits to the facts that satisfy the elements of the crime to which he is pleading guilty.

The holding in *Morgan* is reflective of the requirement that a judge must ascertain that there is a factual basis for the guilty plea and that what the de-

---

39. Although there are alternative guilty pleas in which a defendant does not have to admit his guilt, the discussion here is primarily limited to standard guilty pleas. See Chapter VII dealing with types of pleas.

40. 426 U.S. 637 (1976).

fendant admits to satisfies the elements of the crime to which he has pled. The best way for judges to do this is to ask the defendant exactly what he did that constituted the crime to which he is pleading guilty. Describing it in his own words better assures the defendant actually understands the facts to which he is admitting. Additionally, this makes it more difficult for the defendant to claim later that he did not understand what conduct he acknowledged to having committed. Genuine problems surrounding the defendant's understanding of his guilty plea can arise when judges, perhaps anxious to get through the allocution as quickly and efficiently as possible, pose a series of leading questions to the defendant, seeking only his assent to the questions. Imagine part of such an allocution in an armed robbery case.

Judge: Did you stop him on the street?
Defendant: Yes
Judge: Did you forcibly steal his wallet?
Defendant: Yes

The defendants can later challenge this recitation by claiming he stole the wallet while the victim was looking elsewhere and assumed "forcibly" meant that the victim didn't want him to steal it. It is far better for the judge to ask the defendant what he did, a more open question. Then if the description of the crime omitted a specific element as in the *Morgan* case or was unclear as to its relationship to an element of the crime, the judge could specifically ask him about it.

The next aspect of the plea allocution required to make the defendant's guilty plea knowing is knowledge and understanding of the fundamental constitutional rights he is giving up as part of his plea. In cases that require the right to a jury trial, judges must explain to defendants their guilty plea waives this right. Additionally, he is told that he waives his right to confront and cross-examine those witnesses who would testify against him. The defendant is told he would have the right to be represented at trial and all other significant phases of the criminal justice process by competent counsel. As the reading of these rights by the judge is normally pro forma and in most instances requires only acknowledgment by the defendant, this aspect is rarely the basis for a challenge to the knowing nature of the plea.[41]

A far more likely, and probably the most likely, challenge to the knowing nature of the guilty plea relates to the explanation of the potential sentences that could be meted out based on the charge to which the defendant pled guilty.

---

41. If the defendant had some question about the surrender of these rights and the judge's explanation was inaccurate or misleading, that could form the basis for such a challenge.

The nature of the plea agreement and its elements must be disclosed to the defendant on the record. If the prosecutor and defense attorney agreed to a specific sentence, the defendant must be told that in open court. The judge then must tell the defendant whether she will adhere to the sentence agreed to by his counsel and the prosecutor or whether she will not be so bound. Additionally, the judge must outline for the defendant the minimum and maximum sentences resulting from the charge to which he pled or any additional limitations to which the judge ("the statute allows for a ten-year sentence but I have agreed to sentence you to no more than seven years") or the prosecutor ("in exchange for your guilty plea, the prosecutor has agreed to remain silent at the time of your sentencing") have agreed. When the judge misstates the sentence the defendant will be exposed to on his guilty plea, such a misstatement is likely to lead to an invalidation of the plea. Typical of such holdings is the North Carolina case of *State v. Reynolds*.[42] At the time of his guilty plea, Reynolds was misinformed by the judge of the maximum sentence he could receive as a result of the plea, leading to a decision that the guilty plea was involuntary and unknowing.[43] Potential non-prison aspects of the possible sentence such as probation conditions, fines, and restitution to the victim also must be explained to the defendant.[44] If the sentence for the crime to which the defendant pled guilty can or must be enhanced based on the defendant's background (i.e., recidivist statutes for prior convictions) or there are other significant consequences that can flow from the guilty plea (such as that if the defendant is not a citizen, his conviction can result in deportation), those too have to be explained by the judge.

As well as assuring that the defendant's plea is knowing, the judge must ascertain from the defendant that his guilty plea is voluntary. Most judges will ask if anyone, meaning the prosecutor, his attorney, or anyone else, compelled the defendant into accepting the guilty plea. We have seen above how challenges can arise from the judge's own actions in this regard and in other chapters on how the prosecutor or defense attorney can be the source of such coercion. Unless the judge is made aware of developments during the negotiations that may raise questions of the voluntariness of the guilty plea or unless

---

42. 721 S.E.2d 333 (N.C. Ct. App. 2012).

43. *Id.* See also *State v. McTaggart*, 615 S.E.2d 737 (N.C. Ct. App. 2005), in which the trial judge's failure to inform the defendant of the maximum sentence similarly resulted in a determination that his guilty plea was invalid.

44. In *Commonwealth v. Hart*, 174 A.3d 660 (Pa. Super. Ct. 2017), a guilty plea was invalidated because the defendant was not informed correctly about the requirement to register as a sex offender as part of his plea.

the allocution by the defendant raises such a question, the defendant's acknowledgment is usually enough to allow the plea process to proceed.

3. The judge's options in accepting the plea

After all the protections embodied in statutes to ensure the defendant's plea of guilty is knowing, intelligent, and voluntary are addressed, the judge must formally accept the plea. It is at this moment that the guilty plea takes effect. The judge's acceptance of the plea can include her complete acquiescence to the terms agreed to by the parties or her qualified acceptance (such as by agreeing to sentencing limitations but not the exact terms negotiated by the parties), or it can make clear to the parties that she is keeping open all her options under the statute to which the defendant pled.

Chapter VI

Impact of the Law of Contracts on Plea Bargaining

In addition to the disingenuousness that has pervaded judicial decisions about plea bargaining, jurisprudence on the subject has long been characterized by a lack of clear guidelines, even as to the foundational concepts and principles of plea bargaining. Simply put, the law did not know what to make of plea bargains. What constitutes a plea bargain? More specifically, what elements must be present to make the bargain valid? Does plea bargaining punish and deter the constitutional right to trial, and if so, can the agreement be legal? Are there any limits to what the parties can bargain for? At what stage, if any, is the bargain official? What happens if one of the parties won't or can't fulfill the terms of the bargain? Can that party be compelled to perform as promised? If not, what remedy is available to the party who has been harmed by the failure to perform? When and under what circumstances can a party withdraw from a plea agreement?

Although there was some form of bargaining in criminal cases that existed off and on over time in the U.S., its modern legal history is largely recognized to have begun around 1970 with the Supreme Court's decisions in *Brady v. United States*[1] and *Santobello v. New York*.[2] Only after that did American judges and scholars begin to pay substantial attention to the many legal questions that surrounded bargaining away the right to trial. The combination of the lack of historical precedent, the negative connotation of a system that allows defendants to "cop a plea," and the lack of transparency that accompanies the plea bargaining process itself led to much uncertainty about how the law should

---

1. 397 U.S. 742 (1970).

2. 404 U.S. 257 (1971). Each of these cases gave at least implicit judicial authorization for plea bargaining.

handle issues surrounding negotiating, accepting and enforcing guilty pleas. In such a situation, lawyers and judges fell back on what they were trained to do: find an area of the law that is comparable and apply the principles of that discipline to plea bargaining. Enter the law of contracts.

With a global history said to go back to Plato, the law of contracts has clear similarities to plea bargaining, and well-established contract law principles appear to respond to many of the issues that arise in plea bargaining. American contract law is derived to a great degree from English contract law, the first treatise on the subject having been written in 1790.[3] The principles of American contract law have been pronounced and described in great depth in famous legal treatises such as *The Law of Contracts* written by Samuel Williston from 1920–22 and *Corbin on Contracts*, originally written in 1962, now 16 volumes long, and called "the greatest law book ever written." A Restatement of the law is a series of writings designed to educate judges and lawyers on a specific area of the law. There is a complete and updated *Restatement of Contract Law*.[4] So if plea bargains are comparable to contracts, criminal lawyers and judges certainly have a well-established body of law to call upon. The task, then, is to determine if the similarities between the two disciplines are compelling enough for the reasonable application of contract law to plea bargaining and if so, when and to what degree.

As any first-year law student can tell you, there are three principal elements to any contract—offer, acceptance, and consideration. One party has to make an offer to another party, which the second party must accept and there must be something of value (which can take the form of a promise) that is exchanged. I offer to sell you ten widgets for $39 each. When you accept the offer, we have a contract. In a plea bargaining agreement, the defendant offers to waive his right to trial and plead guilty, resulting in a saving of judicial and prosecutorial resources and assuring a conviction. In return, the prosecutor usually promises to recommend to the judge some diminishment in the seriousness of the charge and/or the length of the sentence the defendant will face. On the surface, the plea bargain seems like a contract. Understand, then, the appeal for lawyers and judges to be able to remove or at least substantially reduce the amount of uncertainty surrounding the law of plea bargaining by turning for guidance to the relative safety and certainty of contract law.

While it makes sense to apply some of what we know about contract law to resolve similar issues surrounding plea agreements, there are several drawbacks

---

3. John Joseph Powell, Essay Upon the Law of Contracts and Agreements (1790).
4. ALI, Restatement 2d of Contracts (1981–2010).

to doing so. Some of these drawbacks relate to the imprecision of some of the comparisons between the two bodies of law. Do we allow for the parties to be bound by oral agreements and promises, and if so, at what stage of the plea bargaining process and in what form? Other than those oral contracts not recognized as binding due to the Statute of Frauds[5] or other specific laws, oral contracts generally have the same force as written ones. Do plea bargains have to be in writing to be binding?

There are three basic remedies for a party who is the victim of a contract that is breached. The most common one is awarding damages to plaintiffs to compensate them for their losses. Other remedies are voiding the contract or requiring specific performance compelling the breaching party to live up to its commitment. How do courts apply these remedies when the prosecutor fails to adhere to a condition of the plea agreement, such as a commitment to make no specific sentencing recommendation? What if the judge at the time of sentencing feels she cannot or will not honor a pledge which she made when the guilty plea bargain was entered? Does the criminal defendant, when the victim of the breach, have his choice between rescission of the plea agreement and specific performance of the plea conditions? If so, how are those remedies actually enforced in a criminal case? What are the remedies when it is the defendant who violates some condition of the bargain?

Superimposed on issues like these is the profound difference between the nature of contracts and plea agreements. Rarely does anyone face criminal sanctions because of a civil contract. If I don't deliver those widgets to you as I was required to do under our above-mentioned contract, I won't be charged with a crime. Specifically, nothing about my sale of those widgets to you will result in the deprivation of a fundamental human value—freedom. The harsh and unique impact of the criminal law means that unlike in most civil contracts cases, a discussion of the remedies attached to the breach of a plea bargain should include in some manner the interests of justice.[6]

---

5. *See, e.g.,* UCC §2-201.

6. Certain civil contracts that are fundamentally unfair due primarily to the presence of duress when they were formed or the substantially unequal bargaining positions of the parties are regarded as unconscionable. Such contracts may be modified by the courts to remove the unfairness. *See* UCC §2-302.

A. The Formation of the Plea Agreement

1. Similarities of plea bargains to civil contracts

The process of negotiating a plea of guilty typically begins with off-the-record, relatively informal conversations between the prosecutor and the defense attorney. If and usually when they come to an agreement, the defense attorney consults with her client about whether he should accept the plea agreement. Assuming the defendant agrees to the terms of the bargain and his consent is communicated to the prosecutor, it seems as if the meeting of the minds necessary for a contract has been formed. Offer, acceptance, and mutual consideration (from the defendant agreeing to forfeit his right to trial or from the prosecutor acquiescing to some charge or sentence reduction recommendation) have now occurred. While the terms of the deal have not actually been performed yet, most contracts do not need to be executed in order to be binding.

2. Differences between plea bargains and civil contracts

This agreement, however, is not a finished plea bargain and its terms and promises are not binding on either party. A plea bargain is not deemed to be binding until it has been entered into in court. In part this is because the judge, in almost all cases, has to agree to the deal. While contract law accounts for third-party agreements in which all parties have to agree, the agreement between the prosecutor and defendant (depending to some extent on how it is framed) should still be binding on those two parties if standard contract law controlled. In fact, however, it is not binding because criminal law does not recognize plea agreements until the prosecutor lays out the terms of the deal in open court, the defendant in most cases admits his guilt to the charge or charges he is pleading guilty to,[7] and the defendant is informed of the fundamental constitutional rights he is surrendering as part of his guilty plea. Known as the allocution, sometimes this is performed in great detail, other

---

7. Two types of pleas do not require an acknowledgment from the defendant of his culpability. See the discussion of Alford and no lo contendere pleas in Chapter VII on types of pleas.

times in a somewhat cursory manner. In all cases, however, this allocution must take place in some form and encompass the requirements above before the defendant's agreement to the deal and plea of guilty is official. Additionally, the judge must declare that he accepts the agreement before it is binding.

Already one can see several differences between plea agreements and contracts. Unlike typical contracts, the presence of offer, acceptance, and consideration alone, at least as they are defined in a civil context, do not make for a binding guilty plea agreement. Additionally, for almost all civil contracts to be binding, unlike guilty plea agreements, the presence and acquiescence of a judge is unnecessary. There are several reasons for this difference, and perhaps most obvious is that the judge is a necessary third party to a finalized plea bargain because she has a critical role to play in its implementation. This requirement points again to a recognition of the difference in stakes between a civil contract and the guilty plea to a crime.

3. One example of the impact of the differences between contract and plea bargaining law regarding the formation of the agreement

At times, however, the requirements that go beyond those of a typical civil contract for a plea bargain to be binding can be harmful to the defendant. The Supreme Court's unanimous decision in *Mabry v. Johnson*[8] offers a clear illustration of this. After Johnson was originally charged with murder, his attorney worked out a plea deal with the prosecutor that permitted Johnson to plead guilty to a reduced charge of accessory after the murder. Critical to the deal was the prosecutor's agreement to recommend a sentence of 21 years' incarceration to be served *concurrently* with the imprisonment time he was serving for other offenses. Johnson accepted this deal. A few days after the deal was agreed to, the prosecutor told Johnson's attorney that he had made a mistake when offering a concurrent sentence. He meant to say that the offer was for a 21-year *consecutive* sentence. While the alphabetical difference between the words concurrent and consecutive might be small, the difference in their significance was huge for Johnson, as for all criminal defendants. Unlike a concurrent sentence, a consecutive one does not begin to be served until the other sentences have been completed. For Johnson, this meant he was to serve 21 years after his other sentences had been served.

8. 467 U.S. 504 (1984).

Ultimately Johnson agreed to the "corrected" plea offer and was sentenced to the consecutive 21-year prison term. Johnson then challenged this new guilty plea arrangement and requested that the deal with the concurrent sentence be honored.

Before looking at the Court's decision in the case, it is first important to understand why the sentencing recommendation of a prosecutor is often critical even though the sentencing decision belongs to the judge. After accepting the plea, unless the judge binds herself to a certain sentence or a maximum possible sentence, she has the discretion to sentence the defendant to anything up to the statutory maximum permitted for the crimes to which the defendant has pled guilty. In actuality, judges generally will not punish a defendant with a harsher sentence than recommended by the prosecutor. There may be several reasons for this. The judge may feel that the prosecutor has better access to the witnesses and facts of the case as well as its strengths and weaknesses — legal, factual, evidentiary and personal (e.g., is the key witness credible, will he show up for trial). When combined with the judge's awareness that prosecutors represent the public and prosecutors often regard this representation as a duty to obtain a substantial sentence that is commensurate with the seriousness of the crime, this can explain a judge's reluctance to sentence more severely than the prosecutor's recommendation. Additionally, many judges view their roles as neutral arbiters of the institutional positions taken by prosecutors and defense attorneys. Sentences that fall between the recommendations of the prosecutor and defense attorney may in part be a reflection of this belief. Finally, although appeals of sentences, especially those following a plea bargain, are usually unsuccessful, a sentence harsher than that recommended by the prosecutor does raise red flags for appellate courts.

It would be unrealistic to fail to recognize that judges are often concerned about the impact their decisions have both within the legal community and outside of it. This is especially true for those whose judgeship is an elected position. There was a time when most believed that the public wanted the severest possible sentence in most criminal cases and judges regarded as "tough" were the most popular. While this belief still exists to a degree, assessing the public's feelings about criminal sentences is far more nuanced now, depending on, among other things, the nature of the crime, the backgrounds of the victim and the defendant, and the community's view of law enforcement. Additionally, as the American criminal justice system incarcerates more people per capita than any other country in the world, there is now a strong movement toward decarceration and away from draconian sentences. For any or all of these reasons, judges' sentences normally do not exceed those recommended by the prosecutor, and thus it is understandable why defense attorneys bargain so hard and so often for a prosecutorial recommendation beneficial to their client.

There were two basic arguments raised by Johnson in claiming that the original offer of the prosecutor that included a recommendation of a concurrent sentence was binding and should be enforced. The first was based on contract law. The elements of a contract — offer, acceptance, and consideration — were all present after the initial offer made by the prosecutor was accepted by Johnson, and therefore when the prosecutor backed out, this constituted a breach. The Court disagreed, holding that, since no plea agreement is official until it is accepted by all parties in court, what occurred at that point was merely an agreement to agree. With no recognized plea agreement having been entered into at that stage, no breach could have occurred. The Court went further in discussing the analogy to contract law by saying that even if a breach did occur, that does not mean the defendant had the civil law right to specific performance of the contract (meaning an accepted plea with the recommendation of concurrent prison time). As will be discussed below, the Court, in a previous case, had rejected giving defendants the absolute choice of remedy even when there is a clear breach of the agreement by prosecutors.

The second argument for enforcing the original plea agreement related to the wrongfulness of the prosecutor's actions in offering the defendant a plea bargain and then taking it back after the offer was accepted. The Court declared that the nature of such conduct was irrelevant, whether it was "negligent or otherwise culpable." The Court reasoned that when the defendant ultimately pled guilty in court to the consecutive-sentence plea offer, his acceptance of the plea was fully knowing and voluntary. Regardless of the purpose and intent of the prosecutor leading up to that plea, the Court said, "[T]he Due Process clause is not a code of conduct for prosecutors."[9] Such a statement by the Court raises the troubling possibility of prosecutors offering a series of escalating pleas, the acceptance of which invites the prosecutor to withdraw the offer and then offer a more punitive plea deal. Knowing that the defendant is willing to plead guilty and accept a substantial sentence rather than go to trial puts the prosecutor in an unfairly advantageous bargaining position.

---

9. *Id.* at 511.

B. When the Prosecutor Violates the Terms of the Plea Agreement

1. What constitutes a breach of a plea bargain by the prosecutor?

Unlike the holding in *Johnson*, there are instances when prosecutors have been found to violate the terms of a plea agreement, the rough equivalent of breaching a contract. We need to examine, therefore, some of the actions of a prosecutor deemed to be such violations and then what remedies are available to the defense should such a breach occur. Perhaps the most common examples of prosecutorial breaches involve matters related to what the prosecutor has promised to say or not say at the time of sentencing. The landmark Supreme Court case on this is *Santobello v. New York*.[10]

Faced with two felony gambling charges, Santobello agreed to plead guilty to a lesser gambling charge that carried a sentence of up to one years' incarceration. As part of the agreement, the prosecutor offered to make no recommendation as to the sentence Santobello should receive. For many reasons, the sentencing date was delayed, and on the date that sentencing did occur, the original prosecutor had been replaced by another. Asked if he wished to be heard, the new prosecutor told the judge that because of Santobello's criminal record and his links to organized crime, he should be sentenced to the maximum one-year imprisonment. Thus the new prosecutor failed to honor the promise made by the original prosecutor of making no recommendation as to Santobello's sentence. The Court held that this failure by the prosecutor constituted a breach of the plea bargaining agreement. As one who became a prosecutor in that very same office a few years after the case was decided by the Supreme Court, I can well imagine why the violation occurred. There were so many felony cases in Bronx County, New York, at this time that prosecutors often had to be shuttled between cases. This made it difficult for the same prosecutor to stay with a particular case all the way through the criminal justice process. Manila folders were used to hold the essential materials of the case, such as the criminal complaint and police reports. Notations about the various court appearances, including plea deals offered and accepted(and their conditions) were usually handwritten on the cover of the folder. The potential for mistake was obvious. The Court in *Santobello* seemed to recognize

---

10. 404 U.S. 257 (1971).

this and observed, "This record represents another example of an unfortunate lapse in orderly prosecutorial procedures, in part, no doubt, because of the enormous increase in the workload of the often understaffed prosecutor's offices." Still, the Court was clearly correct in deciding that "the heavy workload may explain these episodes, but it does not excuse them."[11] The decision in *Santobello* made clear that prosecutors must adhere to the terms of the plea bargain they agreed to in court.

One issue that arises occasionally with respect to the promise a prosecutor made in exchange for the defendant's guilty plea is the precise meaning of the promise. For example, a number of cases have dealt with the meaning of the prosecutor's pledge "to take no position," "to make no recommendation," or "to stay silent." Which of these prohibit the prosecutor, for example, from saying "this is a serious crime" or "the defendant has a significant criminal background"? Judicial opinions in this area are often governed by fine distinctions. In *United States v. Miller*,[12] the U.S. Court of Appeals distinguished between a prosecutor's promise to "make no recommendation," which it regarded as narrow in scope, requiring only that the prosecutor make no request for a specific sentence or sentence range, and a promise to "take no position," which the court said required virtual silence from the prosecutor. The unexpressed implication of the decision apparently is that although such a nuanced distinction might be lost on the defendant, we can count on his attorney to explain it to him sufficiently. In *Miller v. State*[13] (a different Miller), the Maryland Court of Appeals determined that the prosecutor breached his promise at the time of the plea bargain to make no recommendation as to sentence. At the time of sentencing when asked by the court if he wished to say anything, the prosecutor replied, "[n]o, Your Honor. I agreed as part of our plea bargaining that I would not in this case make a recommendation to this Court. I would just state that I am not in full compliance with the recommendation of the Probation Officer, but I have not gone into it that fully."[14] While the prosecutor argued he was merely commenting on the Department of Probation recommendation and not making one of his own, the court said the effect was the same and therefore violated the plea agreement.

The decision in *Miller v. State* is consistent with federal and state court holdings that generally construe any ambiguity in the language of a plea agree-

---

11. *Id.* at 260.
12. 565 F.2d 1273 (3d Cir. 1977).
13. 322 A.2d 527 (Md. 1974).
14. *Id.* at 528.

ment, written or oral, in favor of the defendant.[15] Still, where the language of the promise is fairly clear, the prosecutor will not be held to any version of the promise that goes beyond that language. In *United States v. Benchimol*,[16] in exchange for the defendant's plea of guilty, the prosecutor promised to recommend a sentence of probation with restitution. When the presentence report came back, it incorrectly indicated that the prosecutor agreed to remain silent. At the time of the sentence, the defense attorney pointed out the mistake and told the court that the prosecutor had agreed to recommend the probation sentence. When asked for a comment on the defense attorney's assertion, the prosecutor said, "[t]hat is an accurate representation." In arguing that the prosecutor's statement at sentence breached his earlier promise, the defense claimed that the words above evidenced a lack of enthusiasm for the probation sentence.[17] In rejecting this reasoning, the Supreme Court concluded that even if enthusiasm could be a condition of a plea bargain, because no such promise was made here, the prosecution would not be held to any level of enthusiasm once it acknowledged its original plea promise.

2. What is the remedy for a breach by the prosecutor?

The Court's holding in *Santobello* established categorically that prosecutors must adhere to the conditions they agreed to as part of an accepted plea bargain or they will be deemed to have breached the agreement. The remaining question for that court was to determine what remedy was available to the defendant because of this violation. Sometimes, as exemplified by *Mabry v. Johnson* discussed above, the defendant seeks to have his agreement specifically performed. In that case, it would have meant Johnson's plea to the original offer of a concurrent sentence would be enforced. Because the Court found that the initial agreement was without legal consequence, there was no need to fashion any remedy for Johnson such as specific performance.

At other times, however, a defendant who is the victim of such a breach wants to void his initial plea and start the judicial process again from the beginning.

---

15. With written plea agreements, there is another basis for interpreting any ambiguity against the government. If a contract is in writing, ambiguity in the language will generally be held against the party who drafted the agreement. Thus, ambiguities in written plea agreements, if, as is usually the case, executed in the form of a letter drafted by the prosecutor to the defense attorney, will be held against the prosecutor.

16. 471 U.S. 453 (1985).

17. *Id.* at 465–66.

That was precisely the remedy sought by Rudolph Santobello. Santobello did not want his original plea specifically performed—meaning being sentenced by a different judge with the prosecutor remaining silent. Whether that was because Santobello thought (quite reasonably) it would be unlikely that another trial judge in the Bronx could be found who was unaware of the prosecutor's sentence recommendation detailed in the Supreme Court decision or because his lawyer convinced him he now had a better chance of prevailing at trial, we do not know. We do know, however, that although several members of the Court believed that the choice of remedy should be Santobello's, the majority decided to remand the case back to the New York courts for them to make that determination. The New York court decided that since Santobello knowingly and voluntarily agreed to plead guilty based on the prosecutor's assurance of making no sentence recommendation, assigning the case to a new judge to do just that was in the interests of justice and did not violate due process.[18]

Since the Supreme Court's holding in *Santobello*, which avoided requiring one particular remedy in every case of prosecutorial breach, some courts, like the New York court in *Santobello*, have ordered specific performance of the plea. Others have rescinded the plea and voided the agreement altogether. Among the factors most commonly considered by courts in fashioning remedies in such situations are the nature of the prosecutor's breach (whether it was deliberate or accidental), the wishes of the defendant (to be given weight but not necessarily be controlling), and the interests of justice. This last factor looks to whether circumstances, such as the death or disappearance of witnesses, have occurred which could make starting the case anew unfair to either the prosecutor or the defendant.

C. When the Defendant Violates the Terms of the Plea Agreement

1. What constitutes a breach of the plea bargain by the defendant?

Cases in which the defendant is the party violating the terms of the plea agreement occur less frequently than those involving claims of breach by the prose-

---

18. 39 A.D.2d 654 (App. Div. 1st Dept. 1972).

cutor. In one such case decided by the Supreme Court, *Ricketts v. Adamson*,[19] the defendant promised as part of his plea agreement to testify against others who were charged with the same murder as he was. Adamson testified at the first trial of the others charged but, after those convictions were overturned on appeal, refused to testify against one of the defendants in the retrial. The government claimed this constituted a breach of the plea agreement. In its opinion, the Court considered the nature and meaning of Adamson's agreement to testify, whether its terms were actually violated by his refusal to testify in the retrial, and what the appropriate remedy should be. The Court held that Adamson's refusal to testify violated the language and meaning of the promise he made as part of the plea agreement. Justice Brennan's dissent took issue with the Court's conclusions mentioned above. What is noteworthy about the *Adamson* case is that the majority and the dissent based their positions on both contract principles and those related to criminal law, such as due process fairness and the Double Jeopardy clause of the Fifth Amendment. The case shows that while contract law can help inform how courts should address issues related to the nature, terms, and violations of plea agreements, decisions in this area cannot be made without consideration of constitutional and other criminal law principles as well.

Other cases in which the defendant was alleged to have violated his plea agreement involved promises to cooperate with the prosecution, refrain from participation in criminal activities,[20] plead guilty to an uncharged offense as well as one for which he'd been indicted,[21] waive his right to appeal,[22] testify truthfully,[23] testify in the grand jury,[24] and avoid re-arrest pending sentence.[25] These cases also looked to both contract law and criminal law principles in deciding whether the defendant violated the plea agreement.

2. What is the remedy for a breach by the defendant?

Adamson argued to the Supreme Court that even if the Court considered his failure to testify against others to be a breach of a material condition of the plea bargain, the government could not then try him on the original charges

---

19. 483 U.S. 1 (1987).
20. United States v. Britt, 917 F.2d 353 (8th Cir. 1990).
21. Smith v. Phillips, 865 F. Supp. 2d 271 (E.D.N.Y. 2012).
22. United States v. Lockwood, 416 F.3d 604 (7th Cir. 2005).
23. Brown v. State, 582 S.E.2d 13 (Ga. Ct. App. 2003).
24. United States v. Bryant, 905 F. Supp. 2d 877 (C.D. Ill. 2012).
25. Innes v. Dalsheim, 680 F. Supp. 517 (E.D.N.Y. 1988).

because to do so would violate the Fifth Amendment. Specifically, Adamson claimed that when his guilty plea was accepted, this acceptance constituted a conviction for murder in the second degree in satisfaction of his culpability for the crimes he was charged with. Compelling a withdrawal of that plea against his will and requiring him to face the original first degree murder charge again constituted a violation of the Double Jeopardy Clause of the Fifth Amendment (charging him twice for the same crime). In rejecting this argument, the Court held that Adamson's breach of the terms of the plea agreement meant that double jeopardy was not a bar to the subsequent prosecution.

Cases decided since the decision in *Adamson*, such as the ones referred to immediately above, have largely followed the Supreme Court's reasoning and held that both the prosecution and the court are relieved from any promises made to the defendant as part of a plea agreement if the defendant fails to adhere to his own promise. Consistent with the opinion in *Adamson*, such a breach by the defendant even defeats double jeopardy claims.

D. When the Judge Violates the Terms of the Plea Agreement

1. What constitutes a breach of the plea bargain by the judge?

In order for a plea bargain between the prosecutor and defendant to take effect, it must be accepted by the judge. The judge's acceptance may take several different forms, but it must reflect the terms of the contract agreed to by the parties and expressed in court at the time the plea is entered. The prosecutor may have agreed to make no recommendation as to sentence or another material matter. He may have agreed to recommend a specific sentence, a range of sentences, or a maximum sentence. The decision as to whether to accept the prosecutor's recommendation or sentence above or below the recommended term lies solely with the judge. If she makes no commitment as part of the plea agreement, she may sentence the defendant to any term of imprisonment or other sanction that is authorized under the offense or offenses to which the defendant has pled. Not infrequently, however, in order to enhance the likelihood of a plea agreement, the judge will make some sort of commitment as to what her sentence will be or as to some other matter. Similar to the prosecutor, she may commit to a precise sentence, a limited range of sentences, or a maximum sentence. Additionally, she may require certain conditions for her commitment to be binding. For example, she may condition her promise of no more than five years' imprisonment on the defendant's not committing another offense before sentencing or that a complete and updated record of his prior crimes does not reveal any convictions beyond what is already indicated. As a third party to plea agreements, the judge, like the prosecutor and defendant, is bound to any promises she made. When the judge at the time of sentence mistakenly does not or deliberately will not abide by the commitment she made when accepting the plea, the issue is what remedies are available to the defendant.

Because the judge is a third party to the plea agreement,[26] a material breach by her is similar to that of a breach by the prosecutor or defendant in that it generally voids part or all of the agreement. This breach may be the result of her interpretation and subsequent application of a term of the plea bargain which turns out to be incorrect. In assessing whether the judge breached the terms of the plea bargain, appellate courts again will look primarily to the plain meaning of the promise that was made by the judge. For example, in *Ray v. State*, the defendant argued that the judge's sentence of ten years' incarceration with six suspended violated his plea agreement commitment that Ray's sentence would include a "[c]ap of four years on any executed incarceration." In rejecting the defendant's argument, the appellate court found the language in the plea agreement to be unambiguous in its meaning that the four-year term referred to actual imprisonment.[27] In *People v. Mancheno*, the judge promised as part of a plea agreement that the defendant would not be sentenced without a diagnostic study being performed. When he was ultimately sentenced without that study, Mancheno argued that the judge had breached the plea agreement. Rejecting the government's assertion that the study was merely a step toward the concurrent sentences that the defendant was promised and in fact received, the appellate court said the language requiring the study was clear and the judge's sentence breached the agreement.[28]

---

26. Rather than considering the judge to be a third party to the original plea agreement between the prosecution and the defense, the law of contracts could regard the acceptance of the plea by the judge as a separate contract among all three relevant parties. In any event, the judge's failure to honor any promise she made as part of the plea agreement would allow the injured party out of at least that part of the agreement.

27. Ray v. State, 165 A.3d 408 (Md. 2017).

28. People v. Mancheno, 654 P.2d 211 (Cal. 1982).

2. What is the remedy for a breach by the judge?

As is the case when the prosecutor fails to live up to an agreed term of the plea bargain, the breach of a material term by the judge allows for two possible remedies. The first is specific performance of the bargain with the original condition enforced. The second is a withdrawal of the guilty plea leading to a virtual restart of the judicial process. Due process has not been held to prioritize between those remedies in a manner that applies to every case involving a breach. The Supreme Court's decision in *Santobello* made clear that in cases of breaches by the prosecutor, while the preference of the defendant for one remedy over the other is a consideration as to which remedy courts should apply, it is not necessarily determinative. In considering what factors to apply to breaches by the judge, the California Supreme Court in *Mancheno* enumerated the following:

> Factors to be considered include who broke the bargain and whether the violation was deliberate or inadvertent, whether circumstances have changed between entry of the plea and the time of sentencing, and whether additional information has been obtained that, if not considered, would constrain the court to a disposition that it determines to be inappropriate.[29]

In other words, the interests of justice will play a prominent role in how a court chooses between declaring the entire plea void or enforcing the plea bargain as originally agreed.

A factually different but conceptually similar situation arises when a judge determines she will not or cannot adhere to a term that she committed to as part of a guilty plea agreement. While courts agree that the judge's unwillingness to fulfill a term of the plea bargain she committed to allows the defendant to withdraw from the plea deal, they are divided on whether the defendant should have the unfettered right to choose the remedy to be implemented. This division of opinion can best be seen by comparing the decisions of a court in Maryland with one in New York. In *Banks v. State*, pursuant to Banks' guilty plea to murder in the second degree, the prosecutor agreed to recommend a ten-year prison term for the defendant. In response, the judge committed himself to a sentence of no more than ten years' incarceration but said he might be open to a shorter term after seeing a pre-sentence report.[30]

---

29. *Id.* at 214.
30. Banks v. State, 56 Md. App. 38 (1983).

When he committed to the ten-year sentence limit, the judge was aware of some early convictions, but no recent ones. In fact, the judge said he was told the defendant had no arrests or convictions in the last nine years and agreed to the sentence limitation because of that. He never inquired as to whether there had been other convictions prior to that nine-year period. Five weeks later at the time of sentencing, the judge said he had now read in the pre-sentence report that the defendant had been convicted of two other felonies over nine years earlier. At the sentence proceeding, the judge indicated that knowing of these additional earlier convictions now, he could no longer live up to his promise of a sentence limit of ten years. He offered the defendant the choice of withdrawing his plea and either renegotiating a deal acceptable to the prosecutor and the court or going to trial. Banks argued that he had the right to hold the judge to his commitment and requested a sentence within the agreed-to range. The judge denied the request, and ultimately Banks was convicted at trial and sentenced to 30 years' incarceration.

Banks' trial conviction was overturned on appeal, and the appellate court ordered that Banks' original guilty plea be honored, including the judge's commitment to a sentence of no more than ten years. What made the court's opinion especially noteworthy was how it integrated principles of contract law with those of justice. Initially, the court held that the remedy issue was controlled by a Maryland rule which said that a judge "shall ... embody" the sentence agreed to at the time of the guilty plea in its ultimate sentence. The court then went considerably beyond that statutory interpretation in its analysis of why the terms of the plea bargain should bind the judge. As there are analogies to contract law that readily come to mind when looking at plea bargaining, the court examined and then dismissed one particular argument based in contract law that could be used to free the judge from his commitment. In contract law, if the agreement is induced by a material misrepresentation of fact, even if that misrepresentation is innocent in nature or a unilateral mistake of fact (a mistake of fact known by the other party at the time the contract was formed), a party can seek relief from the contract's terms. While there was no actual misrepresentation of Banks' criminal record here, it is certainly possible that the judge's sentence commitment was based on the mistaken criminal record he relied upon at the time of the plea. In dismissing the relevance of this aspect of contract law, the court said, "rigid application of contract principles is not appropriate in plea bargaining cases" and using the language of contract law in plea bargaining is done only "metaphorically."[31]

---

31. *Id.* at 50.

The reason that contract law should not be applied rigidly to plea bargaining is because the interests of the defendant and the impact of the criminal law upon him go much deeper than in civil cases. Accordingly, the *Banks* court looked next at the interests of justice. The court acknowledged that courts in other states had allowed judges out of such commitments where there was good reason to do so. While the *Banks* court did not detail why, several courts have held that the interests of justice are best served when the defendant's sentence is based on all the information available to a court. Those courts have reasoned that excluding important and relevant information that all would agree should play a role in meting out an appropriate sentence, such as additional prior felony convictions, does not serve the interests of justice. In response, the court in *Banks* discussed the importance of plea bargaining in general and then specifically the importance of certainty in the process of bringing that bargaining to finality. The court alluded to the benefits of certainty in the process for the prosecution, the defense, and the public. Finally, the court claimed that the loss of this certainty "seems inconsistent with the standard of fair play and equity" and with preserving reasonable expectations.[32]

The reasoning of the *Banks* case, specifically as to what is required by the interests of justice in cases where the judge does not fulfill his original commitment to sentence, stands in opposition to opinions such as *People v. Selikoff.*[33] At the time Selikoff pled guilty to second-degree grand larceny in order to satisfy charges based on a real estate swindle, he was told by the judge that based on the facts then known to him, the defendant's sentence would not include imprisonment. After presiding at the trial of Selikoff's codefendants, the judge came to believe that Selikoff's role in the fraudulent scheme was considerably more significant than what he had thought when accepting the plea and committing to a sentence of no imprisonment. On the date of sentencing, the judge informed Selikoff that based on this new information, he could no longer fashion a sentence that did not include imprisonment. He then offered Selikoff the chance to withdraw his plea. Similar to Banks in the Maryland case, Selikoff asked instead for specific performance of the judge's promise of a sentence with no imprisonment. The judge denied this, and sentenced Selikoff to up to five years in prison.

Because the judge in this case indicated at the time of the plea that his "promise" of no imprisonment was based on "the facts known to him,"[34] the New York Court of Appeals could have limited its decision denying Selikoff

---

32. *Id.* at 52.
33. 35 N.Y.2d 227 (1974).
34. *Id.* at 235.

the relief he sought by focusing on that language. As the judge conditioned his promise on what was then known to him at the time of the plea and he learned things later that were previously not known to him, he would be liberated from his promise. But the court went considerably further in its decision, touching on the role of both contract law and the interests of justice in determining the outcome of such cases. In discussing Selikoff's attempt to apply contract law (his request for specific performance), the court observed that to do so would also require a consideration of whether there was fraud by the defendant in inducing the agreement (understating the degree of his involvement in the scheme). Additionally, contract law would require looking into whether there was a unilateral mistake by the judge, which was an issue in the *Banks* case. The court, however, chose not to focus on those issues, observing that "application to plea negotiations of contract law is incongruous."[35]

In rejecting a rigid application of contract law to issues related to plea bargaining, the New York Court of Appeals then turned its attention to the interests of justice in determining whether Selikoff was entitled to specific performance of the non-incarceration sentence. The court found those interests lie primarily in meting out a sentence that accounts for traditional purposes of punishment such as rehabilitation, deterrence, and societal protection. The court stated quite clearly that these interests offer "considerations paramount to benefits beyond the power of individuals to contract."[36] In applying these traditional sentencing purposes, the judge must use all relevant information available to him at the time of sentence. Since that information in this case involved a different understanding of the defendant's role in the crime than the judge had at the time of the plea, the judge was free to impose a sentence that reflected this new information once he offered Selikoff a chance to withdraw his plea.

What is particularly interesting in the different approaches taken by courts regarding whether a judge must sentence a defendant to what she agreed to at the time of the plea is the interplay of contract law and the interests of justice. Both the *Banks* and *Selikoff* courts looked at analogies to contract law principles and relevant state statutes, but at the end of the day their opposing decisions each focused on principles of justice. To the Maryland court, those interests were best served by ensuring the element of certainty is present in plea negotiations. Parties to the bargaining process must bargain in good faith, and in part that means honoring their commitments, including those made

---

35. *Id.* at 238.
36. *Id.*

by the judge. To the New York court, such concerns are trumped by the need to ensure that a defendant's sentence is appropriate based on traditional sentencing considerations.

Of course, one way to avoid the dilemma caused by judges who at the time of sentencing feel they cannot honor the commitment they made when the plea was accepted is to avoid making such a commitment. The problem with this solution can be seen by considering why judges make such commitments in the first place. Put simply, the defendant often seeks such a commitment and in many instances will not agree to plead guilty without one. The chapter on judges (Chapter V) explores why they are motivated to obtain plea bargains and thus make such commitments to get them. As discussed in the chapter on defense attorneys (Chapter IV), it is wise for counsel to seek such commitments whenever possible. Because judges usually don't go above the recommendation from the prosecutor, such a recommendation by the prosecutor can be helpful to the defendant. But as it is the judge who determines the sentence, his commitment has considerably more value for the defendant. This may be a commitment to a specific sentence or a range of sentences that, most importantly for the defendant, contain a maximum beyond which the sentence won't go. Even courts, such as the one in *Selikoff*, that allow judges out of their agreed-to sentencing commitments rarely do so unless the judge has a good reason for wanting out. A change of circumstances (such as a new arrest between plea and sentence) or new important information for one reason or another not available to the judge when the commitment was made are deemed to constitute such good reasons. These changes do not happen that often, and if they do occur are used relatively rarely by judges to avoid the sentencing commitments made during plea bargaining. Thus in the vast majority of cases, such commitments provide defendants with a degree of certainty about how severe their sentences will be — commitments that are almost always honored.

Another means of avoiding the problem created by judges who become unwilling to honor commitments they made at the time of the guilty plea is to place conditions on their commitments. Those conditions can be specific, such as "I will commit myself to sentencing the defendant to no more than three years in prison if he makes full restitution before the date of sentence and is not charged with other crimes." Sometimes the condition can be more general: "Based on the information available to me now, I will sentence the defendant to probation." The latter condition gives the judge more leeway to avoid the proposed sentence. But it is just that flexibility and the uncertainty accompanying the promise that might discourage the defendant from accepting the plea, knowing that the judge can with greater ease avoid the agreed-upon sentence.

When the judge has made no sentencing commitment as part of a plea bargain or adheres to the commitment, the factors regarding the binding nature of the plea are different. If the defendant wishes to withdraw his guilty plea in such situations, it is usually within the judge's discretion whether to allow this withdrawal. In deciding whether to allow the defendant to withdraw his plea in these cases, courts typically look to the timing of the withdrawal request and the reason the defendant is seeking to withdraw his plea. Courts look less favorably on a plea-withdrawal request made after the judge imposes sentence, as that often reflects only the defendant's disappointment in the sentence and is not considered a valid basis for withdrawing a guilty plea. If the reason for the withdrawal request is based on a reasonable misunderstanding of some aspect of the plea agreement (as evidenced, for example, by an ambiguous or confusing allocution when the plea was accepted or supportive representations by defense counsel), courts are more apt to seriously consider the request.

Chapter VII

Types of Pleas Other than Standard Guilty Pleas

The standard guilty plea requires the defendant to acknowledge his guilt for the crime or crimes to which he is pleading guilty. During the plea allocution, usually after discussing the crime with the defendant in order to establish that there is a basis in fact for the guilty plea, the judge is likely to ask the defendant if he is pleading guilty because he is in fact guilty. The defendant normally must respond in the affirmative for the plea to be accepted. There are, however, two types of guilty pleas which obviate the need for the defendant to admit his guilt. Both of these pleas can result in the same sentence as the standard plea, but they contain important differences from standard pleas and from each other. The first such plea is called no lo contendere, and the second, named after the Supreme Court case which authorized it, is an Alford plea.

A. No Lo Contendere Pleas

1. What is a plea of no lo contendere?

No lo contendere is Latin for "I do not contend." A plea of no lo contendere (hereafter no lo) in our criminal justice system is an indication that the defendant does not contest the charges against him. In not contesting the charges, a no lo plea involves neither an admission nor a denial of guilt. It is essentially the equivalent of the defendant's allowing the waters of the criminal justice system to flow over him as he remains motionless. About three-fourths of the states and the federal government allow no lo pleas.[1] The no lo plea is controversial essentially for two reasons. The first results from the defendant's being permitted to derive the benefits of a plea bargain without having to admit his participation in any crime. Reacting to a no lo plea taken by a man who murdered two people in Pennsylvania in 2008, one commentator voiced this criticism:

> [T]he plea "means [he] does not admit guilt but concedes" there is a good case against him. What rubbish. This tactic to avoid accountability is as vile now as when [Vice President Spiro] Agnew used it. If people are accused of crimes, let them either strive to clear themselves or stand up and admit what they did. For criminals who hide behind an imaginary "no contest" middle ground, the penalties should be doubled.[2]

The second reason is that in many jurisdictions a no lo plea prevents the use of the defendant's guilty plea in future civil cases arising out of his criminal conduct.

2. The reasons for the plea

To assess the consequences of no lo pleas, it is first essential to understand in what ways these pleas are identical to standard guilty pleas. Similar to a standard guilty plea, a no lo plea is a criminal conviction and is reflected as such on the defendant's record. The defendant who enters a no lo plea faces exactly the same penalties for the crime or crimes he was convicted of that he would face had he entered a standard guilty plea. For certain defendants who cannot find it within themselves to admit to criminal conduct in the case for one reason or another, there may be some emotional or psychological value in being able to get the benefit of the plea bargain without such an admission. But there is no tangible advantage to entering a no lo plea as opposed to a standard guilty plea with respect to the criminal justice consequences of the defendant's conduct.

The reason why most defendants who plead no lo contendere do so is to avoid the consequences that a standard guilty plea might have in any civil suit arising from their criminal conduct. Standard guilty pleas are generally admis-

---

1. See respectively American College of Trial Lawyers, The Case for No Lo Contendere, https://www.actl.com/docs/default-source/default-document-library/nolo_contendere_website_final_v1.pdf?sfvrsn=4, and FRCP 11 (a)2 and 3.

2. Paul Carpenter, Agnew's "No Lo" Plea Set the Stage for the Corruption of Semantics, The Morning Call, https://www.mcall.com/news/mc-xpm-2009-04-24-4360197-story.html.

sible in civil trials to prove the defendant committed the actions encompassed by the plea, while no lo pleas are not admissible for that purpose.[3] To understand why this is allowed regarding standard guilty pleas, we need to consider the respective burdens of proof in criminal and civil cases. To convict a person of a crime, the prosecutor must meet the burden of proving every element of that crime beyond a reasonable doubt. This is often referred to as the highest standard of proof in our legal system. The burden of proof in most civil cases is a preponderance of the evidence. This means the party who carries that burden (usually but not always the plaintiff) must demonstrate the fact "more likely than not," or by 51% as it is commonly explained. If a defendant is convicted of negligent driving in criminal court (be it at trial or through a standard guilty plea), that means the factfinder has found beyond a reasonable doubt that he drove negligently. If the defendant is later sued civilly by the other driver for damages caused by the defendant's negligent driving, there is no need to re-litigate that issue because the judicial system has already determined that issue to a higher standard of proof than is required in the civil case. The defendant can still contest the amount of damages that should be awarded to the plaintiff because that issue was likely not resolved by his criminal conviction. The ability to use the criminal conviction in the civil case is one important reason why plaintiffs are in no rush to have their civil claims determined before the criminal case against the defendant is resolved. In the far less frequent situation where a civil judgment of liability precedes the disposition of the criminal case, that judgment cannot be used in the criminal prosecution because the burden of proof in civil court is lower than in criminal court.

While there may be civil consequences to certain violent crimes such as rape or assault, lawsuits in such cases are usually limited to those in which the defendant has deep pockets and can afford to pay any judgment that comes about or those involving an employer of the offender who can be sued for the conduct of their employee.[4] The many civil suits filed against alleged sex abusers Harvey Weinstein and Jeffrey Epstein would be examples of the former. Suits seeking money damages from governments for the assaultive behavior of police officers

---

3. *See, e.g.,* Fed. R. Evid. 410(a)2.

4. My personal experience with such a situation occurred when I prosecuted a New York City Department of Parks employee for the rape of a 9-year-old girl. During the trial, I was cheered on by the attorney representing the family of the girl in their civil suit against the city. The conviction of the defendant settled the issue of whether the city employee raped the child, meaning the attorney's only remaining responsibility was to satisfy the issues surrounding the employer-employee relationship and to work out the money damages with the city.

would be examples of the latter. In negligence cases, such as the hypothetical discussed above, the fact that the insurance company is usually the real financial party in interest provides another type of deep pocket that makes the use of the defendant's criminal conviction to show fault a useful piece of evidence for the plaintiff. While defendants might seek no lo pleas in cases of violent crimes, the far more common use of them occurs in instances of white-collar crime — usually non-violent offenses involving some sort of fraud, theft, or improper acquisition of money or other valuable commodities.

Perhaps the most famous such no lo plea involved former Vice President of the United States, Spiro Agnew. As his President, Richard Nixon, was in the midst of battling allegations regarding Nixon's involvement in the Watergate break-in and subsequent cover-up, Agnew was indicted for a series of corrupt actions which began during his time as a politician in Maryland and continued into his vice presidency. In 1973, Agnew was allowed to plead no lo contendere to one count of tax evasion to cover all charges against him. He was sentenced to probation plus a $10,000 fine, a very favorable outcome for Agnew that was undoubtedly agreed to by the government because the plea was accompanied by his resignation as vice president. Agnew was subsequently sued civilly by citizens of Maryland for the money he had stolen from the people of the state. While his no lo plea could not be used in this civil case, Agnew was found liable anyway and forced to pay a quarter of a million dollars on the judgment.

B. Alford Pleas

1. What is an Alford plea?

Every person charged with a crime in the United States possesses important protections guaranteed to her by our constitution. We have seen how the overwhelming number of criminal defendants surrender these protections in order to gain the benefits that come from a plea bargain with the prosecutor. What allows the courts to tolerate this routine and prolific abandonment of constitutional rights deemed essential to our criminal justice system is the defendant's admission that he committed the crime to which he pleads guilty. In other words, we need not actually employ all the protections in our constitution designed to ensure that people will not be convicted of crimes without a fair trial to determine their guilt because they are already admitting that guilt. As we have seen, these guilty pleas are not exceptions to trials–instead, trials are relatively rare exceptions in our system of resolving cases primarily through plea bargaining. No lo contendere pleas as described above provide an exception to the requirement that a defendant must admit his guilt to gain the advantage of a plea bargain. At least the defendant pleading no lo contendere is not affirmatively protesting his innocence before his conviction without a trial is official. Surely our system would not tolerate the conviction of a person who claims he is innocent without first finding that person guilty at a trial. But what of the defendant who maintains his innocence but comes to believe it is in his best interest to plead guilty? Enter the Alford plea.

An Alford plea allows a defendant to plead guilty to a crime while at the same time asserting his innocence of that very crime. Does such a plea serve the interest of the defendant and/or the criminal justice system? Why would a person plead guilty to a crime he did not commit or at least to one for which he is maintaining his innocence? Should the system require him to admit to a crime he claims he is innocent of or be forced to go to trial? Each of these questions must be answered before we examine just how the Supreme Court has permitted the criminal justice system to respond to defendants who maintain their innocence but wish to plead guilty.

2. The reason for the plea

The defendant is charged with rape. He has consistently denied the charge, maintaining that the sex was consensual. At preliminary hearings, the victim proved to be a highly credible witness when she testified that the defendant forcibly attacked her. Her testimony is buttressed by the injuries she incurred during the incident that are thoroughly documented in a hospital report. Additionally, she told a friend immediately after the incident that she had been raped, testimony likely admissible as an exception to the rule normally prohibiting hearsay. In response, the defense can offer only the testimony of the defendant that he met the woman at a club and she agreed to invite him into her home with the idea of having sex. The problem with his taking the witness stand is that the defendant has previous convictions which are usable to cross-examine him, thus reducing his credibility. The prosecutor will surely say to the jury on summation something like, "Against the entirely believable testimony of Ms. Jones, you have that of the defendant, whose previous convictions for larceny and robbery tell you all you need to know about the value he places on honesty. Whose testimony is more worthy of belief?"

One of the primary responsibilities of a criminal defense attorney is to use all the materials at her disposal to offer her client a reasonable assessment of the likelihood he will be convicted if the case goes to trial. Any competent attorney faced with the information above will tell her client that while no prediction of a verdict comes with certainty, his chances of acquittal are not good.

Next, the attorney will make her best educated guess as to what sentence the defendant will receive if he is convicted at trial. Assume rape carries a maximum penalty of 25 years' incarceration in this state and with the defendant's prior record there is a good chance he will have to serve substantial prison time if convicted, perhaps in the neighborhood of 15 years. For whatever reason (possibly because the victim wishes not to relive events), the prosecutor is offering to recommend and the judge to commit to a term of five years of prison time if the defendant pleads guilty. Faced with the likelihood of conviction at trial followed by a long prison sentence, the defendant's decision to plead guilty and avoid a decade behind bars, notwithstanding his continued assertion of innocence, is certainly not unreasonable.

3. Should the criminal justice system allow Alford pleas?

This tells us why a defendant who maintains his innocence might want to plead guilty but leaves open the question of whether the criminal justice system should allow this. That was precisely the issue when the Supreme Court decided the case of *North Carolina v. Alford* in 1970.[5] Henry Alford was charged with Murder in the First Degree and faced a maximum sentence of capital punishment under this indictment. After negotiations between his attorney and the prosecutor, a guilty plea agreement was reached. In order to avoid the potential death sentence, Alford agreed to plead guilty to Murder in the Second Degree, a crime which had a maximum term of 30 years' imprisonment. What made Alford's plea different than most was that before, during, and after the allocution and formal acceptance of his guilty plea, Alford proclaimed his innocence of the charges. Sometime after Alford's guilty plea in 1963, he changed his mind about wanting to so plead, and he challenged his plea as being involuntary. While the importance of this case derives from how the Court handled the issue of whether a person who consistently maintains his innocence should be allowed to plead guilty, it is instructive to look first at the exchange between Alford and his attorney during the allocution.

> 'I pleaded guilty on second degree murder because they said there is too much evidence, but I ain't shot no man, but I take the fault for the other man. We never had an argument in our life and I just pleaded guilty because they said if I didn't they would gas me for it, and that is all.'

---

5. 400 U.S. 25 (1970).

In response to questions from his attorney, Alford affirmed that he had consulted several times with his attorney and with members of his family and had been informed of his rights if he chose to plead not guilty. Alford then reaffirmed his decision to plead guilty to second-degree murder:

'Q. (by Alford's attorney). And you authorized me to tender a plea of guilty to second degree murder before the court?

'A. Yes, sir.

'Q. And in doing that, that you have again affirmed your decision on that point?

'A. Well, I'm still pleading that you all got me to plead guilty. I plead the other way, circumstantial evidence; that the jury will prosecute me on — on the second. You told me to plead guilty, right. I don't — I'm not guilty but I plead guilty.'[6]

The Court did not spend much time discussing whether this colloquy itself suggested Alford's guilty plea may be less than voluntary but instead turned to the broader issue of whether a person can simultaneously plead guilty while protesting his innocence. This question had been lingering for a time in state and federal courts leading to different results.

In holding that Alford's plea was valid, the Supreme Court offered two justifications for its conclusion that a guilty plea by a man who claims innocence can still be voluntary. While noting that Alford's claims of innocence set up a factual dispute with the guilty plea, the Court implied that this factual dispute was less significant because of the strength of the prosecution's case. Specifically, the government's case against Alford would have included, "information from Alford's acquaintances that he had departed from his home with his gun stating his intention to kill and that he had later declared that he had carried out his intention."[7] The second indicia of voluntariness came from the fact that Alford understood what the guilty plea entailed and ultimately made clear that he wanted to plead guilty to avoid the death penalty. Factual issues related to the guilt of a defendant are traditionally resolved at criminal trials. The Court acknowledged that the defendant's admission of guilt at the typical plea allocution is what normally obviates the need for a trial to resolve that dispute. But according to the Court, there is nothing in the constitution or previous Supreme Court decisions that requires such an admission. Where

---

6. *Id.* at 28–29 n.2.

7. *Id.* at 32.

the defendant seeks to get the benefit of a plea deal and the evidence showing his guilt is strong, courts should not stand in the way of his pleading guilty.

Related to this reasoning about voluntariness is the policy argument offered by the Court in support of its decision. In a tribute to pragmatism, the Court wrote, "The prohibitions against involuntary or unintelligent pleas should not be relaxed, but neither should an exercise in arid logic render those constitutional guarantees counterproductive and put in jeopardy the very human values they were meant to preserve."[8] By "arid logic," the Court was apparently referring to the notion that in the American system of criminal justice, people who say they are innocent should not be found guilty without a trial. Phrased in that way, such a guilty plea should make us all swallow hard. On its face it runs contrary to our fundamental beliefs about what constitutes due process in criminal cases. Alford pleas are the ultimate triumph of pragmatics over principle in our plea bargaining system. They represent the criminal justice system's recognition of the free-marketplace ethics of caveat emptor (let the buyer beware), and then afford him the freedom of his choices. But consider the alternative.

Should we prohibit defendants who want the benefit of a plea bargain from getting that benefit because we insist upon their acknowledgement of guilt? Had the Court so decided, defendants wishing to take advantage of a guilty plea offer who protest their innocence would have to nevertheless admit their guilt and thus in some instances be compelled to lie to the court. This smacks of the same hypocrisy we largely banished decades ago by abandoning the requirement that defendants deny the existence of those promises that all parties know induced the plea bargain. Combine that with all the other motivations that encourage disposing of cases through guilty pleas rather than trials where possible and the systemic argument for allowing Alford pleas is strong. Additionally, if either the prosecutor or the judge believes the interests of justice will not be furthered if the defendant is allowed to plead guilty while denying his guilt, the Alford plea will not be accepted.

The argument is stronger still when considering the criminal justice system's role in relationship to the defendant. This book has discussed how prohibiting judges from providing any information to defendants before they plead guilty concerning the judge's thoughts about a post-trial sentence is paternalistic. Such a ban presumes the system knows better what is in the defendant's best interest than does the defendant himself with the aid of his counsel. Preventing a defendant from doing what he believes is in his best interest by forbidding him the benefit of a plea bargain he wants without an admission of guilt is similarly paternalistic. Should we force a defendant against whom the evidence of guilt is

---

8. *Id.* at 39.

compelling to go to trial and face a much heavier sentence because we think that is in his best interest? Consider Alford himself. Should the court have compelled him to risk the death penalty by taking to trial a case in which the evidence clearly pointed to a conviction and in which the prosecutor believed a non-capital sentence was warranted in exchange for avoiding a trial? The safeguards now required by Alford pleas — the presence of counsel, a demonstratively strong prosecution case pointing to the defendant's guilt, and the defendant's acknowledgment of the likelihood of his conviction at trial — seem to be adequate protections against the plea being any more involuntary than traditional guilty pleas.

An interesting case dealing with Alford pleas decided by the Supreme Court of Iowa in 2005 exposes one of the shibboleths of plea bargaining jurisprudence. In Chapter II on punishment for exercising the right to trial, we examined the traditional reasons offered by courts for why the sentences imposed after trial do not constitute punishment even though they are almost always harsher than those sentences offered to a defendant as part of a plea bargain . Among the reasons mentioned most often is the claim that through a plea of guilty, the defendant expresses remorse for his commission of the crime. Since remorse is claimed to accelerate and make the defendant's rehabilitation more likely, those who demonstrate such remorse through their guilty plea should be sentenced to less time than those who apparently display no remorse by opting for a trial. Under federal law this somewhat related justification for lower sentences for those who plead guilty is referred to as "acceptance of responsibility." As discussed in that same chapter, if defendants who plead guilty happen to feel remorse for their crimes or a desire to accept responsibility for them, such feelings are likely to be mere appendages to their understandable and primary reason for the plea — to minimize punishment.

In *State v. Knight*,[9] the defendant entered an Alford plea to three charges involving the sexual exploitation of a minor. The judge sentenced the defendant to consecutive terms of imprisonment (meaning he had to serve one after another as opposed to serving them at the same time). One of the reasons offered by the judge for sentencing the defendant harshly was because Knight failed to show any remorse for his crime. The trial judge reasoned that although he pled guilty, Knight's continued claim of innocence belied any notion of remorse. Of course the definition of an Alford plea is one in which the defendant denies his guilt and therefore will never be able to express remorse for committing the crime. The Iowa Supreme Court then had to determine if the demonstration of remorse and likelihood of rehabilitation that is said to be part of a guilty plea comes from the plea itself or from the admission of guilt

---

9. 701 N.W.2d 83 (Iowa 2005).

that accompanies standard guilty pleas. Feel sorry for the Iowa court — it had to choose between two fictions.

The idea that remorse should play a role in sentencing at all is a debatable one. That judges can distinguish genuine remorse from the kind that most attorneys attempt to convince their clients to show in order to gain favor from the judge is highly questionable.[10] People exhibit remorse in different ways. Factor in the added difficulty of trying to determine whether remorse is genuine when coming from defendants of different ages, social, economic, and racial backgrounds than the judge and the difficulty is magnified. Finally, who is more likely to show remorse, an 18 year old from the inner city or a typical white collar defendant? The former may wish to save face among some in his community by refusing to say he is sorry. The latter, more focused on saving another part of his anatomy, will undoubtedly be deeply remorseful after being advised by his lawyer of the possible benefit of such "remorse."

Assuming arguendo that remorse is a proper sentencing factor, should an Alford plea be treated more like a standard guilty plea (indicating remorse) or more like a trial because similar to a trial the defendant is denying his guilt (thus showing no remorse)? The Iowa court chose the latter and affirmed Knight's sentence. But if showing remorse or acceptance of responsibility is not indicated by an Alford plea, the justification for the reduced sentence (reduced from what the sentence will be if the defendant is convicted at trial) that accompanies almost all Alford pleas loses its force. Additionally, courts can't fall back on the rationale that differential sentencing is a benefit and not a punishment because the issue as expressed by the court in *Knight* is whether the defendant's lack of remorse as demonstrated by a guilty plea in which he maintains his innocence can be an aggravating sentencing factor (a punishment). Of course, if we openly acknowledge that defendants who plead guilty receive reduced sentences because of the savings and other benefits that the parties to the criminal justice system receive from avoiding trials and not from any bromide about remorse, we negate this problem.

---

10. I tell my students that should they become judges and I appear before them as a criminal defendant, I want to express my deep remorse for any crime I have committed or will commit. I want to apologize to the victim, even in victimless crimes, to the court for taking up its time, and to anyone else who has read about my crime, be it murder, tax evasion, reckless driving, or littering. I am deeply, deeply sorry and will never offend again.

I have made this same "sincere" plea to groups of judges I taught about sentencing in Maryland's judicial education program. Some judges said they would surely have seen through my insincerity while others honestly admitted that had I shown a little less sarcasm, they might have reduced my sentence because of the remorse I exhibited, genuine or not. Their reactions were similar to those of my students.

C. Fictitious Guilty Pleas

We have now seen that defendants can plead guilty to crimes they claim they did not commit because substantial evidence points to their guilt. What about pleading guilty to crimes to which their guilt cannot be proven? Known as fictitious pleas, the issue here is whether the defendant can plead guilty to a crime he was not originally charged with and for which there is insufficient or no evidence whatsoever that he committed. The fictitious plea is not linked to the discovery of new evidence but instead is accepted to achieve the goals of the parties to the bargaining process. An example of this occurred in the 2012 Nevada case of *Melton v. State*.[11] Melton was charged with burglary and attempted grand larceny and ultimately pled guilty to grand larceny, a crime he was not originally charged with and apparently did not commit. At the time of the plea, Melton acknowledged in writing that his plea was fictitious, yet the plea was accepted by the court anyway. In affirming the legality of the plea, the Nevada Supreme Court noted this acknowledgment by Melton and that at the time of the plea he waived any "defects to the charge." Apparently the defect to the charge was that he did not commit the crime to which he pled guilty and there was no proof suggesting otherwise. Oh well.

An entirely different approach to fictitious pleas was taken by the Iowa Supreme Court, not with respect to invalidating the plea, but in a disciplinary proceeding against the prosecutor who used such pleas. In *Iowa Supreme Court Attorney Disciplinary Board v. Howe*,[12] the court considered whether the repeated practice of prosecutor Howe to reduce misdemeanor driving charges to the fictitious charge of violating the cowl light law in furtherance of guilty pleas constituted the unethical practice of seeking a conviction to a charge for which there is no probable cause of the defendant's guilt. Although I am certain that everyone reading this is intimately familiar with Iowa's cowl light law, I'll share it with you anyway. Iowa law states that a motor vehicle "may be equipped with not more than two side cowl or fender lamps which shall emit an amber or white light without glare."[13] The problem with pleas to this charge was that as Howe knew, "vehicles have not been equipped with cowl or fender lamps 'for a considerable number of years.'"[14]

---

11. 381 P.3d 641 (Nev. 2012) (table in unpublished disposition).
12. 706 N.W.2d 360 (Iowa 2005).
13. Iowa Code § 321.406.
14. 706 N.W.2d at 367.

Howe argued that in these cases the defendant and her attorney always agreed to and sometimes proposed the fictitious plea because the plea was to the defendant's benefit. The magistrate who accepted these fictitious pleas testified that she knew there was no basis for the cowl light charge when the pleas were accepted. The court took a literal approach to the prosecutor's ethical responsibility of not filing a charge for which there is not probable cause and sanctioned Howe for doing so.

The *Howe* case should be regarded as the rare instance when a guilty plea agreed to by all parties and not challenged as being unknowing or involuntary served as the basis for a critical analysis by a court. Not only is the decision an exception, but even Howe's actions in these cases did not invalidate the pleas. They merely resulted in the prosecutor being disciplined.

D. Impossible Pleas

1. Pleas to crimes that are logical impossibilities

For those of you still in doubt regarding the application and triumph of marketplace principles regarding plea bargaining, consider situations involving guilty pleas to impossible charges. In these cases, the defendant pleads guilty to a crime that cannot logically exist. Take the New York case of *People v. Foster*,[15] for example. Foster was indicted for the crime of Manslaughter in the First Degree, but as part of a bargain was allowed to plead guilty to Attempted Manslaughter in the Second Degree. The problem with this plea is that logic makes this charge of "attempted manslaughter" impossible. The New York manslaughter charge was based on reckless conduct in killing a human being. Attempting to commit a crime requires a showing that the conduct was intentional. One cannot attempt to act recklessly. The New York Court of Appeals acknowledged that attempted manslaughter was both "legally impossible" and "logically repugnant"[16] yet still affirmed the plea. In doing so, the court relied upon the fact that the defendant not only accepted the plea offer but "induced" it and that the deal accrued to his benefit regarding the sentence he received. More recently, a New York court cited the holding in *Foster* in declaring the validity of a guilty plea to Attempted Reckless Endangerment while conceding it too was a legally impossible crime.[17]

---

15. 225 N.E.2d 200 (N.Y. 1967).
16. *Id.* at 201.
17. People v. Stanley, 78 N.Y.S.3d 851 (App. Div. 4th Dept. 2018).

While not all states allow pleas to fictitious crimes, many do. One Kansas court summed up the approach typically taken most courts:

> We hold that a criminal defendant who is originally brought into court on a valid pleading may, pursuant to a beneficial plea agreement knowingly entered, plead guilty to a nonexistent crime. We further hold that if a defendant enters into a plea agreement voluntarily and intelligently, he or she forfeits the right to attack the underlying infirmity in the charge to which he or she pled.[18]

It is undisputed that were a jury to convict a defendant of an impossible crime, such a conviction would be overturned. But where the defendant makes a knowing and voluntary plea to such a crime, most courts will not stand in the way of his doing what he deems to be in his benefit.

2. Pleas to crimes that are factual impossibilities

It is not merely crimes that are logical impossibilities to which defendants are permitted to plead guilty. They are also allowed to plead guilty to crimes which are factual impossibilities. In the recent case of *Commonwealth of Pennsylvania v. Imbalzano*, the defendant was charged with and pled guilty to statutory sexual assault.[19] A required element of this crime was that the defendant had to be at least 11 years older than his victim. In fact, Imbalzano was 10 years 10 months older than his victim and therefore his conviction of the statutory sexual abuse charge was factually impossible. In his attempt to invalidate his plea, Imbalzano argued that his lawyer's recommendation to accept a plea to a crime he could not have committed constituted ineffective assistance of counsel. In rejecting the defendant's argument, the Pennsylvania Superior Court noted that his lawyer told Imbalzano that the guilty plea was to a charge he could not have committed and then correctly explained the substantial sentencing benefits that would accrue from such a plea. According to the court, counsel's advice to his client was reasonable and the fact that the plea was to a crime that defendant could not have committed is immaterial.

So we see that courts have approved guilty pleas when the defendant does not admit his involvement in the crime, affirmatively denies his involvement, pleas to a fictitious crime, or the plea is to a crime that is a logical and/or factual impossibility. Reasonable people can disagree as to whether one or all of these pleas improperly exalts pragmatism over principle. What is beyond dispute,

---

18. Spencer v. State, 942 P.2d 646, 649 (Kan. Ct. App. 1997).
19. 237 A.3d 457 (Pa. Super. Ct. 2020).

however, is that our criminal justice system in its desire to encourage disposition of cases without a trial has adopted a largely marketplace approach to plea bargaining. If an agreement entered into by the parties was known, understood, and not coerced, there is little reason to invalidate those agreements. In practice, it is not hard to understand why such is the case.

Plea bargains challenged on appeal by defendants represent a very small minority of the guilty pleas accepted in American courts every day. In examining the cases discussed above, we have seen that challenges to those pleas, barring egregious behavior by one or more of the parties, are likely to be unsuccessful. The thousands and thousands of plea bargains entered into annually take effect without legal challenges and incorporate all sorts of conditions and requirements. We once again look to normal human behavior regarding how it plays a role in the disposition of criminal cases through non-traditional and impossible pleas. We have seen that almost no guilty plea is entered without the approval of the three parties to the process — the prosecutor, defendant/defense attorney, and the judge. If all three decide their best interests are served through disposing of a case in a certain manner, it is the rare occasion that such a plea is not implemented. When I was a prosecutor, New York had a draconian drug law which required, among other things, a minimum sentence of 15 years' imprisonment and a maximum of life for possession of four ounces of marijuana.[20] I am not ashamed to admit that working with like-minded defense attorneys and judges, I often sabotaged those laws by working out guilty pleas of questionable factual accuracy that clearly frustrated the unduly harsh sentencing approach that was the stated purpose of the laws. I point this out not to suggest that what I did is beyond criticism, but only that where all three parties to a process agree on the best outcome, that outcome is generally achieved.

---

20. Rockefeller Drug Laws, Wikipedia, https://en.wikipedia.org/wiki/Rockefeller_Drug _Laws.

Chapter VIII

The Impact of Racial Disparity in Plea Bargaining

A. Introduction

It should come as a surprise to almost no one that racial disparity plays a role at every point in the criminal justice system. It would be virtually impossible considering the manner in which we respond to crime and the people who do so to be free of the systemic racism and implicit biases that pervade much of society. For some time, a great deal of evidence has existed, both empirical and anecdotal, that confirms this unfortunate reality. We have heard stories and seen evidence of African Americans being stopped and frisked in far greater proportions than their numbers in the total American population would suggest. The deaths of George Floyd and others have highlighted the tragic effect of some police overreactions and outright criminal behavior that disproportionately victimizes African Americans. We have seen statistics that demonstrate how the so-called war on drugs had targeted people of color, resulting in disproportionate numbers of drug arrests for these minorities. In fact, overall arrest rates for blacks show the same disparity. The United States imprisons a greater percentage of our population than any nation in the world.[1] Statistics for many years have shown that African Americans comprise a proportion of prison inmates well beyond their overall share of the population. Studies have also revealed that African Americans receive longer sentences than white Americans who have committed the same or similar crimes.

---

1. The U.S. has approximately 5% of the world's total population yet 21% of its prison population. Criminal Justice Fact Sheet, NAACP, https://www.naacp.org/criminal-justice-fact-sheet/.

What had been largely lacking in materials dealing with racism in the criminal justice system was information about its impact on plea bargaining specifically. We can only speculate on the reason for this relative inattention to the effect of racism on the part of the criminal justice process that accounts for the disposition of 95% of criminal cases. I think the best guess as to this inattention is due once again to the negative reputation plea bargaining has had since its inception and its treatment as the bastard child of the criminal justice system. We know we do plea bargaining—we know we do it a lot, in fact—but "the less said about it the better" was the prevailing view for many decades.

With respect to racism in plea bargaining, the following questions need to be asked: Is there a difference among the offers prosecutors make and judges accept to secure guilty pleas based to some extent on the race of the defendant? Breaking that question down requires a careful examination of the two most frequent benefits defendants are offered and receive as part of plea deals. First, is there a difference based on the race of the defendant regarding the reduction in the charge a defendant pleads guilty to? Second, is such a difference reflected in the sentence offered and actually imposed after the bargain is accepted?

B. Racial Disparity in the Overall Criminal Justice System

In order to understand the likelihood that racism plays some role in plea bargaining, it is instructive to examine briefly its impact on the various interactions between those accused of crimes and the two American institutions charged with enforcing our criminal laws—the police and the courts.

In 1968, the Supreme Court handed down a landmark opinion allowing the police to make limited seizures of a person and limited searches based on a standard of proof less than traditional probable cause.[2] These limited seizures and searches that came to be known as "stop and frisk" were permitted based on reasonable suspicion of criminal activity (for the stop) and of weapon possession (for the frisk). In the early part of the 21st century, New York City thought it could reduce violent crime by instituting a much more aggressive approach to stop and frisk. That meant stopping more people and searching them for weapons. At its peak in 2011, 605,000 people in the city were subjected

---

2. Terry v. Ohio, 392 U.S. 1 (1968).

to stop and frisk by the police. Of those stopped, 55% were black and 9% white.[3] At that time, the ethnic breakdown of those groups in New York City's population was 25% black and 35% white.[4] Thus blacks were stopped more than double the number of times of their share in the overall population, while whites were stopped about one-fourth of their total population numbers. Vast amounts of anecdotal evidence is testament to the increased likelihood that you are more likely to be detained by the police if you are a person of color. Think about the only slightly sarcastic claim of being stopped for driving while black.

In addition to being stopped and investigated more, blacks are more likely to be arrested than whites. "In 2016, black Americans comprised 27% of all individuals arrested in the United States—double their share of the total population."[5] Black youth constituted 15% of all U.S. children yet made up 35% of juvenile arrests in that year. In a study of arrests in New York, New Jersey, and Connecticut in 2018, on average blacks were five times more likely to be arrested than whites.[6] Although they comprised only 6% of the total population of San Francisco, blacks accounted for 41% of the arrests in that city between 2008 and 2014.[7] The disparity in arrest rates between whites and blacks for some crimes, such as those linked to the war on drugs, is especially noteworthy. "In every year from 1980 to 2007, blacks were arrested nationwide on drug charges at rates relative to population that were 2.8 to 5.5 times higher than white arrest rates."[8] An NAACP report found that although the percentage of blacks who use drugs is estimated to be about equal to the percentage of whites who use drugs, the imprisonment rate for blacks on drug-related crimes is six times higher.[9]

---

3. Stop-and-Frisk Data, New York Civil Liberties Union, ACLU of New York, https://www.nyclu.org/en/Stop-and-Frisk-data.

4. Sam Roberts, Slower Racial Change Found in Census of City, N.Y. Times (July 28, 2011), https://www.nytimes.com/2011/07/29/nyregion/census-finds-slight-stabilizing-in-new-york-city-racial-makeup.html.

5. Report to the United Nations on Racial Disparities in the U.S. Criminal Justice System, The Sentencing Project (Apr. 19, 2018), https://www.sentencingproject.org/publications/un-report-on-racial-disparities/.

6. John Kelly, Analysis of Police Arrests Reveals Stark Racial Disparity in NY, NJ, and CT, ABC7 New York (Jun. 10, 2020), https://abc7ny.com/police-racial-bias-profiling-disparity-in-arrests-black-arrest-rates/6241175/.

7. Timothy Williams, Black People Are Charged at a Higher Rate Than Whites. What if Prosecutors Didn't Know Their Race?, N.Y. Times (Jun. 12, 2019), https://www.nytimes.com/2019/06/12/us/prosecutor-race-blind-charging.html.

8. https://www.hrw.org/report/2009/03/02/decades-disparity/drug-arrests-and-race-united-states#.

9. https://www.naacp.org/criminal-justice-fact-sheet/.

Once arrested, blacks are more likely to be denied bail than white defendants and more likely to remain in jail until their trial.[10] A study that looked into the entire pretrial jail population in the U.S. in 2002 found that the percentage of blacks among this group was 3½ times their percentage in the overall population of blacks in the nation.[11] A more recent examination found that blacks in urban areas are 25% more likely to be jailed pretrial than white defendants and that young black males are 50% more likely to be detained than their white counterparts.[12] Aside from the obvious downsides to being in jail, preparing for and participating in a trial is both easier and likely to be more productive when the defendant is not incarcerated.

Racial disparity is reflected at the end of the judicial process as well. For the years 2008 and 2009, the average prison sentence meted out in federal courts was 55 months for white defendants and 90 months for black defendants.[13] From 2012 through 2016, the United States Sentencing Commission reported that blacks convicted of federal crimes received sentences 19% longer than "similarly situated" whites.[14] All of the above data leads to the obvious conclusion that blacks are significantly over-represented in the American prison population. In 2016, for example, although there were 5½ times more white than black Americans, the total number of blacks and whites incarcerated in state prisons throughout the U.S. was about the same. If there is hopeful news from this data, it is that, disproportionally high as it is, the percentage of blacks among the total state prison population has diminished since 2000.[15]

C. Racial Disparity in Plea Bargaining

In examining the issue of race in plea bargaining, we need to consider the offers made by prosecutors and especially the terms and ultimate results of the

---

10. Traci Schlesinger, Racial and Ethnic Disparity in Pretrial Criminal Processing, 22 Just. Q. 170, 181–83 (2005).

11. Wendy Sawyer, How Race Impacts Who Is Detained Pretrial, Prison Policy Initiative (Oct. 9, 2019), https://www.prisonpolicy.org/blog/2019/10/09/pretrial_race/.

12. Id.

13. Sonja B. Starr & M. M. Rehavi, Racial Disparity in Federal Criminal Sentences, 122 J. Pol. Econ. 1320, 1321 (2014).

14. Demographic Differences in Sentencing, U.S. Sentencing Comm'n (Nov. 14, 2017), https://www.ussc.gov/research/research-reports/demographic-differences-sentencing.

15. William J. Sabol, Thaddeus L. Johnson, & Alexander Caccavale, Council on Criminal Justice, Trends in Correctional Control by Race and Sex (Dec. 2019), https://cdn.ymaws.com/counciloncj.org/resource/collection/4683B90A-08CF-493F-89ED-A0D7C4BF7551/Trends_in_Correctional_Control_-_FINAL.pdf.

guilty plea. Almost all the data analyzing the role that race plays in the plea bargaining process is of fairly recent vintage. While there is nowhere near as much information on the influence of race in plea bargaining as there is regarding other aspects of the criminal justice process, what does exist is revealing. In part that is because this data encompasses widely diverse court systems. A 2014 study by the Vera Institute of Justice of criminal cases in the New York City borough of Manhattan found that black defendants were 13% more likely to receive plea offers from prosecutors that involved jail or prison time than were similarly situated white defendants. The disparity was even more stark in misdemeanor drug cases where the difference between the races regarding custodial plea offers was 27%.[16]

A 2018 law review article in which the author studied the statistics from Wisconsin circuit courts revealed that there was a significant difference between the plea bargain dispositions for black and white defendants. Specifically, the plea deals obtained by white defendants were 25% more likely to lead to the dismissal of the most serious charge or its reduction to a lower charge than for black defendants in the same circumstances. The result of this was that the convictions of white defendants initially charged with felonies were 15% more likely to be for less serious misdemeanors than the convictions of their black counterparts. The disparity between the races in cases initially charged as misdemeanors is even more pronounced. When looking at the ultimate dispositions of these cases, this study found that whites were 75% more likely than blacks in the same category to be convicted of offenses carrying no jail time or convicted of nothing at all.[17]

A 2017 report in *Justice Quarterly* examined over 900 felony cases in a large Florida county. Its conclusions were that "whites have a significantly greater probability of charge reduction when they plead guilty" and that "pleading guilty increases the probability of a charge reduction by 50.1% for blacks, as opposed to 55.8% for whites."[18] The Daily Press reviewed 474,000 criminal cases over a ten-year period in the courts of Hampton Roads, Virginia, to determine if there were disparities in the plea bargains obtained by white and

16. Esiki Kutateladze, Whitney Tymas, & Mary Crowley, Race and Prosecution in Manhattan, Research Summary, Vera Inst. of Justice (July 2014), https://www.vera.org/downloads/Publications/race-and-prosecution-in-manhattan/legacy_downloads/race-and-prosecution-manhattan-summary.pdf.

17. Carlos Berdejó, Criminalizing Race: Racial Disparities in Plea-Bargaining, 59 B.C. L. Rev. 1187, 1191 (2018).

18. Derek Gilna, Study's Data Show Racial Disparity in Plea Bargaining Outcomes, Crim. L. News (Nov. 16, 2017), https://www.criminallegalnews.org/news/2017/nov/16/studys-data-show-racial-disparity-plea-bargaining-outcomes/.

black defendants for certain specific crimes. Plea bargains for white defendants charged with drug possession resulted in non-incarceration sentences 65% of the time, but for black defendants it was only 56% of the time. For drug distribution, those same numbers, respectively, were 48% and 22%. For grand larceny, the numbers were 55% and 48%, respectively.[19]

The racial disparities that exist in plea bargaining can be viewed as yet another reflection of racism in the criminal justice system, which in turn can be seen as another reflection of racism in society. The causes of racism are of course many and varied and well beyond the purview of this book. Even controlling for non-racial variables, it would be incomprehensible not to regard the disparities that exist throughout the criminal justice system as evidence that among those charged with crimes, blacks are treated differently than whites. With respect to plea bargaining, it is probably fair to say that to a significant extent, the disparities we see above are due to the implicit biases of the parties to the process. Do prosecutors see black defendants as more dangerous than white ones and offer stiffer plea deals? Do the preexisting views of some defense attorneys make them willing to recommend acceptance of plea offers to black clients that they might not for their white clients? Do judges apply the justifications for sentencing in a way that is different for blacks than whites? For example, might race play a direct or indirect, albeit unconscious, role in how long a judge believes it will take for a defendant to be rehabilitated and sentence accordingly?

In attempting to confront racial disparities in plea bargaining, some approaches are consistent with overall suggestions for improving plea bargaining that will be discussed in the next chapter. For example, we should develop ways of limiting the vast discretion possessed by prosecutors regarding the charges they file and the plea deals they offer. More transparency in how plea offers are made by prosecutors and accepted by judges would be helpful as well. Maintaining plea bargaining statistics based on race would aid in illuminating the existence of disparate treatment. Informing prosecutors, defense attorneys, and judges about these statistics and educating them about the often subconscious manner in which racism affects plea bargaining would help as well. Such illumination should make the parties to plea bargaining who are anxious to achieve racial fairness more motivated to correct it. As for those less anxious to correct the problem, making bias less implicit and more statistically verifiable can embarrass them into taking action. Still, it would be un-

---

19. Dave Ress, Blacks More Likely to Get Prison Time in Plea Deals, Hampton Roads Court Data Show, Daily Press (Mar. 17, 2016), https://www.dailypress.com/news/dp-nws-sunshine-disparities-20160317-story.html.

realistic to expect we can resolve the disparate treatment blacks receive in plea bargaining without making meaningful improvements to achieve fairness and equality in other areas of criminal justice. That reality, however, should not prevent the judicial system from taking meaningful steps to minimize racism in plea bargaining wherever possible.

Chapter IX

Reforming Plea Bargaining

Although most of the significant concerns arising from a criminal justice system that does not merely include plea bargains but depends upon them are apparent to all who participate in the system, the responses to these concerns have often been non-existent, random, or completely haphazard. Some have been sensible but minimal in their impact, while others have been far more ambitious but either unrealistic in their assumptions and/or unsuccessful in practice.

The previous chapters have focused to a large extent on the parties involved in the criminal justice system, specifically those involved in settling cases through plea agreements. Because the criminal justice system, and most especially the plea bargaining process, is so fundamentally a human endeavor, attempts to examine the nature of the process, its problems, and possible reforms without such a focus is at best unrealistic and at worst a complete waste of time. So as we explore proposed reforms to plea bargaining, the book will again emphasize its two themes. What role can each of the parties to the plea bargaining system play in improving it, and are these proposed reforms realistic? In other words, do the proposed reforms comport with what we understand about human motivations and specifically what we expect of people in their institutional roles as prosecutors, defense attorneys, and judges? Then we will take a look at changes in plea bargaining that are systemic in nature and require action by lawmakers and law schools. Most critically, the discussion of these proposed reforms will look beyond their goals and assess the likelihood that those goals will be accomplished.

A. Suggestions for Prosecutors

1. Avoid overcharging

As we have seen, prosecutors have enormous power regarding when a plea bargain is arrived at, the terms of that agreement, and what happens if the terms of that agreement are not fulfilled. This power is exercised in several ways. Initially, the prosecutor chooses from a menu of possible charges to file against the defendant. The charges he chooses to file may warrant vastly different sentences than the charges he forgoes. He may opt to file one charge that covers the offense or several charges for the same offense. If he opts for filing multiple charges, the sentences for those charges can run concurrently, meaning the prison time for each crime is served simultaneously or consecutively, allowing the sentence on the second charge to be added on to that of the first charge. Because of the significance of such a determination to the length of the sentence and the normally critical factor of sentence length to the defendant's decision whether or not to accept a plea offer, it is important that attempts to reform plea bargaining begin with consideration of the charging and overcharging practices of prosecutors.

The problems with plea bargaining caused by the virtually unlimited power of prosecutors to choose what crimes to charge the defendant with were discussed in Chapter III on the role of prosecutors. To review, this authority reallocates the roles and hierarchy among the parties to the criminal litigation process. In so doing, it allows the prosecutor to wield enormous leverage over the process and in a sense become an adjudicator as well as the party seeking to convict the defendant. This results in an unwarranted and unfair transfer of authority from the judge to the prosecutor.

Legislatures are the governmental bodies tasked with deciding the appropriate range of sentences for each crime. Such determinations are based on reasonable assumptions about how the facts of particular crimes constitute one statutory offense as opposed to another. If a prosecutor decides that she is likely to gain leverage during plea negotiations by charging a crime for which there may be probable cause but is clearly not the focus of the statute, this may diminish the role of the legislature in establishing the appropriate relationship between crime and punishment.

Given the almost total authority prosecutors have over the charging decision, any current attempts to avoid or at least limit overcharging rests largely with prosecutors themselves. While each jurisdiction is somewhat different, cases that proceed through the system as purely misdemeanors usually begin with charging instruments decided upon and drafted by prosecutors. Felony cases may begin the same way, but the ultimate charge the defendant faces in these more serious cases is usually handed down by a grand jury through an indictment. As I realized during the nine months I spent doing nothing but presenting cases to the grand jury, the prosecutor has immense discretion regarding what charges to seek in connection with an indictment.[1] While it is the grand jurors who make the ultimate decision regarding precisely what charges to bring in cases presented to them, they invariably follow the advice of the prosecutor who presents the evidence and acts as their legal advisor.

Recently, reform-minded prosecutors have been elected in places such as Philadelphia, St. Louis, and Boston. It would be consistent with their stated mission of achieving a fairer and more just system to attempt to limit overcharging by enumerating relatively clear guidelines regarding which factors should play a role in deciding what crimes to charge and the extent of the role each factor should play in that decision. Publishing those guidelines would add a much needed element of transparency to the plea bargaining process. Having supervisors review the charges brought to ensure compliance with the guidelines would make them more effective. I suggest such guidance from above would benefit even less reform-minded prosecutors. When I was a prosecutor, the Bronx was faced with many serious crimes. As in almost all jurisdictions, especially urban ones, there were nowhere near enough prosecutors (or, for that matter, judges, courtrooms, or public defenders) to take even a substantial minority of those cases to trial. So we prioritized and triaged cases. For example, although the misdemeanor of petit larceny became the low-level felony of grand larceny if the value of the theft exceeded $250 back then, we were instructed not to seek a felony indictment unless the value exceeded $1500. This approach allowed our office to avoid several procedures required in felony cases; sped up resolution of those cases; facilitated the application of limited resources to more serious crimes such as arson, rape, and murder; and led to fewer and shorter prison sentences for non-violent crimes. With the push for decarceration coming from many different quarters these days, such a limitation on overcharging could be politically beneficial for prosecutors as well.

---

1. If the reader gets nothing else from this book, please be careful before attributing too much significance to the number of charges in an indictment. I remember routinely handing down multicount indictments in cases involving one basic crime because I was advised to make sure I missed nothing in the way of criminal behavior.

2. Provide discovery materials more quickly and make them more complete

As has been discussed throughout the book, our approach to criminal justice is dominated by the adversary system. With clearly designated opposing parties and a structure that reinforces their adversarial roles, it is not surprising to see numerous examples of actions taken for purely strategic purposes, sometimes taking on the characteristics of game playing. The implementation of discovery rules, whereby the parties are obligated to reveal certain aspects of their cases to the opposing party, is one area where this game playing is common practice. Although the defense is generally required to reveal such things as any expert testimony it plans to elicit during trial or the names of witnesses who will provide the defendant with an alibi,[2] the prosecution understandably has greater discovery responsibilities.[3] Each state and the federal government have discovery statutes which are different from one another in terms of exactly what is discoverable and when that discovery must be provided. In some states, for example, a document that can be used to impeach a witness on cross-examination does not have to be turned over to the defense until the witness is actually on the stand. This gives the defense attorney a very limited time to determine if and when to use the document.

Some prosecutors have an "open folder" discovery policy, allowing the defense access to all pertinent material as soon as it is available. Others limit discovery in terms of what material they provide and when it will be provided to meet the minimal requirements of the local discovery statute. Within the range of those two approaches, there are all sorts of policies related to revealing information about witnesses, oral statements, reports, tangible evidence, and the times when those matters will be revealed. With respect to plea bargaining particularly, the more discovery and the earlier it takes place, the better. As we again focus on what happens in the real world, there will be some things the prosecutor, for one reason or another, does not want to reveal to the defense and certainly does not want to do so early on in the process. Sometimes that inclination not to reveal until and unless it is necessary is justified. Think, for example, of a prosecutor wanting to hold off as long as possible on revealing the name of a witness to a defendant who has made threats to anyone planning on testifying against him. Given the amount and seriousness of witness intim-

---

2. *See, e.g.*, ABA Criminal Justice Standard 11-2.2.
3. *See, e.g.*, ABA Criminal Justice Standard 11-2.1.

idation in some urban areas especially, this hesitancy is warranted.[4] At other times, the prosecutor's reasons may make strategic sense but compromise the fairness of the plea bargain. If there is a material inconsistency in a police report or statement of a witness, that should be revealed to the defendant before acceptance of a guilty plea whether it qualifies as Brady material (exculpatory evidence) or not. Our system depends on fair treatment even for guilty people, and obtaining a guilty plea from a defendant who is blind to important aspects of the case against him is unfair.

For a system that depends on plea bargaining to survive and is loath to undertake actions likely to increase the number of cases that go to trial, there is admittedly a possibility that revealing aspects of the prosecution's case may have just that undesired effect. On the other hand, bringing such matters out into the open might encourage prosecutors to make plea offers both more reflective of their actual case and more appealing to the defendant. Additionally, some discovery material if revealed early will convince the defendant of the strength of the case against him and incline him to accept a guilty plea offer.

3. Avoid a vindictive response to a plea offer that is rejected

The natural feeling of a prosecutor who has made what she thinks is a reasonable, even generous, offer to a defendant and has had that offer rejected can range from minor disappointment to outright anger. As a former prosecutor, I can recall quite well those occasions where I recommended a strong sentence for a clearly guilty defendant who was convicted at trial after earlier rejecting what I thought was a reasonable guilty plea offer. These sentence recommendations took into consideration that the defendant's rejection of the plea offer resulted in putting witnesses through the sometimes traumatizing ordeal of a trial. Still, clearly guilty or not, the defendant has the right to a trial. While his post-trial conviction sentence will undoubtedly be longer than that contained in the guilty plea offer, it should still correspond to the traditional sentencing factors we use to determine punishment and not prosecutorial vindictiveness.

A judge can of course ignore the sentencing recommendation of the prosecutor if she believes it to be unduly punitive. Other actions by the prosecutor in response to the rejection of a plea offer, however, are largely insulated from

---

4. Witness intimidation unfortunately can transcend individual cases and become part of a community's culture. The infamous Stop Snitching DVD, first released in Baltimore and then nationwide, is an example of how such a culture can develop and become a tangible threat to the workings of the criminal justice system.

any modifying decision of the court. A prosecutor can seek to re-indict a defendant who rejects a plea offer and if convicted on the re-indicted offenses, the defendant will face considerably more severe and at times mandated sentences that he did not face in the original indictment. As discussed earlier in the book, in *Bordenkircher v. Hayes*, the defendant was charged with uttering a forged instrument for $88 — an offense that called for a statutorily defined sentence upon conviction of between two to ten years in prison. Given his two prior felony convictions, Hayes was offered a plea including a five-year prison sentence, which he rejected. The prosecutor re-indicted Hayes as he said he would do if the plea bargain was rejected. Upon his conviction at trial, Hayes was sentenced to life imprisonment, a sentence mandated by Kentucky's habitual offender law. The prosecutor's actions resulting in a life sentence for a minor forgery would seem to be a vindictive response for rejecting the plea offer under any plain meaning of the word vindictive. The Supreme Court, however, held it was all part of the give-and-take negotiations inevitable in plea bargaining and was not a violation of due process.[5]

While the decision in *Hayes* authorizes such behavior by a prosecutor, it is behavior that should nonetheless be avoided. Of course, the defendant will almost inevitably receive a heavier sentence after being convicted at trial than had he accepted the plea, and if the prosecutor makes a sentence recommendation after trial, it too will undoubtedly be harsher than that which accompanied the plea offer. As we have seen, such differential sentencing (or charge reduction) is essential for plea bargaining to succeed and to some degree it will always occur. As in *Hayes*, one way of virtually ensuring a considerably heavier sentence if the defendant is convicted at trial is to re-indict the defendant where possible with a crime involving a mandatory minimum sentence, a recidivist punishment statute, or to just add more or more serious charges to the original indictment. Even without a obtaining a new indictment, the prosecutor can choose to exhibit his vindictiveness for the rejection of his plea offer by making an unduly harsh sentence recommendation after the trial conviction. While judges are free to ignore that recommendation, the view of the prosecutor often plays a significant role in the sentence meted out.

In response to this real problem stemming from an understandable but counterproductive human reaction to a plea offer rejection, prosecutors need to develop a mechanism for seeing that reaction does not turn into

---

5. 434 U.S. 357 (1978). A more recent case in which the defendant was punished in a similarly vindictive manner is *United States v. Haynes*, No. 93 CR 1043 (RJD), 2020 WL 1941478 (E.D.N.Y. Apr. 22, 2020). Haynes, too, rejected a plea offer and was then re-indicted, resulting in a sentence 40 years longer than he was offered as part of a guilty plea.

overreaction. In other words, whatever factors played a role in what the prosecutor believed was an appropriate sentence prior to her guilty plea offer should still, for the most part, be the same factors governing her sentence-related actions after the rejection. The seriousness of the offense and the background of the defendant should be the primary sentencing factors as well as other information that bears on the traditional sentencing justifications of retribution, deterrence, rehabilitation, and incapacitation. While these factors and punishment justifications are likely to be the same before and after the plea bargain is rejected, this does not mean that the prosecutor cannot seek a heavier sentence than that included with the guilty plea offer. As explored earlier in the book, such a heavier sentence represents punishment for the defendant's choice to opt for a trial (even as the courts struggle to describe it otherwise), but it is punishment deemed acceptable and necessary for the functioning of the criminal justice system.

When factoring in all appropriate information that should go into a sentence, there is almost always a range of appropriate sentences that would fit the offense and the offender. While the sentence offered as part of the plea deal is usually at the bottom of that range, the sentence the prosecutor recommends after trial may be more toward the middle or top of that range. Any sentence beyond the top of that range should be considered improperly vindictive. Of course these are somewhat subjective determinations and the ranges will be subject to different opinions, but an honest application of these principles should avoid sentences that are wildly disproportionate to the offense and the offender. As the first duty of all prosecutors is to seek justice, placing limits such as these will help them achieve that goal without putting them at a strategic disadvantage by making their plea offers meaningless.

4. Be careful about off-the-record and vague comments, promises, and recommendations

Because the negotiations that result in plea bargains are conducted almost completely off the record, it is easy to see how such informal discussions can lead to comments by prosecutors (and defense attorneys) that are general expressions of their thoughts and intentions: "I will promise not to recommend more than ten years for your client, but I'm leaning to something in the area of five years," or, "If your client seems genuinely remorseful when discussing the crime, I'll go below the sentence recommendation in the agreement." While statements such as these may honestly and accurately reflect the prosecutor's intentions, they can create false expectations about the ultimate disposition of the case.

Looking at the motivations of the parties illustrates why such comments happen and why they could prove problematic. Usually, prosecutors want the defense to accept the plea bargain they have offered. Comments such as those above, in the mind of the prosecutor and perhaps in actuality, may contribute to that acceptance. If the defense attorney believes the plea offer is a good one for her client, communicating these prosecutorial intentions is a way to aid her in persuading her client to accept the deal.

Such statements of the prosecutor's qualified intentions are rarely put on the record and included in the terms of the bargain when the plea is accepted in court. Accordingly, they are almost never held to be binding in the face of the defendant's acknowledgment as part of the allocution that no promises were made to him other than those already on the record.

One solution to this problem would be for the prosecutor to choose between not making the comment at all or, if she felt it was important, to place it on the record as part of the deal. Human behavior during relatively informal discussions being what it is, however, such off-the-record comments will never be entirely eliminated. What this means is that prosecutors should be careful what they say regarding their intentions and that defense attorneys should be even more careful about how they communicate such intentions to their clients.

B. Suggestions for Defense Attorneys

1. Do more preparation for plea negotiations and do it early

Defense attorneys, where possible, need to conduct more of their investigation into the case and into their client earlier in the criminal justice process. For public defenders who get assigned new cases while already overloaded with existing ones, this is easier said than done. Private attorneys, who must keep an eye on the economics of managing their practices as well as handling legal matters for other clients, have their own obstacles to spending extra time on cases that likely will be disposed of through a guilty plea. But given that almost all cases at one point or another are settled through plea bargains, attorneys have to develop a systematic approach to preparing for such negotiations similar to their preparations for trial.

This entails spending some time assessing the strength of the government's case that goes beyond speaking once to their client and reading the indictment and police report. Work to obtain discovery from the prosecution as quickly as possible. If permitted, interview the key witnesses. Identify the most important legal issues and conduct at least a modicum of research to determine if it is worth pursuing the issue further. Get a sense from your client what his primary concerns are with respect to plea bargaining the case. Is he more worried about how much time he will spend in prison than what charge he pleads guilty to? Is he willing to cooperate and provide information about other criminal cases if it will get him a better disposition? Does he want the attorney to talk with his family when the time comes to make decisions about a plea offer? Is he so adamant about going to trial that no plea offer will be acceptable or perhaps only one which is so generous he cannot refuse?

This is a criminal justice system whose default disposition of a case is a plea bargain not a trial. The plan and preparations of a defense attorney should reflect this reality. To pursue plea negotiations in some form or another with the prosecutor without being fully prepared is as bad as going to trial unprepared. Attorneys who would never do the latter often do the former. The negotiation of a guilty plea is a dynamic process that takes on a life of its own depending not just on the pertinent facts of the case but also on the human interactions between the parties. Defense attorneys who enter plea negotiations absent important information about the case or their client start off at a disadvantage from which they may never recover.

2. When counseling about the plea, include a discussion of the collateral and other significant consequences of a guilty plea that go beyond the agreement itself

Beyond the actual charge to which the defendant pleads guilty and the sentence he receives as a result, the attorney must be aware of consequences that accompany the conviction within the criminal justice system and outside of it. Even if the current guilty plea does not implicate recidivist or mandatory minimum sentence repercussions, the client should not plead guilty without understanding that the plea might have such a result should he be convicted of a crime in the future. A conviction for certain sex offenses requires a defendant to register as a sex offender. In certain jurisdictions there are other aspects to this requirement that can create challenges and concerns for the defendant. Attorneys should discuss these potential guilty plea consequences with their clients before recommending acceptance of a guilty plea.

If probation is part of the sentence that could be meted out after the guilty plea, counsel should ascertain to discover as much as possible before the plea is accepted about what the potential conditions of that probation could be.[6] Judges have wide latitude in determining probation conditions and at times come up with quite creative requirements that a defendant must adhere to. Counsel should explain as precisely as possible what she knows about those conditions and learn whether the client anticipates any significant problems complying with them before the guilty plea is accepted. One type of probation condition that a defendant might have problems with involves attempts by judges to include a requirement designed to shame the defendant in the hopes that he, she, or others who witness this shame will be deterred from committing similar crimes in the future. For example, in *United States v. Gementera*,[7] the defendant pled guilty to mail theft which included a term of supervised release to be served following his short jail sentence. One of the conditions of his release required Gementera to "perform 100 hours of community service," to consist of "standing in front of a postal facility in the city and county of San Francisco with a sandwich board which in large letters declares: 'I stole mail. This is my punishment.'"[8] Gementera's statutory and constitutional objections to the shaming requirement were rejected by the court. In other cases, shaming requirements have included sharing a sty with a pig, marching down the street with a donkey (for vandalizing a statue of the baby Jesus), and carrying sign reading "only an idiot would drive on a sidewalk to avoid a school bus." Whenever possible, counsel should inform their clients of shaming and other conditions within their probation period that the client might find overly difficult to carry out.

In the *Padilla* case, the Supreme Court made clear that attorneys have a responsibility to advise their clients about the collateral consequences of a guilty plea that are of critical importance, such as the impact of a conviction on the defendant's immigration status. Criminal defense attorneys should endeavor to learn of other aspects of their client's lives that could be impacted by a criminal conviction. Regardless of whether a court determines that a collateral matter is of critical importance or not, it is ineffective lawyering not to inquire about the problems outside the criminal justice system that could materially affect the client's life. What licenses does the client possess or will seek to possess that may prove difficult if not impossible to have if there is a criminal conviction on his record? Is the client's position in a custody dispute likely to

---

6. Although the conditions of probation are tied directly to the sentence, because the conditions of probation can involve many aspects largely unconnected to the criminal justice system, I included it here.

7. United States v. Gementera, 379 F.3d 596 (9th Cir. 2004).

8. *Id.* at 598.

be impacted detrimentally by a conviction? Will a conviction affect the client's current employment or future job possibilities? The attorney needs to inquire from his client about the existence of these and other matters and then help the client factor those concerns into the decision about whether to accept the plea offer.

3. Be careful about how you advise the client whether to accept the plea offer

Chapter IV on the role of the defense attorney discussed the problems that can arise from attorneys who refuse to advise their client about whether to accept a plea bargain or who go to the other extreme and pressure the defendant to accept their opinion of the offer. Attorneys must find a place between those two extremes, keeping in mind on the one hand that the purpose of a counsel is to counsel about important matters and nothing is more important than the defendant's choice of whether to surrender the right to trial by accepting the offer of a guilty plea. An attorney should not abandon that role. On the other hand, as the decision impacts the client, it is his decision to make. No matter how confident the attorney is regarding her belief about the best outcome of the case, she must not try to take the decision away from the defendant through pressure or manipulation.

In providing that advice, the attorney must take care not to make statements suggesting he has certainty about the outcome of a trial should the defendant elect that option. He is well advised to avoid mathematical probability estimates of success at trial as the dynamics of a trial and its attendant uncertainties (especially if it is a jury trial) don't lend themselves to such precision, even when couched in the terms of an estimate. The attorney should assess for his client the evidence against the defendant, any legal arguments that can keep damaging evidence from the factfinder, the strength of the defendant's case, any other matter that might influence the verdict, and the range of anticipated sentences should the defendant reject the plea and be convicted at trial. Based on this assessment and what he knows about his client's goals and concerns, he should make a recommendation about whether the defendant should accept the plea offer and answer any question posed to him. Then he must let the defendant decide what action to take on the plea offer.

Attorneys should do what they can to gauge the judge's view of the case and particularly the judge's sense of what a proper sentence entails. In most cases, attorneys should seek a commitment from the judge to a specific sentence or sentence maximum. A tougher task, although one worth taking, is to try to get at least a rough idea of what the sentence will be if the defendant rejects the plea offer and is convicted at trial. For reasons discussed previously and below, although this would be valuable knowledge for the attorney to possess before recommending acceptance or rejection of a plea offer, the judge is unlikely to provide such a pre-trial assessment. Still it is worth a try.

C. Suggestions for the Conduct of Judges

1. Allow judicial participation in the negotiation process

I have two somewhat related suggestions for improving plea bargaining through permitting more judicial involvement. The first is to allow judicial participation in plea negotiations. As discussed in Chapter V on the role of judges, the Federal Rules of Criminal Procedure and many state rules and court decisions prohibit judicial participation in the plea bargaining process. In other states, judges are allowed to participate in the negotiations as long as their participation does not become coercive in nature. In almost all court-rooms, judges are permitted to commit to a certain sentence or sentence range to be imposed should the guilty plea offer be accepted by the defendant. Before examining the benefits to judicial participation, let's review the arguments that have been raised in opposition and the responses to those arguments.

The federal courts and those states that have prohibited judges from participating in plea negotiations do so for several reasons. They are understandably concerned that such involvement may lead to judicial coercion both real and perceived. Defense attorneys are the first protection that defendants have against such coercion. An objection on the record by the attorney to any such coercive behavior by the judge should act as both a deterrent and remedial device, helping to either prevent or successfully appeal any such behavior by the judge. In states that permit judicial involvement in plea negotiations, appellate courts have invalidated pleas where there is evidence of coercion by the judge.

A second concern with judicial participation in the negotiations involves cases in which the defendant ultimately challenges his guilty plea as being unknowing or involuntary. As such a claim is likely to come before the same judge who helped negotiate the plea, a defendant may believe he will not get an unbiased ruling on his challenge. Whether the judge is actually biased regarding a challenge to the plea or the defendant merely perceives that is the case, the issue is real. The solution is to make sure a different judge handles such challenges at the trial level, though in any event an appellate court is likely to be the ultimate arbiter of the challenge.

The last significant argument against judicial participation in plea negotiations relates to the sentence the defendant receives after trial if he has rejected a plea deal negotiated by the judge. A concern may arise that the sentence at least in part reflects the judge's resentment of the defendant's rejection of that plea offer. In responding to this concern, the plea offer rejected by the defendant should be placed on the record. As the ultimate sentence imposed after trial will also be on the record, appellate courts can see if the difference between the two is beyond the normal penalty imposed on defendants for being convicted at trial rather than accepting a plea bargain. A robust proportionality analysis should be done to determine if the punishment no longer has a reasonable relationship to the crime and the criminal. Unless the judge can offer a sound reason for such an exceptional difference between the sentence the judge helped negotiate in exchange for a guilty plea and the one actually imposed after trial, the sentence should be modified.

The benefits of permitting judges to participate in plea negotiations can be seen from the perspectives of each of the parties to the bargaining process. In an important recent study of the role of judges in the plea bargaining system, Professors Nancy King and Ronald Wright interviewed prosecutors, defense attorneys, and judges throughout the United States.[9] Through these interviews, the authors were able to enumerate the advantages of a more robust role for judges in plea negotiations for all the parties involved. Prosecutors reported that judicial participation helped them manage their relationships with the police, victims, and public. By shifting some of the responsibility for the plea deal to judges, there is less chance that the prosecutor will receive negative publicity, and victims are assuaged by the knowledge that no efforts of the prosecutor could have led to a greater sentence for their victimizer. Defense attorneys reported that judicial involvement leads to more appropriately lenient sentences, in part because the judge gives the prosecutor a face-saving way to admit the weaknesses in her case. Judges saw their contribution as a means to correct errors by perhaps inexperienced attorneys on either side and to offer options that may not have been considered by the attorneys. There was substantial agreement that the more a judge could offer to the settlement of a criminal case, the more the system could

---

9. Nancy J. King & Ronald F. Wright, The Invisible Revolution in Plea Bargaining: Managerial Judging and Judicial Participation in Negotiations, 95 Tex. L. Rev. 325 (2016).

achieve a greater degree of certainty regarding the resolution of the case, a benefit to all parties.[10]

2. Permit judges to comment on likely post-trial sentence during plea negotiations if requested to do so by the defense

The second, perhaps more controversial, suggestion is to end the prohibition on judges being able to respond to requests by defendants or their attorneys for any meaningful information about the likely sentence should the plea offer be rejected and the defendant later convicted at trial. Regardless of the various approaches to judicial participation in plea negotiations taken by individual states and the federal government, judges are not permitted to tell defendants what the sentence or sentence range will be if they reject the plea and are convicted at trial or even that the post-trial sentence will be sterner than that offered in conjunction with the guilty plea. Judges do advise defendants of the sentence possibilities that would result from a conviction at trial (i.e., "If convicted by the jury of Robbery 1, you face anywhere from 2 to 25 years' incarceration"), but any competent attorney would already have provided that information to her client. The result of this prohibition on providing the defendant with meaningful information about his likely post-trial sentence if convicted means that he is compelled to make the life-altering decision about whether to accept a plea bargain or go to trial while half blind. He is often permitted to know his sentence or at least a limited sentence range if he chooses to plead guilty, but is not offered the comparative information about his sentence should be convicted after trial.

Worse still is that this ignorance forced on the defendant by our laws and judicial decisions is rationalized as being done in his best interest, done to avoid coercing the defendant into accepting the plea deal. The reasoning here is that when the defendant hears that his sentence if convicted at trial will be longer, at times significantly longer, than that which accompanies his plea bargain, he will be pushed into accepting the offer against his free will. Of course the post-trial sentence almost always will be longer, and but for exceptional circumstances the enhanced post-trial sentence will survive any challenge. The claimed problem is not with that difference in sentences but with the defendant's being told of it at the moment when he needs that knowledge to

---

10. *Id.* at 365–73. This paragraph was adopted from the article I wrote in the *Nevada Law Journal* and cited earlier.

make a fully informed life-changing decision. In Chapter V on the role of judges, I compared this to being forced to make a decision about having a surgical procedure when told of the likelihood of success with the procedure but refused any information about the degree of danger in not having the surgery.

Judges should be permitted to comment about their likely post-trial sentence as long as several protections are put into place to minimize the possibility that their comments will coerce the defendant into either accepting or rejecting a plea offer. First is that the comments should be offered only when requested by the defendant or his attorney. The danger that the judge's comments will put undue pressure on the defendant increases exponentially when the judge volunteers those comments without being asked. When the request for a sentencing range comes from the defense, however, prohibiting judges from providing this information on the basis that the refusal is for the defendant's own benefit is absurdly paternalistic. Not only should that be the defendant's choice with the advice of his counsel as are other crucial decisions he makes, but I believe in most cases it makes good sense to make such a request of the judge. As defense counsel, I know my advice to a client about whether to accept a guilty plea was always better informed if I had a sense of what the sentence would be following a trial conviction. Regardless, though, of the approach the defendant and her counsel choose to take about having such information provided to them, it should be *their* choice.

The second protection for the defendant is that the judge's statements about the likely post-trial conviction sentence range should be on the record. This will help to minimize confusion and uncertainty and in doing so protect the interests of all parties. Putting everything in writing where possible also helps in this regard. For this to happen, appellate courts will have to change their view that providing such information to the defendant is always improperly coercive.

If the judge agrees to the defense request for her thoughts about a post-trial sentence at the time of the guilty plea, except in rare situations the response should offer a range of sentences rather than a specific one. As discussed in Chapter II on punishment for exercising the right to trial, while judges generally know most of what they need to regarding what an appropriate sentence range is for a particular case when a proposed plea deal is put before them, there are those times when new information comes out during or after trial that could impact the judge's sentence. Judges should always make this clear to the defendant by conditioning their sentence range comments on their not learning anything new and significant during the trial or in other ways. Such a condition is already permitted with plea bargains in which judges condition their sentencing commitments on not learning any significant fact about the crime or the defendant unknown to them when the plea was accepted. The same could be done when the judge offers her thoughts about a possible post-trial conviction sentence. Should the judge in rare instances feel unable to sentence the defendant after a trial conviction to within the range he indicated during plea negotiations, he should make his reasons clear. That "upon hearing the evidence at trial, I understood the seriousness of what happened" is both vague and unverifiable. The judge should detail specifically what was revealed at trial or other significant information that was unknown or incorrect when he made his commitment and why that revelation should impact the sentence. For example, "The information I had during plea negotiations was that the defendant was merely a lookout, but at trial I learned he pointed a gun at the merchant and demanded money." Conversely, the belief that the judge has during plea negotiations that the defendant was the shooter in the murder case may be changed by what he hears at trial and result in a sentence lower than the range the judge committed to.

Additionally, judges should condition their post-trial sentence range intentions on no event of significance taking place between his comments offered pre-plea and the time for sentencing after trial. For example, a sentence range commitment of one to two years for robbery may turn out to be insufficient if the defendant is arrested for armed robbery again before sentence. A commitment to a post-trial conviction sentence of six months to a year in jail for harassing his ex-wife a second time may need to be changed if the defendant violates a protection order and harasses her again. Placing conditions on the sentence commitment does raise a degree of uncertainty, but is necessary to avoid an unjust or incorrect sentence.

D. Systemic Reforms

1. Should plea bargaining be abolished?

With the realization that the differential sentencing that is required for any plea bargaining system is in essence punishment for exercising the constitutional right to trial, and considering the many other problems associated with plea bargaining, some have come to recommend abolition of the practice in one form or another. Abolitionists claim that in addition to resolving the many problems ingrained in plea bargaining, its abolition will lead to more trials, the method through which criminal cases should be decided. Responding to critics of abolition who say that there are not enough resources to deal with the massive increase in trials that would follow, abolitionists respond in basically two ways. The first advocates for fewer cases to be prosecuted, especially those related to victimless crimes such as drug possession. Resources then will require less stretching to try the remaining cases. If more resources than currently exist are required for the remaining cases, it is worth the price to allocate them in order to make the criminal justice system fairer to all involved. Second, if prosecutorial practices such as over-charging are avoided, we should be able to expect a significant number of guilty pleas anyway and thus reduce the number of trials required.

There have been a few attempts over the years to abolish or at least limit plea bargaining. The most significant in terms of its totality — both with respect to its application for an entire state and its abolition of all bargaining at any stage of the criminal justice process — was instituted in Alaska in 1975. The state at-torney general prohibited prosecutors from engaging in charge or sentence bar-gaining at any stage of the process, and he instituted procedures that would prevent overcharging. In apparent support of the policy, the judiciary banned judges from engaging in any form of charge or sentence bargaining as well.[11] The claims by critics that Alaska courts would be flooded with more trials than they could handle turned out mostly not to be true as a substantial number of defendants still pled guilty even without an explicit reward for their plea.

Although the abolition experiment received some positive reviews, statistics showed that those who pled guilty still received lower sentences than those who were convicted at trial, suggesting, in the words of one commentator, "some form of implicit bargaining still occurred."[12] The claim that adequate resources still existed to handle the increase in trials after Alaska banned plea bargaining is questionable (although limiting both cases brought into the system and overcharging certainly could have contributed to this relative suc-cess) and, if true, perhaps unique to Alaska. El Paso, Texas, also tried to abolish plea bargaining, "but the experiment foundered when the courts were flooded with additional trials and could not cope with the added load."[13] Perhaps most telling about Alaska's total ban is that it was essentially ended in 1980, only five years after it was instituted.[14] Bronx County, New York, tried a ban on

---

11. State v. Buckalew, 561 P.2d 289 (Alaska 1977).

12. Douglas Guidorizzi, Should We Really Ban Plea Bargaining?: The Core Concerns of Plea Bargaining Critics, 47 Emory L.J. 753, 775–76 (1998).

13. Josh Getlin, Plea Bargain Issue: The Jury's Still Out: County D.A.'s Crackdown on Practice Reassessed as Controversy Rages On, L.A. Times (Aug. 30, 1987), https://www.latimes.com/archives/la-xpm-1987-08-30-me-4836-story.html.

14. "A few jurisdictions have attempted abolition, at least in part, but those experiments have produced no lasting successes and certainly have not inspired widespread emulation."

post-indictment plea bargaining in 1992, but that too was largely regarded as a failure for many reasons.[15]

At the end of the day, one lesson learned from all attempts to abolish plea bargaining is that where the prosecutor, defendant/defense attorney, and judge all believe disposing of a criminal case accrues to their benefit, a way will be found to make such a disposition happen. Although certainly not their only goals in plea bargaining, prosecutors want the certainty of a conviction, defendants want the reduction in charge or sentence, and the court wants to dispose of the large number of cases on its docket. The method to accomplish these and other goals necessary to satisfy all three parties almost always will require some differential treatment for defendants who plead guilty vis-à-vis those convicted at trial. In the real world then, some form of bargaining is inevitable.

2. Eliminate laws that establish mandatory minimum sentences

Much has been written about the impact of criminal statutes that contain mandatory minimum sentences. Often those writings enumerate the many problems that accompany implementation of such statutes. Primary among those criticisms is that such laws create unfairness, are overly harsh, and place too much control in the hands of prosecutors. Mandatory minimums can lead to what has been referred to as the "cliff effect," allowing something of relatively minor significance to trigger the significantly harsher minimum sentence. This occurs most obviously in drug cases, where a small difference in the amount of the substance possessed or sold can lead to a vastly different sentence that is grossly disproportional to the crime committed.[16] At other times, the presence of a certain fact can be the distinguishing factor although that fact

---

Russell D. Covey, Fixed Justice: Reforming Plea Bargaining with Fixed Base Ceilings, 82 Tul. L. Rev. 1237, 1240 (2008).

15. *See generally* Roland Acevedo, Is a Ban on Plea Bargaining an Ethical Abuse of Discretion? A Bronx County, New York, Case Study, 64 Fordham L. Rev. 987 (1995).

16. See, for example, 21 U.S.C.S. §841, enumerating minimum sentences for federal defendants based on, among other things, the amount of drugs they possessed. A very slight difference in that amount can result in a substantially different sentence involving considerably longer time in prison. Because of the mandatory minimum nature of the sentence, the judge cannot modify the sentence to make it more fairly proportional to the amount possessed.

If a defendant in Florida state court is convicted of possessing 1999 pounds of cannabis plant, he must serve at least three years in prison. If he was unfortunate enough to have one more pound, he faces a seven-year minimum. *See* Fla. Stat. §893.135.

may be present in minor as well as more serious cases.[17] Mandatory minimum sentences contribute significantly to our being the most overly incarcerated per capita nation in the world.[18] Aside from being an unfortunate statement about how we treat our citizens, maintaining such a large prison population is very expensive. Making these unfair mandatory minimum sentences even more of a problem is that they impact minority defendants to a greater degree than others.

With respect to plea bargaining specifically, mandatory minimums skew the negotiations too much in favor of the prosecution in two ways. First, the difference between a non-mandatory sentence and one with a mandated minimum can be extreme. This creates pressure on the defendant to accept the prosecutor's guilty plea offer even more than would the normal sentence penalty for rejecting a plea and being convicted at trial. Second, where such a mandated minimum does result in an unduly harsh sentence, the judge no longer has the ability to modify the trial penalty to something that still corresponds to the offense and the offender.

E. Increase Education about Plea Bargaining

At the time I started teaching a course called Sentencing and Plea Bargaining several decades ago, there were very few law schools that taught about the manner in which the criminal justice system, even back then, disposed of the overwhelming number of cases before it. This attention to plea bargaining in law schools has increased, but the subject should not be taught as an afterthought in criminal law or criminal procedure courses. The law of plea bargaining deserves every bit the curricular attention that we pay to search and seizure or confession law. Similarly, the process of engaging in plea bargaining deserves

---

17. Many states have statutes that require a judge to impose additional minimum prison terms on anyone delivering or possessing to distribute drugs within a certain distance of schools, colleges, or playgrounds. *See, e.g.,* 18 Pa. C.S. §6317. If the illegal activity involves the school or playground or exposes a child to the activity, such additional prison time might be warranted. But if it if occurs late at night, as many such drug deals do, the reason for the higher sentence largely vanishes. Once again, because the sentence is mandatory, a judge cannot incorporate that distinction into her sentence.

18. Countries with the Largest Number of Prisoners per 100,000 of the National Population, as of June 2020, Statista.com, https://www.statista.com/statistics/262962/countries-with-the-most-prisoners-per-100-000-inhabitants/.

to be afforded consideration comparable to that which law schools give to trial advocacy.

Professional education classes for lawyers that deal with trial skills abound, but far fewer exist with respect to plea bargaining. There are classes in negotiations, but these often focus on negotiations in civil cases, which although requiring some of the same skills, can be markedly different in nature and degree. Nobody goes to jail as a result of negotiations in civil cases, and such negotiations are not affected by constitutional protections such as the right to competent counsel in the Sixth Amendment and the protection against cruel and unusual punishment in the Eighth Amendment as well as certain aspects of due process.

Many prosecutor's and public defender's offices now embody thorough training in plea bargaining. All should. Most states now have programs for judicial education, some of which touch only tangentially on all the aspects of plea bargaining that judges will encounter. Such programs need to explore whether and to what degree judges should have a role in the various stages of plea bargaining and how they should perform in that role.